"In taking us straight to the hea
us magnificently. We so need t
Scriptures get into us. The fact t
such submission to Biblical reve
helped to be shaped by the Bible's teaching."

– Terry Virgo

"Phil makes the deep truths of Scripture alive and accessible. If you want to grow in your understanding of each book of the Bible, then buy these books and let them change your life!"

***– PJ Smyth** – GodFirst Church, Johannesburg, South Africa*

"Most commentaries are dull. These are alive. Most commentaries are for scholars. These are for you!"

– Canon Michael Green

"These notes are amazingly good. Lots of content and depth of research, yet packed in a Big Breakfast that leaves the reader well fed and full. Bible notes often say too little, yet larger commentaries can be dull - missing the wood for the trees. Phil's insights are striking, original, and fresh, going straight to the heart of the text and the reader! Substantial yet succinct, they bristle with amazing insights and life applications, compelling us to read more. Bible reading will become enriched and informed with such a scintillating guide. Teachers and preachers will find nuggets of pure gold here!"

***– Greg Haslam** – Westminster Chapel, London, UK*

"The Bible is living and dangerous. The ones who teach it best are those who bear that in mind – and let the author do the talking. Phil has written these studies with a sharp mind and a combination of creative application and reverence."

***– Joel Virgo** – Leader of Newday Youth Festival*

"Phil Moore's new commentaries are outstanding: biblical and passionate, clear and well-illustrated, simple and profound. God's Word comes to life as you read them, and the wonder of God shines through every page."

***– Andrew Wilson** – Author of* Incomparable *and* GodStories

"Want to understand the Bible better? Don't have the time or energy to read complicated commentaries? The book you have in your hand could be the answer. Allow Phil Moore to explain and then apply God's message to your life. Think of this book as the Bible's message distilled for everyone."

– Adrian Warnock – *Christian blogger*

"Phil Moore presents Scripture in a dynamic, accessible and relevant way. The bite-size chunks – set in context and grounded in contemporary life – really make the make the Word become flesh and dwell among us."

– Dr David Landrum – *The Bible Society*

"Through a relevant, very readable, up to date storying approach, Phil Moore sets the big picture, relates God's Word to today and gives us fresh insights to increase our vision, deepen our worship, know our identity and fire our imagination. Highly recommended!"

- Geoff Knott – *former CEO of Wycliffe Bible Translators UK*

"What an exciting project Phil has embarked upon! These accessible and insightful books will ignite the hearts of believers, inspire the minds of preachers and help shape a new generation of men and women who are seeking to learn from God's Word."

- David Stroud – *Newfrontiers and ChristChurch London*

For more information about the Straight to the Heart series, please go to **www.philmoorebooks.com**.

STRAIGHT TO THE HEART OF

Revelation

60 BITE-SIZED INSIGHTS

Phil Moore

MONARCH BOOKS

Oxford, UK & Grand Rapids, Michigan, USA

First published in the UK in 2010 by Monarch Books
(a publishing imprint of Lion Hudson plc)
Wilkinson House, Jordan Hill Road, Oxford OX2 8DR, England
Tel: +44 (0)1865 302750 Fax: +44 (0)1865 302757
Email: monarch@lionhudson.com
www.lionhudson.com

ISBN 978 1 85424 990 6

Distributed by:
UK: Marston Book Services, PO Box 269, Abingdon, Oxon, OX14 4YN
USA: Kregel Publications, PO Box 2607, Grand Rapids, Michigan 49501

The text paper used in this book has been made from wood independently certified as having come from sustainable forests.

British Library Cataloguing Data
A catalogue record for this book is available from the British Library.

Printed and bound in the UK by JF Print Ltd.

This book is for my wife Ruth.

You amaze me more and more every day.

CONTENTS

THE SIXTH OVERVIEW OF AD HISTORY

THE VISION OF THE AGE TO COME

About the *Straight to the Heart* Series

On his eightieth birthday, Sir Winston Churchill dismissed the compliment that he was the "lion" who had defeated Nazi Germany in World War Two. He told the Houses of Parliament that *"It was a nation and race dwelling all around the globe that had the lion's heart. I had the luck to be called upon to give the roar."*

I hope that God speaks to you very powerfully through the "roar" of the books in the *Straight to the Heart* series. I hope they help you to understand the books of the Bible and the message that the Holy Spirit inspired their authors to write. I hope that they help you to hear God's voice challenging you, and that they provide you with a springboard for further journeys into each book of Scripture for yourself.

But when you hear my "roar", I want you to know that it comes from the heart of a much bigger "lion" than me. I have been shaped by a whole host of great Christian thinkers and preachers from around the world, and I want to give due credit to at least some of them here:

Terry Virgo, David Stroud, John Hosier, Adrian Holloway, Greg Haslam, Lex Loizides, and all those who lead the Newfrontiers family of churches; friends and encouragers, such as Stef Liston, Joel Virgo, Stuart Gibbs, Scott Taylor, Nick Sharp, Nick Derbridge, Phil Whittall, and Kevin and Sarah Aires; Tony Collins, Jenny Ward and Simon Cox at Monarch books; Malcolm Kayes and all the elders of The Coign Church, Woking; my fellow elders and church members here at Queens Road Church, Wimbledon;

my great friend Andrew Wilson – without your friendship, encouragement and example, this series would never have happened.

I would like to thank my parents, my brother Jonathan, and my in-laws, Clive and Sue Jackson. Dad – your example birthed in my heart the passion that brought this series into being. I didn't listen to all you said when I was a child, but I couldn't ignore the way you got up at five o'clock every morning to pray, read the Bible and worship, because of your radical love for God and for his Word. I'd like to thank my children – Isaac, Noah, and Esther – for keeping me sane when publishing deadlines were looming. But most of all, I'm grateful to my incredible wife, Ruth – my friend, encourager, corrector, and helper.

You all have the lion's heart, and you have all developed the lion's heart in me. I count it an enormous privilege to be the one who was chosen to sound the lion's roar.

So welcome to the *Straight to the Heart* series. My prayer is that you will let this roar grip your own heart too – for the glory of the great Lion of the Tribe of Judah, the Lord Jesus Christ!

Introduction: God is on the Throne

And they cried out in a loud voice: "Salvation belongs to our God, who sits on the throne, and to the Lamb."

(Revelation 7:10)

The President of the United States rules from the Oval Office. He sits on a chair behind the impressive Resolute desk and in front of the carpeted Seal of the President. The whole room is designed, in the words of President Bartlet in the TV series *The West Wing*, *"to remind guests that this is the office of the President of the United States, and that the person on this side of the desk is the President"*.[1] Even in a democracy, there is no doubt that one chair tops them all.

Ancient kings were less subtle in the way they demonstrated this fact. King Solomon made a throne of ivory and gold so that he could sit at the top of six magnificently decorated steps, with his feet resting on a footstool of pure gold.[2] The Persian King Xerxes appears in the film *300* at the top of a massive throne reached by twenty ivory steps, with the whole structure transported at his bidding on the shoulders of several dozen slaves. His herald loudly proclaims him to be *"the ruler of all the world, the god of gods, king of kings"*, but his throne already conveyed this claim without words.[3] It tells us that Xerxes is in control; Xerxes will prevail; Xerxes is to be obeyed.

---

[1] *The West Wing*, Season 5, Episode 8: "Shutdown".

[2] 2 Chronicles 9:17–19.

[3] *300* (Warner Brothers, 2007).

That's why thrones and their modern, democratic equivalents play such an important role in times of great crisis. It's why President Reagan addressed America from his chair in the Oval Office after the explosion of the Space Shuttle *Challenger*, and why President Bush addressed America from the same chair on the day that two passenger jets crashed into the Twin Towers in New York. Both presidents chose to address the nation from their "throne" in a show of force that they were still seated in the Oval Office and that they would prevail. In George W. Bush's words: *"They have failed; our country is strong… The functions of our government continue without interruption."*

We need to understand all this if we are to grasp the message of the book of Revelation. The last book of the Bible is not primarily about weird beasts, strange allegories, or encoded detail about the final years of Planet Earth. It's a book which focuses on one great fact which trumps all others throughout the whole of AD history. It's a simple fact, but a fact which changes everything: God is on the Throne of the universe.

The Greek word *thronos*, from which we get our English word *throne*, is only used fifteen times in the New Testament leading up to the book of Revelation. It's in the background in the gospels when Jesus proclaims that the Kingdom has come, and it moves to the foreground in Acts when the apostles go into all the world to preach the Gospel of the Kingdom.[4] But it's in the book of Revelation that the Throne of God moves centre-stage. The word is used forty-seven times and in seventeen of the twenty-two chapters. Again and again John's vision picks up on the many Old Testament references to the *Throne of Heaven*, and tells us that one fact is central to the Christian worldview and to how Christians must live within AD history. God is on the Throne; God is in control; God will prevail.

John received this vision while exiled on the Greek island of Patmos in about 95 AD. He was aged about a hundred, the

[4] Matthew 12:28; 24:14; Acts 8:12; 28:23, 31.

last surviving disciple, and his exile hadn't dented his position as the elder statesman of the Church. Times were bad, very bad, and the Church stood at a moment of extreme crisis. The early apostles had all been killed by beheading, crucifixion or worse. Thousands of ordinary Christians had been martyred in wave after wave of persecution, either as human torches in Nero's gardens or as fodder for the lions at the public games. Even worse than this persecution from the outside was the way that the Church had also become riddled on the inside with false teaching, immorality and corruption. Even the faithful had begun to flounder in disappointment and despair. Whatever had happened to Daniel's picture of the Kingdom of God filling the whole earth?[5] What had happened to the Parable of the Mustard Seed and the unstoppable advance which Jesus promised to the Church?[6]

It was in this tumultuous context that Jesus appeared to John to give him answers for the Church. The first word of the book in Greek is *apokalupsis*, which means *Revelation* or simply *Apocalypse*, and which literally means *disclosure, laying bare,* or *unveiling*. The Revelation John received is Jesus' message to his suffering and bewildered Church, which lays bare his plans and purposes for the period between his ascension and his triumphant Second Coming. If at first it seems daunting, inaccessible, and frankly a bit weird, that's because it is packed with divine secrets which are meant *for our eyes only*. Daniel received an apocalyptic vision like John's several hundred years earlier and was told that he received it in a series of strange pictures so that *"none of the wicked will understand, but those who are wise will understand"*.[7] We need to understand John's

---

[5] Daniel 2:35, 44.

[6] Matthew 13:31–32.

[7] Daniel 12:10. The book of Revelation is "apocalyptic" literature in the same style as parts of Daniel, Ezekiel and Zechariah. Such writings were deliberately cryptic and obscure so as to hide their meaning from unfriendly eyes. We should not be surprised, then, that we need help to understand Revelation.

Revelation in the same way, as a deliberately baffling series of pictures and portents, which reveal God's purposes and strategies to his People alone. If the Holy Spirit brings them to life, they provide answers to our deepest questions, but if he does not, they will only yield ideas for fantasy novelists and the writers of computer games. The book can be divided simply along the following lines:

Chapter 1
John's vision of Jesus and the start of the Revelation

Chapters 2–3
A first overview of AD history: The Seven Churches

Chapters 4–5
John's vision of Heaven and the continuation of the Revelation

Chapters 6–7
A second overview of AD history: The Seven Seals

Chapters 8–11
A third overview of AD history: The Seven Trumpets

Chapters 12–14
A fourth overview of AD history seen from three perspectives

Chapters 15–16
A fifth overview of AD history: The Seven Bowls

Chapters 17–20
A sixth overview of AD history which expands on the Seventh Bowl

Chapters 21–22
John's vision of the Age to Come and the end of the Revelation

I have written this book because we still live in the time of John's crisis and because the Revelation he received from Jesus is still the definitive answer to today's big questions. It's God's answer to the questions which face us every day of our lives, and it's time for us to rediscover the book of Revelation and its message of hope.

In a world where an estimated 170,000 Christians are martyred for their faith each year, we still need the Revelation which Jesus gave to John.

In a world where the Church remains terribly flawed and where every week sees another church close down and its building turned into a nightclub, a restaurant or a mosque, we need the Revelation which Jesus gave to John.

It's a Revelation which changes everything. It's a Revelation that God is on the Throne. And he is working out his strategies from the control room of Heaven.

The Vision of Jesus

The Revelation of Jesus Christ (1:1)

> *The revelation of Jesus Christ, which God gave him to show his servants what must soon take place... that is, the word of God and the testimony of Jesus Christ.*
>
> (Revelation 1:1–2)

The book of Revelation is about Jesus Christ. I know that some people will tell you that it's all about beasts, barcodes, timelines, trumpets and judgments, but they've missed the point. It's much more than an encrypted account of the last days of Planet Earth. It's a book about Jesus, and John starts it with words intended to clear that up once and for all. He entitles his book very simply, *"the revelation of Jesus Christ"*.

On one level John is telling us that this is the revelation which belongs to Jesus because the Father has given it to him. That's true, but it's not all that John is saying here. He is also telling us that this is *"the revelation **about** Jesus Christ"*, and that makes a massive difference. It prevents us from majoring on minors, fascinated but confused, and it turns Revelation into a book which can really change our lives.

Before John ever arrived on Patmos, he knew all about Jesus the baby and Jesus the child. He had read Matthew, Mark, and Luke's gospels, and he even counted Jesus' half-brothers among his friends. Jesus had asked him to take his mother Mary into his home and to look after her as if she were his own mother,[1] so no one alive knew more about Jesus the baby and Jesus the child than John.

John also knew more about Jesus the man than anyone

---

[1] John 19:26–27.

else on earth. He had been one of the first people to follow Jesus, chosen to be one of his twelve disciples, and later to be a member of his inner circle of three.[2] He knew so much about Jesus' adult life that he even wrote the last of the four gospels about him, a gospel in which Jesus gets excited, tired, thirsty and so sad that he weeps.[3] No one knew more about Jesus' humanity than John, yet Jesus knew that he needed more than this if he were to live the Christian life to the full.

John also knew first-hand Jesus crucified and raised to life. He was the only one of the twelve disciples who had watched Jesus' trials and who had stood at the foot of the cross to watch his crucifixion.[4] Later that same weekend, he had raced with Peter to find Jesus' tomb empty except for his grave clothes.[5] Jesus had appeared to him, risen from the dead: twice in a locked room, once at Lake Galilee with a miraculous catch of fish, once on a mountain in Galilee, and once on the Mount of Olives where he ascended to heaven.[6] No one alive knew more about Jesus crucified and raised to life than John did – and yet Jesus still knew that he needed more.

Something was missing from John's view of Jesus, and we need it ourselves if we are to live as Christ-followers today. Knowing Jesus the baby, Jesus the man, Jesus the suffering sacrifice, and Jesus the risen Son of God is essential – that's why he is revealed in such detail in the four gospels – but our view of him is too small unless we also see him ascended and in heavenly glory. Without this view, John reclined happily on Jesus' chest at the Last Supper.[7] When he saw Jesus in his post-

[2] Mark 3:17; 5:37; 9:2; 14:33.

[3] John 2:17; 4:6; 19:28; 11:35.

[4] John 18:15; 19:26.

[5] John 20:1–8.

[6] John 20:19–25, 26–31; 21:1–25; Matthew 28:16–20; Luke 24:50–53.

[7] John 13:23–25. The KJV captures the intimacy expressed in these verses in Greek.

ascension glory, however, he tells us in 1:17 that *"I fell at his feet as though dead."*

We need to grasp that Revelation is as much a book about Jesus as the gospels of Matthew, Mark, Luke, and John. Although *"Jesus Christ is the same yesterday, today and forever"*,[8] he appeared humbly as a man at his incarnation and received glory and power at his ascension.[9] There is a real danger that unless we see Jesus in the pages of Revelation, we will worship him as he walked on the earth yesterday and not as he reigns in heaven today. That's the great tragedy when Christians treat this book like a fantasy novel or a secret code for someone other than themselves. They have missed the point as much as a person who watches the movie *Jaws* and thinks it is about the seaside. *Jaws* is about a movie about a shark. Revelation is a book about Jesus Christ, the King of Glory.

We need the book of Revelation to save us from the sin of idolatry – from worshipping Jesus as someone less than he really is. It takes the baby who sleeps in Bethlehem's manger and reminds us that he has grown up and is coming back to judge the earth in his wrath. It takes the great teacher and healer from Galilee and tells us he is now riding out to victory wearing a robe dipped in blood. It reminds us that Jesus is not just the weak and suffering Saviour depicted on a crucifix, because he is also the one who holds the keys to Death and Hades, and who rules over the whole earth with irresistible strength.[10]

Is your view of Jesus too small? It may well be too small for you to worship without being guilty of idolatry, and too small to sustain you through the ups and downs of AD history. That's why Jesus appeared to John to give us a complete picture of the real Jesus. That's why we need *"the revelation of Jesus Christ"*.

---

[8] Hebrews 13:8.

[9] Some key verses on this are John 17:5; Philippians 2:5–11; Acts 2:36; Hebrews 2:9.

[10] Revelation 6:15–17; 19:13; 1:18.

One Like a Son of Man (1:12–18)

I turned round to see the voice that was speaking to me. And when I turned I saw seven golden lampstands, and among the lampstands was someone "like a son of man".

(Revelation 1:12–13)

I love Agatha Christie novels. I particularly enjoy the chapter at the end of her Hercule Poirot mysteries where he reveals a solution so breathtakingly unexpected that it leaves the reader speechless with amazement. Some passages in the Old Testament book of Daniel are like a mystery novel, and these verses in Revelation 1:12–18 act as their grand dénouement.

One of the great mysteries of the book of Daniel is the identity of the shadowy figure who appears in the middle of chapter 7. It's the year 553 BC and Daniel dreams of four terrifying beasts, which represent the great empires of the next few centuries of history. First comes a beast which looks like a cross between a lion and an eagle, representing the Babylonian Empire which ruled until 539 BC. Next comes a beast like a bear, representing the Persian Empire whose power lasted until 331 BC. Next is a beast like a leopard, representing Alexander the Great and his Macedonian Empire. Worst of all is the fourth beast, a beast with large iron teeth to crush and devour anyone in its path, and which speaks ominously of the merciless Roman Empire.

But then Daniel sees something unexpected in the midst of those rising and falling empires. It is not a fifth beast but a human being, one whose empire will be truly global, larger than all the empires of the Babylonians, Persians, Greeks and Romans put together. It will not simply last longer than its predecessors, it will last forever. Daniel tells us that

> *I looked, and there before me was one like a son of man, coming with the clouds of heaven. He approached the Ancient of Days and was led into his presence. He was given authority, glory and sovereign power; all peoples, nations and men of every language worshipped him. His dominion is an everlasting dominion that will not pass away, and his kingdom is one that will never be destroyed.*[1]

So who is this *"One Like a Son of Man"*, whose empire will vastly exceed all its rivals? That's the great mystery.

So are you ready now for John's Hercule Poirot moment? One Sunday on Patmos, full of the Holy Spirit and lost in praise and worship, John hears a voice as loud as a trumpet calling him from behind. He wheels round to look at the speaker, and is staggered to recognize the person Daniel described as *"one like a son of man"*. Jesus had often called himself *"the Son of Man"*,[2] but this had still not prepared John for what he saw. Jesus perfectly matched Daniel's identikit picture of the *"One Like a Son of Man"*, and that could only mean one thing. The carpenter's son from Galilee was the one greater than Nebuchadnezzar, Cyrus, Alexander and Caesar, and whose global empire would never end.

In 536 BC, seventeen years after the dream of chapter 7, Daniel had seen the *"One Like a Son of Man"* for a second

---

[1] Daniel 7:13–14.

[2] Jesus is called *"the Son of Man"* eighty-two times in the four gospels, but God also calls Ezekiel *"son of man"* ninety-three times in the Old Testament so it might simply have meant that he was human. John knew from Jesus' words in Matthew 25:31 and 26:64 that it was probably a reference to Daniel 7, but this confirmed it beyond doubt.

time up close and personal.[3] He gave a detailed account of his appearance in 10:5–6, which is startlingly similar to John's description of Jesus in these verses. Daniel saw a man dressed in a linen garment with a belt of gold around his waist, and John sees Jesus dressed in a long garment with a sash of gold around his chest. Daniel saw his face as bright as lightning, and John sees Jesus' face shining as brightly as the noonday sun in its dazzling white purity. Daniel saw his eyes like flaming torches and his arms and legs like burnished bronze, and John sees Jesus' eyes like flames of fire and his feet like burnished bronze. Daniel compared his voice to the sound of a massive crowd, and John compares Jesus' voice like the sound of a loud trumpet and a rushing waterfall. John recognized him instantly, and so should we. Overcome with awe, he does the same thing before Jesus that Daniel also did before the *"One Like a Son of Man"*. He falls face down before him.[4]

We sing songs about Jesus the King of kings, but few of us grasp what this statement really meant to John and the churches of Asia. They lived in a world where Rome ruled supreme and where Caesar was the great king of all the earth. The Roman Empire was not portrayed as a beast with iron teeth for nothing, and Christians had been powerless to resist wave after wave of imperial persecution. Daniel's vision had promised them *"One Like a Son of Man"* in the future, but they needed his reign to begin now – and John's vision issued the revolutionary proclamation that it had. This was sedition of the highest order against Caesar, an insecure ruler who tolerated no rivals,[5] but John saw three things which Daniel had not seen, which convinced him that it was true.

Jesus held the keys of Death and Hades in his hand, because

---

[3] In Daniel 10:16 the Hebrew phrase *kidmuth beni adam* means literally *one according to the likeness of a son of man*. Daniel identifies his visitor very clearly as the *"One Like a Son of Man"* whom he saw in 7:13–14.

[4] Compare Revelation 1:17; Daniel 10:9.

[5] See Luke 23:2; John 19:2; Acts 17:6–7.

he had defeated these two great enemies through his death and resurrection. He wielded a sharp double-edged sword in his mouth, because his Gospel message had gone out to the nations with a command to submit to him as King.[6] He held seven stars in his right hand, because he had founded the Church as the agent of his Kingdom whom even the gates of Hell could not resist.[7] Daniel had seen a picture of the coming King, but John saw the reality of the King who had come. He fell on his face and got up with a confidence that God's Kingdom would overcome every setback, every obstacle and everyone who opposes it. The rest of Revelation explains world history in the light of this glorious fact.

The early Christians were not persecuted because they believed that Jesus was King of their private lives, their families and their churches. They were persecuted because they refused to state that *"Caesar is Lord"* and because they insisted that Jesus was the true King before whom Caesar, his empire, and every nation, tribe and tongue needed to bow the knee. They might be persecuted, exiled and even killed, but they would not be silenced. They had a Gospel message of a new King and a new Empire which would never stop growing and would never pass away. They faced up to Caesar and allied themselves with the one who had once been nailed to a Roman cross, and amazingly it was their voice which still sounded long after Rome had been sacked and the last of its emperors had fallen.

Hercule Poirot never grasped a mystery as great as this one, but we can. Jesus calls his followers to proclaim the Good News of his Kingdom, and to call people from every nation and every language to receive him as their King. Many will hate us, persecute us and even kill us, but they will never silence us. Because Jesus is the *"One Like a Son of Man"*, and his Kingdom has now come.

---

[6] This fulfils the Messianic prophecy of Isaiah 49:2 and ties in with Hebrews 4:12. Note how Paul expresses the Gospel in Acts 17:30.

[7] Revelation 1:20; Matthew 16:18.

The First Overview of AD History

The Seven Churches (2:1–3:22)

Write on a scroll what you see and send it to the seven churches: to Ephesus, Smyrna, Pergamum, Thyatira, Sardis, Philadelphia and Laodicea.

(Revelation 1:11)

Jesus gave his Revelation to John and addressed it to seven churches. Now that's interesting. He didn't address it to an individual, he didn't address it to Christians in general, and he didn't address it to a parachurch organization. He addressed it to seven churches on the west coast of what is now modern-day Turkey.

This wasn't just a throwaway comment or a literary device. In chapters 1 to 3, Jesus tells John nine times that his message is *"for the churches"*,[1] and right at the end of the book he returns to his theme to remind John that *"I, Jesus, have sent my angel to give you this testimony for the churches"*.[2] Jesus wants us to see that he places great value on the local church, and that so should we.

This is important because he calls anyone who loves him to show it by pouring out their lives for their Christian brothers and sisters. He told Peter in John 21:15–17 that anyone who loves him will care for his People, and he takes care to address his Revelation in such a way that this priority stares us in the face. Jesus speaks to local churches, he walks among local churches, and he expects each of us to be engaged right at the heart of a local church. He knows that church life is often full of disappointments, let-downs and hypocrisy – as these two

[1] Revelation 1:4, 11; 2:7, 11, 17, 29; 3:6, 13, 22.

[2] Revelation 22:16.

chapters show only too well – but despite all this he does not give up on the local church, and nor should we. The writer C.E.B. Cranfield puts it this way: *"The freelance Christian, who would be a Christian but is too superior to belong to the visible Church upon earth in one of its forms, is simply a contradiction in terms."*

The grand finale of Revelation will not focus on Jesus coming back for large numbers of individual Christians. It will describe him coming back for a *Bride*, pure, ready and united for her Husband.[3] It will describe him coming back for a *People*, vast, innumerable, and yet united and ready for their King.[4] It will describe the People of God as a great *City*, vast, glorious, and built together with walls so strong that their depth is twice the length of a basketball court.[5] We may not be comfortable with the Church Father Cyprian's conclusion that *"It is impossible to have God as Father without having the Church as mother"*, but we must grasp the core of what Jesus is saying here. He addresses each local church as *you singular*[6] to remind us that he sees each local church as one Body and that casual commitment is utterly out of place for a child of God. The Christian Gospel is a call to give ourselves first to the Lord and second to his People, and not to do so is to swindle our brothers and sisters out of all that we owe them.[7]

It's this high value which God places on the local church which makes the second and third chapters of Revelation so troubling. Jesus promised that *"I will build my Church and the gates of Hell will not overcome it"*,[8] but the seven churches of

---

[3] Revelation 19:7; 21:2, 9; 22:17.

[4] Revelation 18:4; 20:9; 21:3; 22:21.

[5] Revelation 3:12; 20:9; 21:2, 10–27; 22:2–3; 22:19.

[6] Unlike the English language, Greek has the word *su* to mean *you* when it refers to only one person, and the word *humeis* to mean *you* when it refers to many. Jesus speaks to each of these local churches as *su*.

[7] See Paul's words in 2 Corinthians 8:5 and also in Romans 12:5 where he tells us that *"in Christ we who are many form one body, and each member belongs to all the others"*.

[8] Matthew 16:18.

Asia present a sorry and disappointing view of the Church throughout AD history.[9] Jesus tells us that sometimes the Church will be characterized by *coolness* towards God (the first and seventh churches), that sometimes she will be *corrupted* by false teaching and immorality (the third, fourth, and fifth churches), and that only sometimes will she be *commended* for her faithfulness towards God (the second and sixth churches).[10] She has glorious promises in the Old and New Testaments, but she will often fail to enter into them.

She will succumb to sin and compromise, but he will see it and will root it out at the proper time. Her leaders will be weak, but he holds those leaders in his hands, and he will open doors for them which no one can shut. She will see times of defeat and decline like Old Testament Israel, but she will also see times of revival and restoration; and anyone who perseveres to the end will see reward beyond their wildest dreams.[11] There will be times when churches close down and their buildings are turned into wine bars and Bingo halls, but he tells us that even this is a sign of victory and not defeat. He tells us in 2:5 that the Devil cannot close down a church, only Jesus himself can do that, and this changes our view of the present. When a church closes down, it is not in spite of Jesus and in spite of our

---

[9] There is much debate over whether these words refer only to seven literal churches in the first century or to the Church in general throughout history. I take the view that since the number *seven* is used repeatedly in Revelation to refer to the complete span of AD history, Jesus uses aspects of those seven real churches in order to paint a general picture of the highs and lows of churches throughout history. I don't agree with the (mainly Western) commentators who argue that these are "seven stages" of church history and that we are now in the "Laodicean age". This seems to me to be a very Eurocentric view – the Church certainly isn't Laodicean in some parts of China, Africa, and South America! – and a better way is to see the Church going through these stages again and again at various times and in various places.

[10] Note that this stylized "A–B–C–C–C–B–A" symmetry is another reason to assume that Jesus is addressing general issues throughout Church history beyond the initial issues in the seven literal churches.

[11] Revelation 2:7, 11, 17, 26–28; 3:5, 12, 21.

prayers. Jesus answers our prayers for the Church not just by blessing existing churches and new church plants, but also by closing down some churches which bring disgrace to his Name. The Father prunes unfruitful branches so that the whole vine can be more fruitful.[12]

In February 2007 *The Times* newspaper in London ran a story with the headline that *"Thousands of [British] Churches Face Closure in Ten Years"*. Giving the example of one Methodist church in Yorkshire which had been turned into a mosque, it announced that while 1,700 Anglican churches had closed since 1969, about the same number of mosques had opened across the same period. It quoted the view of a Professor of Social Geography at Oxford University that, *"The new cultural landscape of English cities has arrived. The homogenized, Christian landscape of state religion is in retreat."* So how does Jesus want us to react to such news?

The pessimistic Christian retreats inwards towards an attitude of "holding on until the end" until Christ appears. The triumphalistic Christian remains upbeat for a while, chanting Scripture promises to himself, but eventually no amount of positive thinking can offset his sense of disappointment that the Kingdom of God just doesn't appear to be advancing as he thinks Jesus promised it would.

But the Christian who understands Revelation chapters 2 and 3, and who grasps that this is Jesus' first overview of AD history, is able to cope with the setbacks and disappointments of church life and Kingdom mission. He sees the Church with all her faults and he recognizes the hand of the Gardener, pruning his vine so that in due course she may be more fruitful. He is able to look such news full in the face because he sees something even bigger in the background.

He sees that God is on the Throne.

[12] Jesus tells us in John 15:1–2 tells us that radical pruning is the only way to yield the lasting fruit of 15:16.

The Tree of Life (2:7)

To him who overcomes, I will give the right to eat from the tree of life, which is in the paradise of God.

(Revelation 2:7)

The Bible is a collection of sixty-six books, but it is also one book. We can see this in the symmetry of Genesis 1–2 and Revelation 21–22, the first and last two chapters of the Bible, which both describe God's perfect and sinless paradise on earth. Genesis describes the garden-paradise of Eden at the start of creation, and Revelation describes the city-paradise of God's renewed creation. So when Jesus refers here to the tree of life, he is giving us a clue that the Bible will end with a paradise more beautiful and more glorious than Eden.

Genesis 2:9 tells us that there were two trees, not one, in the middle of the Garden of Eden. The more famous tree was the forbidden one, *the tree of the knowledge of good and evil*, but there was also a second one, *the tree of life*. Most of us know the story. The Lord forbade Adam and Eve on pain of death from eating the fruit of the first tree,[1] but at Satan's goading Eve trespassed by eating its fruit, and Adam foolishly followed her lead. The human race fell, their relationship with God was broken, and they found themselves ejected from Paradise and cast out into a fallen world. They had literally eaten themselves out of house and home.

But the reason that Adam and Eve were thrown out of the garden-paradise of God was *not* because God wanted to prevent them from eating more fruit from the tree of the knowledge of

[1] Genesis 2:16–17.

good and evil. The Lord had a different concern: *"The man has now become like one of us, knowing good and evil. He must not be allowed to reach out his hand and take also from the tree of life and eat, and live forever."*[2] Adam's sin was to eat from the first tree, but the reason he was quickly ejected from the Garden was due to the second tree. We don't exactly know what effect the tree of life had upon Adam and Eve, but it seems from this verse that it was the God-given food which enabled them to live and never die. When we come across the metaphor of *a tree of life* later in the Old Testament, it always speaks of refreshing and prosperity,[3] and it looks back to the fruit which was so powerful that angels stood at the entrance to the Garden of Eden specifically *"to guard the way to the tree of life"*.[4]

If Adam and Eve had been able to eat the fruit of the tree of life, even after they sinned, they would have used its life-giving fruit to defy God's just ruling that *"when you eat of [the fruit of the tree of the knowledge of good and evil] you will surely die"*. They would have lived as rebels against God, fallen yet immortal, forever barred from the city-paradise of Revelation 21 and 22 because *"corruption does not inherit incorruption"*.[5] It was only because they were barred from the tree of life that they understood their frail mortality and responded with humble faith when God preached to them the first Gospel sermon. Since then, our own fragile bodies serve as a constant reminder to us that God judges sin and calls us to repent before it is too late. God did not just exile Adam and Eve from the tree of life as an act of judgment; he also did so to prepare them for his act of loving mercy.

He paved the way for Jesus to redeem humankind and to save them into God's new paradise and his great tree of life. He's the one God referred to as *"the seed of Eve"* when prophesying

---

[2] Genesis 3:22.

[3] Proverbs 3:18; 11:30; 13:12; 15:4.

[4] Genesis 3:24.

[5] 1 Corinthians 15:50.

about him to Adam and Eve,[6] and he's the one Paul refers to as the *"Last Adam"* in 1 Corinthians 15:45.

The First Adam chose to disobey God in the Garden of Eden by eating from the tree that brought death. The Last Adam chose to obey God in the Garden of Gethsemane by embracing the cross that brought death, even though it was the path of shame and dishonour.[7] The First Adam brought a curse on humankind by eating from the forbidden tree, but the Last Adam lifted the curse from humankind by shedding his blood on the tree of Calvary.[8] The First Adam ate food which bore death for humankind, but the Last Adam ate death itself, and as he gulped it down he broke its power through his resurrection from the dead.[9] It was God's grace which barred Adam and Eve from the tree of life, because only if the First (fallen) Adam perished could each of us can be saved into Jesus, the Last Adam.

That's why Jesus expects us to be excited when he mentions the *tree of life* here for the first time in the New Testament. He is telling us that God has a new paradise for us, not the garden-paradise of Eden, but the city-paradise of the New Jerusalem. He will go on to tell us in 22:2 that the *tree of life* stands right in the middle of this city-paradise, yielding fruit every month so that God's People will never exhaust its life-giving power, and bearing leaves so powerful that they can heal nations. And he will tell us that this garden is to be our home, and this fruit is to be our food, forever.

Jesus expects us to be so excited by this prospect that the

[6] When God says *"your seed"* in Genesis 3:15, he uses the Hebrew feminine word for *your* to make it clear that he means *Eve's* seed, not Adam's. You don't have to be a biology teacher to know that women don't produce the *seed* – men do. That's why this may well be the first biblical reference to the virgin birth of Jesus.

[7] Mark 14:35–36; Hebrews 12:2.

[8] Galatians 3:13. Some people even see the fact that Jesus wore a *crown of thorns* as a vivid statement that he carried the curse laid upon Adam in Genesis 3:18.

[9] Hebrews 2:9; 1 Corinthians 15:54–57.

thought of eating its fruit in 2:7 will be enough to spur us on to persevere in our faith and never lose our first love. He expects us to value its fruit so highly that we consider it the worst curse imaginable in 22:19 for someone to be told that God will *"take away from him his share in the tree of life"*.

You may be serving the Lord with tireless perseverance like the Ephesian Christians, resisting false teachers and toiling for his sake, but make sure you don't lose your first love for Jesus, his presence, his Church and his mission. Don't lose it for the sake of all that the Last Adam has done for you. Don't lose it for the sake of all the promises that he makes to you. Don't lose it because you hunger to eat the fruit of the tree of life.

True Jews (2:9)

I know... the slander of those who say they are Jews and are not, but are a synagogue of Satan.

(Revelation 2:9)

John grew up in multiracial Galilee and was very proud of being a Jew. It was what separated him from the mixed-race Samaritans and from the Gentile Roman soldiers whose empire had swallowed up his beloved homeland. On one occasion John was so irritated by a Samaritan village's disdain towards Jerusalem that he wanted to call down fire from heaven to destroy them.[1] As for the Gentiles, John knew that *"it is against our law for a Jew to associate with a Gentile or visit him"*.[2] Call it racism or call it legitimate first-century religious purity, the fact remains that John had learned from an early age the importance of his Jewish ethnic identity.

John was not alone in this. Every Jewish child would be taught that God had chosen the nation of Israel out of all the nations of the earth to be his chosen People.[3] He had chosen Abraham out of Ur of the Chaldees, he had chosen Isaac and not his elder brother Ishmael, and had chosen Jacob and not his elder brother Esau. Armed with Old Testament verses such as *"I have loved Jacob, but Esau I have hated"*,[4] John was raised in a

---

[1] Luke 9:52–56.

[2] These are the words of John's good friend and fellow-Galilean Peter in Acts 10:28.

[3] For example in Exodus 19:5. See the later chapter on "God's Private Treasure Collection" and how Jesus' point in 2:9 runs through the whole book of Revelation.

[4] Malachi 1:2–3.

community proud of its Jewishness and dismissive towards the Gentiles.

That's why Jesus' words here cut straight to the heart of Jewish national pride, and tell them that they need to find a greater hope in the Gospel. They warn them that not all Jews are *true Jews*, and that it's even possible for a Jewish synagogue to become a *"synagogue of Satan"*. In fact, this message is so important that Jesus says it once here and then once again in 3:9.

John had already hinted at this when he wrote his gospel many years earlier. He told us Jesus taught there is such a thing as a *"true Israelite"* and a *"false Israelite"*.[5] He recorded Jesus' clash with the Jewish leaders in which he told them that being a biological child of Abraham was no guarantee of being his spiritual child as well, and that for all their ethnic pride they were actually children of the Devil.[6]

Paul, the *"Hebrew of Hebrews"*,[7] had expanded on Jesus' teaching in his letters. He wrote that *"not all who are descended from Israel are Israel"*, and that *"It is not the natural children who are God's children, but it is the children of the promise who are regarded as Abraham's offspring."*[8] He explained this further in Galatians 3:16, telling us that *"The promises were spoken to Abraham and to his seed. The Scripture does not say 'and to seeds', meaning many people, but 'and to your seed', meaning one person, who is Christ."* This same Christ speaks to John in the last book of the Bible to complete our picture of his Gospel message.

It is not that the Church has *replaced* Israel in God's purposes – far from it. Paul devotes a large part of Romans 11 to his teaching that Gentiles are only saved through the Church

---

[5] John 1:47.

[6] John 8:37–59. Jesus tells the Jewish leaders that it is possible to be a child of Abraham ethnically (v. 56) and yet not be a spiritual child of Abraham at all (vv. 39, 44).

[7] Philippians 3:5.

[8] Romans 9:6–9.

because they are branches grafted into Abraham's Jewish tree. But nor is it that Israel can enjoy the covenant promises of God through their race without reference to their Messiah. The Gospel message offends Jewish national pride and tells them that *"Abraham's seed"* is not primarily Isaac, it's primarily Christ, and that a true Jew is not someone who is part of Abraham's Jewish nation, but anyone who is part of Christ's Holy Nation.

Tragically, many Christians who understand this Gospel have little heart for the Jews, while many Christians who love the Jews have little understanding of this Gospel. Jesus stands appalled at some of the flattery which Christians pay to Jews in the hope of winning them to Christ, and he offers a very different strategy to win them. He tells us not to fool them that they are the People of God unless they turn and receive him as Messiah. He tells us not to mislead them that the promises of the Old Testament belong to them unless they receive them through Jesus, and he emphasizes this in 2:27 and 3:7 by taking two of the great promises made to Israel in the Old Testament and applying them to the Church. He tells us not to flatter Jews that they are saved unless they put their faith in the death and resurrection of Jesus the Messiah, the thing which Paul in Acts 28:20 calls *"the hope of Israel"*.

It's not a message which will make us popular within the Jewish community because it tells them they are no better off than Gentiles unless they repent and turn to Jesus. It's the message which provoked a Jewish mob to try to lynch Paul because they thought he *"taught all men everywhere against our people and our law and this place"*.[9] It caused them to kill Stephen because they believed that *"this fellow never stops speaking against this holy place and against the law"*.[10] It caused them to slander the Christians in Smyrna, and to persecute the

[9] Acts 21:28.

[10] Acts 6:13.

Christians in Philadelphia.[11] It will probably cause some of them to hate us too.

But it's also the message which created a megachurch in Jerusalem, and which caused its leader to exclaim *"how many thousands of Jews have believed, and all of them are zealous for the law!"*[12] Evidently, when it comes to the Gospel, flattery gets us nowhere, and Jesus wants us to know this for our own sake and for the sake of the Jewish race into which he was born.

We will soon be shown a great vision in chapter 7 of people from every nation, tribe, and language worshipping Jesus the Messiah as the Seven Seals are opened. God wants the Jewish people to be among them, worshipping their Messiah alongside Abraham, Isaac, Jacob, David and the other heroes and heroines of Old Testament history.

But that won't happen through flattery or pretence, or through Christians pretending that Jews can be true Jews through Isaac without Jesus. Nor will it happen through the Church ignoring the Jewish race and leaving them to their doom.

It will only happen through Christians who dare to preach Jesus as the true *"hope of Israel"* and who make Jews jealous that non-Jews are now heirs to the promises which should be theirs.[13] It will only come through a Church which says with conviction: *"I am not ashamed of the Gospel, because it is the power of God for the salvation of everyone who believes: first for the Jew, then for the Gentile."*[14]

---

[11] Revelation 2:9; 3:9.

[12] Acts 21:20. The Greek word *murias* actually means *ten thousand*, so James is literally exclaiming *"how many tens of thousands of Jews have believed!"* Whilst undoubtedly more offensive to Jews, the Gospel which Jesus shows us here is also much more effective in winning them to faith.

[13] See Romans 11:11, 13–14. This may also be what Jesus has in mind in Revelation 3:9 when he promises to cause the Jews of Philadelphia to fall at the church's feet and to confess that Jesus loves them.

[14] Romans 1:16.

The Iron Sceptre (2:26–27)

To him who overcomes and does my will to the end, I will give authority over the nations – "He will rule them with an iron sceptre; he will dash them to pieces like pottery" – just as I have received authority from my Father.

(Revelation 2:26–27)

My wife, Ruth, is a doctor and she visits patients in their own homes. Her least favourite task was always visiting one man who lived in absolute squalor. As she climbed past piles of rubbish to reach the door of his tiny house, she always took deep gulps of fresh air to prepare her for the stench inside. He had long since abandoned the upstairs of the house and now slept on a dirty mattress in the lounge, surrounded by soiled and unwashed clothing. Ruth pressed him to pay for a cleaner for the sake of his health, but he refused point blank, saying that he could not afford such luxuries. Since he had no friends and no family except for an absent nephew, she could never force the issue, and in due course he died in the stink and filth of his squalid lounge.

Ruth wasn't there when his nephew arrived to begin the clean-up job. She was only told later what he saw when he became the first person in almost a decade to go upstairs. There, in boxes under his uncle's bed, he found large bundles of banknotes worth £100,000. The old man had always distrusted banks, but no one knew that for years he had stashed money in a secret hiding place under his bed. No one knew to remind him when senility took him and he forgot that the money was even there. No one ever told him that he was dying like a pauper when he could have been living like a king.

That's a tragic story, but if you skim too quickly over these verses, the story will be your own. There is tremendous wealth hidden for you in these two verses, and Jesus wants you to stop, uncover it and claim it as your own. Are you ready?

There are thousands of promises in the Bible, but some of the greatest are the ones which God makes to Jesus his Messiah. One of my favourites is in Psalm 2:8 where he promises: *"Ask of me, and I will make the nations your inheritance, the ends of the earth your possession."* Another is in Isaiah 49:6 where he promises: *"It is too small a thing for you to be my servant to restore the tribes of Jacob and bring back those of Israel I have kept. I will also make you a light for the Gentiles, that you may bring my salvation to the ends of the earth."* God made some amazing promises to people in the Old Testament, but none are more breathtaking than the ones he made to his Messiah.

That Messiah is Jesus, the one who is speaking here and making promises of his own to his People. He has already promised believers *"the crown of life"*, deliverance from *"the second death"*, *"a white stone with a new name"*, and a chance to eat his *"hidden manna"*,[1] but now he promises them something even greater.

If you don't know the Old Testament, you might miss it, like Ruth's patient missed the riches under his bed. But if you read Psalm 2:9 in its context, you will see that Jesus is quoting from one of God's greatest promises to his Messiah. This requires a double-take. Jesus is not just quoting it as a great promise which the Father gave to him.[2] He's quoting it to tell us that this promise also belongs to *us*.

Let's hold that thought and join Paul as he preaches to the

---

[1] Revelation 2:10, 11, 18.

[2] John quotes the same promise again later and applies it to Jesus in Revelation 19:15.

city of Antioch in Pisidia in 48 AD.[3] The whole city has gathered to hear the Gospel, and Paul preaches it clearly and powerfully. When the Jews of the city abuse him and attack his message, Paul quotes from Isaiah 49:6 to tell them that he is turning to preach to the non-Jews of Antioch because *"this is what the Lord has commanded* ***us****: 'I have made you a light for the Gentiles, that you may bring salvation to the ends of the earth.'"*[4] That little word *"us"* is important. Paul is sharing exactly the same insight as Jesus in Revelation 2. Through the Gospel, believers do not merely possess the promises which God made to the heroes of the Old Testament, but also the promises which God made to his Messiah. When the New Testament tells us that we are *"heirs of God and co-heirs with Christ"*, it really means it.[5]

Understand what this means. There are Christians all around you who are battered by the spiritual fight, who are too afraid to stand up for Christ, and who make little attempt to advance the Kingdom of God. You may even be such a Christian yourself. Jesus urges you to remember the riches upstairs, and not to live like a pauper downstairs.

You may feel weak, but God tells you that he has made you *"into a polished arrow"* with a *"mouth like a sharpened sword"*.[6] He promises that you will be dangerous to the kingdom of darkness the minute you recognize who you are in Christ. You may feel inferior to other Christians in a thousand ways, but the Lord tells you that you are *"honoured in the eyes of the Lord"* because he is your strength and he has decided that you are one of those *"in whom I will display my splendour"*.[7] You may feel as though you could never win a friend, colleague or neighbour for Christ, but God encourages you to *"ask of me, and I will make the*

---

[3] Luke gives us an account of this in Acts 13:13–52.

[4] Acts 13:47. Paul also applies the Messianic promises of Isaiah 49:8 and 52:7 to ordinary Christians in 2 Corinthians 6:2 and Romans 10:15 respectively.

[5] Romans 8:17.

[6] Isaiah 49:2.

[7] Isaiah 49:3, 5.

nations your inheritance, the ends of the earth your possession". You can expect to be fruitful, because he has determined *"that you may bring my salvation to the ends of the earth"*.[8] You may feel fruitless and discouraged, saying *"I have laboured to no purpose; I have spent my strength in vain and for nothing"*, but the Lord reminds you that *"What is due to you is in the Lord's hand, and your reward is with your God"*.[9] You may feel as though the forces of evil are too strong in your life and that you will never know victory over sin or Satan, but Jesus assures you that, if you stick with him, *"you will rule them with an iron sceptre; you will dash them to pieces like pottery"*.[10]

You can see why Satan doesn't want you to grasp this. He knows his fragile position all too well, and works hard to cloud your mind to the promises which are yours in Christ. He is afraid of the moment when you rise up and use them to challenge his pretended authority and to advance God's Kingdom on the earth.[11] He hopes that you will leave them in a box under your bed, or at the very least reduce them to doctrine in your notebook or lines in a song which you sing on Sundays.

Because if you take them out of the box, you will wield an iron sceptre which shatters his kingdom of clay. You will be one of those who overcome, and in whose service God fulfils his great promises to Jesus his Messiah.

[8] Psalm 2:8; Isaiah 49:6.

[9] Isaiah 49:4.

[10] Psalm 2:9.

[11] The *"morning star"* in v. 28 refers to the great star which signals that darkness is about to flee and that day is about to dawn. Jesus tells us in 22:16 that he is the morning star, but he also tells us here that he wants us to share in his promises so that we can shine like him. See also 2 Peter 1:19; Philippians 2:15.

The Key of David (3:7)

These are the words of him who is holy and true, who holds the key of David. What he opens no one can shut, and what he shuts no one can open.

(Revelation 3:7)

On the evening of Monday 25th September 2006, four masked gunmen burst into the home of Marie O'Neill, a few miles north of Dublin. Shouting and brandishing their weapons, they quickly tied up her husband and her two daughters with plastic cables, bundled them into a car and sped off into the night. Left alone, paralysed with fear, Marie O'Neill was about to discover why they had chosen her home that night. It was because she owned a small piece of metal, no more than eight centimetres long, a piece of metal which would furnish her kidnappers with €800,000 before they safely released her family. Marie O'Neill was a bank manager. The piece of metal was her key to the safe of the bank where she worked.

I own keys and you own keys, although none of them are probably worth €800,000. Our keys may well be more beautiful than Marie O'Neill's key, but (thankfully) they aren't worth kidnapping us for. The value of a key depends entirely upon what it is that the key unlocks.

That is why we need to understand what Jesus means when he introduces himself as the one who holds *"the key of David"*. There can be no doubt that he is referring to his great ancestor King David, the first of three clear references in Revelation to him being the *"Son of David"*, the great heir to David's throne, the Messiah promised in the great Davidic Covenant of 2 Samuel 7.[1]

---

[1] For the other two, see Revelation 5:5 and 22:16.

But what does he mean by *"the key of David"*? It's something quite distinct from *"the keys of Death and Hades"*, which he mentioned in Revelation 1:18, so what does he mean? Unless we can answer that question, we cannot gauge the value of the key of David. It might only be as valuable as the key to my garden shed. Or it might be as valuable as Marie O'Neill's bank key... and far more.

In answer to our question, Jesus sends us on a treasure trail.[2] He lays down a clue for us by quoting from Isaiah 22:22 and a prophecy that someone called Eliakim would become King Hezekiah's palace administrator in the last years of the eighth century BC. The Lord promised regarding Eliakim that *"I will place on his shoulder the key to the house of David; what he opens no one can shut, and what he shuts no one can open."* It proved a great promise for Eliakim when his rival Shebna fell and he was awarded his job, but it's a promise which Jesus tells us is only truly fulfilled in himself.[3]

On Eliakim's first day as palace administrator, David's descendant and heir Hezekiah gave him the key to all the treasure rooms of the royal palace. We're not left guessing what King Hezekiah kept in those locked and vaulted treasure rooms. The next stop on our treasure trail is Isaiah 39:2 where Hezekiah foolishly showed off their magnificent contents while bragging to the visiting king of Babylon. We can just imagine Eliakim's first day on the job as he unlocked the doors and examined *"the silver, the gold, the spices, the fine oil, his entire armoury and everything found among his treasures"*. So now we're getting close to grasping the difference it should make for us to know that Jesus holds "the key of David".

No longer is it simply literal *silver and gold*, which fluctuate daily in their value. These Old Testament shadows have been trumped and superseded by the reality of God's Messianic Kingdom. Jesus holds the key to the royal riches of the Kingdom

[2] I am indebted to my friend Stef Liston for starting me off on this treasure trail.

[3] Isaiah 22:25 stresses that Eliakim is only an imperfect picture of the one who will truly fulfil this promise.

of God – the riches of his grace, of his kindness, of his mercy, of his Gospel and of his glory[4] – and he offers them freely to us as *"heirs of God and co-heirs with Christ"*.[5]

Nor is it literal *spices*, since Revelation will continue in 5:8 and 8:3–4 to disclose that this was an Old Testament picture of answered prayer. Jesus assures us seven times in only three chapters in John 14–16 that, if we dwell in him and let him dwell in us, we will most certainly receive whatever we ask for in prayer.[6] Now John sees a mighty picture of the promises he reported in his gospel.

Fine oil had been used in Old Testament times as a picture of someone being anointed with the Holy Spirit, normally as a sign of the Lord appointing a new high priest or king.[7] It was even used as a picture of the Holy Spirit in New Testament times as the disciples anointed people with oil to heal them from their sicknesses, and as James encouraged church elders to anoint with oil any within the church who were sick so that they could be healed.[8] Now Jesus uses this picture to promise us that we can be filled with the Holy Spirit every day to overflowing, so much so that in chapter 22 John will see the Holy Spirit depicted as the *"the river of the water of life"*.

Finally, the *royal armoury* refers to the full armour of God, which Paul lists in Ephesians 6:13–18 and which is God's gift to us to protect us from the Devil's attacks. It also refers to the offensive weapons which the kings of Judah stored up to slaughter their enemies on the battlefield. These include the power of godly character,[9] but they also include the Word of God, the gifts of the Spirit, and the faith which knocked down the walls of Jericho. Truly an arsenal fit for the King.

---

[4] Riches mentioned in Romans 2:4; 9:23; 11:33; Ephesians 1:7, 18; 2:7, 3:8, 16; Philippians 4:19; Colossians 1:27; 2:2.

[5] Romans 8:17.

[6] John 14:13, 14; 15:7, 16; 16:23, 24, 26.

[7] Exodus 29:7; 30:30–31; 1 Samuel 16:13; 1 Chronicles 29:22; 2 Chronicles 23:11.

[8] Mark 6:13; James 5:14–15.

[9] Romans 13:12–14.

Our treasure-hunt through Scripture has revealed Jesus as the True Eliakim, the true holder of the key to God's royal treasure rooms. They contain treasures which make Marie O'Neill's key look really very second-rate. This was the message which the Christians of Philadelphia needed to hear, and it's what we need to hear too.

The Philadelphians were reeling from persecution at the hands of the Jewish leaders, and they were very conscious of their own feeble strength for the fight. Whatever our own troubles and persecution, these words bring terrific comfort when we recognize our weakness.

The truth is that none of us can ever grow strong enough to prevail in the spiritual battle through our own strength. Weakness is actually strength in the fight, because it is only when we admit our own weakness that we can receive Jesus' strength.[10] The persecuted church in Philadelphia was not suffering in spite of Jesus' love, but because of Jesus' love. It was their troubles which lifted their heads to see Jesus, the True Eliakim, and the doors he had opened to the treasure rooms of God's Kingdom. It is often our own troubles which are God's messengers to lift up our heads too.

You will never be a strong enough Christian to receive God's riches, God's answered prayer, God's Spirit or God's weapons through your own strength. But if you can admit your great weakness and confess Christ's great strength, there is nothing to stop you receiving them right now and every day of your life.

In the words of Martin Luther, the sixteenth-century leader of the greatest revival in Europe, when he looked back on his life and sought to explain all that God had done through his efforts: *"First you must become nothing, then consolation and strength will come. This happened to me, Martin Luther, who against my will came up against the whole world, and then God helped me."*[11]

---

[10] 2 Corinthians 12:7–10.

[11] This quotation comes from Martin Luther's commentary on Isaiah and the promise in 40:29–31.

God's Signature (3:12)

I will write on him the name of my God and the name of the city of my God, the new Jerusalem, which is coming down out of heaven from my God; and I will also write on him my new name.

(Revelation 3:12)

Every year the Stanley Gibbons company publishes its suggested price list for stamps and signatures. The 2008 list valued Neil Armstrong's autograph at £5,500, Winston Churchill's at £6,950, Princess Diana's at £8,500, and James Dean's at £9,500. The most expensive item on the list was a photo signed by all four of The Beatles, which changed hands for around £24,500. Autographs can be worth a lot of money.

But the Stanley Gibbons list misses out another collection of signatures, which is worth far more than all the others put together. Jesus tells us here that the most valuable collection of signatures in the world is not written on a photo or an album sleeve, but on us if we persevere as his followers. It's a collection of three names, and it's not "Father, Son, and Holy Spirit" (as we might have expected) but "Father, Son, and Church", as Jesus invites his People to share in his rule.[1] Jewish law demanded two or three witnesses to establish a matter in court, and so Jesus writes three names on his followers to state his promise beyond any doubt.[2] Stanley Gibbons overlook their value, but we must not.

---

[1] A later chapter in this book explores the way that "The New Jerusalem" refers to the Church.

[2] See Deuteronomy 17:6; 19:15. The three signatures may also be linked to the way that Hebrew expresses superlative certainty – for example, "*holy, holy,*

First, a signature speaks of *authenticity*. The famous advert reminded us that *"One hundred years ago, W.K. Kellogg perfected his first cereal. So proud, he signed every box to guarantee it contained his unique recipe. This trusted sign of quality still stands today. So if you don't see Kellogg's on the box, well, it won't be Kellogg's in the box."* There have always been cults, sects and Christless churches which steal credibility by calling themselves "Christians". One of the churches in Asia had *"a reputation for being alive"* but was actually dead, another church contended with *"those who claim to be apostles but are not"*, and two churches struggled with a group of Jews who claimed to be the people of God but were *"the synagogue of Satan"*.[3] The real People of God desperately need his mark of authenticity. He promises to give it them at his Second Coming, but he also promises to give it them now by filling them with his Holy Spirit so that their words and their works can only have come from him.[4]

A signature speaks secondly of *ownership*. If you have seen the *Toy Story* movies, you will remember the honour and gravity which Woody, Buzz Lightyear, and friends pay to the fact that their owner, Andy, has written his name on their feet. His signature is the bedrock of their faith that they are owned, loved, protected and cherished, not destined for a museum or a yard sale. God wants us to savour this promise and to let these three names shape our lives even more than Andy shapes Buzz or Woody's.[5]

Third, a signature communicates *authority*. Every time we sign a cheque, a letter or a legal document, we testify that a message comes in our name. Ancient rulers used signet rings for this purpose, and their wax seal told the recipient that to

---

holy" to mean "*very holy*" in Isaiah 6:3 and Revelation 4:8.

[3] Revelation 2:2, 9; 3:1, 9.

[4] Hebrews 2:3–4; 2 Corinthians 1:21–22; Matthew 25:31–46.

[5] God does far more than promise us that he will write his name on us. He also promises us in Isaiah 49:15–16 that he has our names on his hands. Woody and friends have nothing to compare with this!

ignore the message was to defy the sender.[6] The Philadelphian Christians had *"little strength"* of their own, but Jesus tells them that he will write names of authority on them so that no door will be shut to them.[7] This promise belongs to us too, and we are made into signet rings, inscribed with the names of the Father, the Son and the New Jerusalem, a mark which cannot be resisted.

Jesus is simply telling us explicitly what is stated elsewhere in Scripture implicitly. Jeremiah told us that the Messiah would be called *Yahweh-Tsidkenu* or *The-Lord-Our-Righteousness*, and then he told us that this name would also be given to the New Jerusalem.[8] Ezekiel told us that the name *Yahweh-Shammah* or *The-Lord-Is-There* would not just belong to the Lord but also to his New Jerusalem.[9] Jesus called himself *"the Light of the World"* and then told his People that he had made them *"the Light of the World"*.[10]

When Jesus tells us that he will write these names on us, he means that he will vindicate us for what we are now, not turn us into something that we are not in this present age. God tells us clearly in Jeremiah 33:9 that he has written his names on us already, because his plan for this age is that *"this city will bring me renown, joy, praise and honour before all nations on earth"*. Like the crowns in verse 11 which are ours to lose, God's names are already written on us, and this makes a world of difference. If God is truly on the Throne, and if he writes these three names on us, it has to.

Whatever our past, our sins, our looks, our race, our history or our hang-ups, all of them are superseded by our identity in

---

[6] For example, see Genesis 41:42 or Esther 3:10–12; 8:2; 8:8.

[7] Revelation 3:7.

[8] Jeremiah 23:6; 33:16. The second verse says that this name will be given ***"to her"***. This must refer to the city of Jerusalem, because the Messiah and the "shoot" are both masculine nouns in Hebrew.

[9] Ezekiel 48:35.

[10] John 8:12; 9:5; Matthew 5:14.

Christ. Whatever the demon, the opposition, the sickness or the stronghold, all of them are forced to yield before the authority we have in Christ. God has written his names on us so that *through* us he can assert his rule on earth as the great Shepherd, Saviour, Healer, Forgiver, Deliverer, Helper and Provider. These are not signatures for us to hang on the wall in a picture frame like a signed photo of The Beatles. They are to be on our lips and in our prayers as we prove their value in each day's new battle. Their value did not register with the analysts at Stanley Gibbons, but it must register with us. This is the currency which Christians use to conquer the darkness and to advance the Kingdom of God.

Vomit (3:16)

So, because you are lukewarm, and neither cold not hot, I am about to vomit you out of my mouth.

(Revelation 3:16)[1]

Last week, my wife gave birth to a beautiful baby daughter. I am madly in love with my newborn little girl, but there's something that I just can't get used to: the vomit. I'll spare you the details, but vomit has become such an unpleasant and repulsive part of my daily life that it is just about the last thing I would expect Jesus to mention to one of his churches. He does so because he wants our rapt and urgent attention.[2]

Laodicea, was a church with impeccable credentials. Planted by one of Paul's trainee church-planters in the 50s AD, it had grown to a good size and had even received its own letter from Paul.[3] It was affluent and respectable, well thought of and well respected within the wider Christian community. If it were around today, it would probably export its excellent church programmes around the world, and be about to launch its own TV ministry. That's the background; now for Jesus' verdict. He tells them, in effect, *"you make me sick, and I'm about to vomit you out of my mouth"*.

Some readers assume that Jesus must be telling the

---

[1] Green's Literal Translation.

[2] The Greek word *emeō* means *to vomit*, but most English translations prefer to render it *to spit*. That's still pretty repulsive, but perhaps less so than *to vomit*. Since Jesus chooses to speak about *vomit* to arrest the full attention of the smug and self-deluded church at Laodicea, I think we should translate his words with their full force. After all, we can also get "Laodicean" at times and we need to feel the shock of Jesus' message.

[3] Colossians 4:12–16.

Laodiceans that he would rather they were *"cold"* non-Christians than *"lukewarm"* Christians, because only red-hot Christians are acceptable to him. Other readers (excuse the pun) find it a bit hard to swallow that Jesus should prefer an out-and-out rebel to a half-hearted son, and they have some great background to support their alternative. They tell us that the nearby city of Hierapolis was famous for its hot springs, and that many people bathed in them to be healed of their ailments. Laodicea had neither hot nor cold springs, but only a shallow river which dried up in the summer. By the time the cold water of Colosse passed through the hot viaduct down to Laodicea, it became lukewarm and distasteful. Therefore, they argue, Jesus is telling the Laodiceans that they need to decide to become a *healing* church or a *refreshing* church, but not to dither in the middle without any clear sense of purpose. The problem with both of these views is that they try to understand Revelation in a vacuum, when the rest of Scripture often provides clues to unlock the book's meaning.

Let me take you back to 622 BC and to one of the greatest spiritual revivals of the Old Testament.[4] Its climax was when King Josiah

> *renewed the covenant in the presence of the Lord – to follow the Lord and keep his commands, regulations and decrees with all his heart and all his soul, and to obey the words of the covenant written in this book. Then he made everyone in Jerusalem and Benjamin pledge themselves to it.*[5]

It was an amazing revival, during which the people of Judah made more promises and sang more songs of devotion than at almost any other point in their history. It must have come as a terrible shock to them only ten years later when God gave them

[4] See 2 Kings 23:1–20; 2 Chronicles 34:29–35:18.

[5] 2 Chronicles 34:31–32.

his Old Testament equivalent of Revelation 3:16. He told them shockingly in Jeremiah 3:10–11 that *"Judah did not return to me with all her heart, but only in pretence... Faithless Israel is more righteous than unfaithful Judah."*

The northern kingdom of Israel had never seen any spiritual revival. In fact, they were so wicked that in 722 BC, a full century before Josiah's revival, they were destroyed and exiled by the kings of Assyria. Israel never made a pledge like Judah to follow the Lord with all their heart and soul, and so God lets Judah know what he thinks of their unfulfilled pledges. He tells them that he would have preferred it had they never made them at all, because their subsequent actions have exposed them as lies. This Old Testament precursor to Revelation 3:16 helps us to understand what Jesus is actually saying to the church in Laodicea. He hates it when Christians make great professions of faith but then follow up with cold apathy. He would prefer us to be up front about our spiritual lethargy than to offer him a sickening mixture of fervent promise and half-hearted disobedience. God hates lying. Even lies sung on a Sunday.

Jesus told a story in Matthew 21:28–32 to make sure that we don't miss this message. Do you remember the Parable of the Two Sons, where a father asks both of his sons to work in his vineyard? The first one refuses point blank but later changes his mind and obeys. The second one readily agrees but never turns up for the job. Jesus commends the son who *does* and not the one who merely *promises*, and presses home his clear, unwavering message. He is not impressed by our promises unless we prove them by our lives. False promises simply make him gag and want to vomit us all over his burnished-bronze feet.

So Jesus is not telling you here that he wishes you were a non-Christian, or that he wishes your church had a more decisive mission statement. He is telling you something far more radical and important than that. He is telling you that your actions as a church must live up to the promises you sing on a

Sunday, or else you he would prefer you not to sing at all. At the church I lead, we regularly sing lines such as *"Lord, I give you my heart, I give you my soul; I live for you alone"*. Jesus tells us that, unless we then do as we have sung, our worship meetings make him retch. He gives us two choices: either to scale down the promises we sing on Sunday, or to scale up the way we honour them from Monday to Saturday. Otherwise he will issue the same verdict over our worship services as he did through the prophet Amos: *"'I hate, I despise your religious feasts; I cannot stand your assemblies... Away with the noise of your songs! I will not listen to the music of your harps... Therefore I will send you into exile beyond Damascus,' says the Lord, whose name is God Almighty"*.[6]

One of my friends is involved in a church-plant into the modern Turkish city at Laodicea. As far as we know, this will be the first strong church in the city since Jesus vomited a smug and self-deluded church out of his mouth many centuries ago. My prayer is not just for the new church in Laodicea, but for the churches you and I belong to, that they will not go the way of the old church at Laodicea. Its congregation genuinely thought that God was impressed with their rich professions of devotion, and they had no idea that every Sunday Jesus was struggling not to vomit because of their barefaced lies.

I'm so grateful that Jesus has a second desire which is even stronger than his urge to vomit. He ends his message to Laodicea with a message of great hope. He is knocking on the door of their church, urging them to invite him back inside so that he can eat, drink and fellowship with them. They make him gag and retch, but he would prefer to wine and dine.

Does your church invite Jesus to feast or to vomit? *"Here I am! I stand at the door and knock. If anyone hears my voice and opens the door, I will come in and eat with him, and he with me."*

---

[6] Amos 5:21–27.

Those Whom I Love I Rebuke and Discipline (3:19)

Those whom I love I rebuke and discipline. So be earnest, and repent.

(Revelation 3:19)

One of the most popular reality TV shows in the UK is *Supernanny*.[1] Millions of people watch each episode with voyeuristic pleasure, both appalled and entertained by the undisciplined children and their terrible parents who enlist the Supernanny's help. Here is one example:

Mother: If you do that one more time I will confiscate all your toys.
Daughter: It doesn't matter!
Mother: It does matter, 'cause you won't have anything to play with.
Daughter: I'll buy more toys from the shop!
Mother: And who will pay for them?
Daughter: You.

It's funny but it's also tragic, because the daughter is right. Her mother loves her and thinks the world of her, yet she is unaware that she expresses her love foolishly and destructively. The daughter has learned that if she shouts loudly enough

[1] Supernanny Jo Frost began her show on Britain's Channel 4, but its success has now spread to nearly fifty other countries.

and throws a tantrum, her mother will back down, give in, make concessions, and dance to her tune. The Bible has its own version of *Supernanny* in some of the pages of the Old Testament, and perhaps one of the worst episodes features King David's sons and their indulgent father. Even though he wrote that *"one generation will commend your works to another"*,[2] he failed to master the art of fatherhood, and consistently failed to rebuke or discipline his sons. The consequences are recorded in 2 Samuel, as one son rapes his sister, two other sons die trying to usurp their father's throne, and even the best son becomes a polygamist and an idolater. Sting sang that *"if you love somebody, set them free"*, but David learned the hard way that true love is more complicated than that. Sometimes love means rebuke and discipline.

I'm not particularly advocating Jo Frost's techniques in *Supernanny*. I'm more interested in the words of Jesus, the true and perfect Son of David, who speaks to us here about how God parents those he loves. Jesus is of course speaking from experience, because he is the Son of God. He lived an earthly life under the Father's loving parenting, and it meant being a displaced refugee as a toddler, then enduring temptation, suffering, and agony as an adult, before being tortured and murdered by his enemies.[3] This is not the fate we would have expected for the one the Father described as *"my Son, whom I love; with him I am well pleased"*.[4] It gives us a clue not to expect an easy ride ourselves.

Hebrews explains God's parenting philosophy very simply: *"Although he was a son, he learned obedience from what he*

[2] Psalm 145:4.

[3] Matthew 2:13–20; 4:1–11; 26:37–38; 27:17–50. Note also John's experience, since in Revelation 1:9 he reminds us from exile on Patmos that he is our *"brother and companion in the suffering and kingdom and patient endurance that are ours in Jesus"*.

[4] Matthew 3:17; 17:5.

suffered."[5] The writer wants us to understand that, if discipline was necessary for Jesus, it will certainly be necessary for us too, and so he quotes the words of Proverbs 3:11–12. *"Do not make light of the Lord's discipline, and do not lose heart when he rebukes you, because the Lord disciplines those he loves, and he punishes everyone he accepts as a son."*[6] He encourages us to welcome God's discipline, and even to see it as a mark of true love. He tells us that,

> *If you are not disciplined (and everyone undergoes discipline), then you are illegitimate children and not true sons... God disciplines us for our good, that we may share in his holiness. No discipline seems pleasant at the time, but painful. Later on, however, it produces a harvest of righteousness and peace for those who have been trained by it.*[7]

Jesus is simply taking the consistent teaching of the Old Testament, Gospels and Letters, and restating it in stark and urgent terms.

This teaching does not sit well with the laissez-faire parenting of the Western world, but Jesus is very clear that it is true. Perhaps *Supernanny* even owes some of its success to the fact that deep down we *know* it is true. Children should be disciplined. Parents who love their children do not just set them free. And the God who loves us will not just set us free either.

Jesus' teaching in this verse has major implications for anyone who is blessed with being a parent. I have three children, and even though I have many faults and shortcomings as a father,

---

[5] Hebrews 5:8.

[6] Hebrews 12:5–6.

[7] Hebrews 12:8, 10–11.

I know that if it were not for the teaching of Scripture, I would have many, many more.[8]

It also has major implications for anyone involved in church leadership, whether they lead a whole church or just a home group. If God's love for us is expressed by rebuke, confrontation, challenge and discipline, this must shape how we lead our churches. Sting's song tells us that *love equals tolerance*, but Jesus warns us that no one can ever pastor a church that way. Shepherds hold crooks, which are basically big sticks for reminding sheep that they are not shepherds and for hooking them back out of harm's way. If God has made you a shepherd – whether of twelve or twelve hundred – you need to pick up your crook and use it for the good of the sheep.[9]

But the main message which Jesus conveys to us as Christians in this verse is that we must expect and rejoice in his discipline. His plan for us is massive, because he intends for us to share his Throne and to rule over the universe with him.[10] Unsurprisingly, we are going to need training for this, and Jesus wants us to embrace rebuke and discipline as modules in his school of leadership. The church at Laodicea was so far from being ready to rule with Christ that only his discipline would bring her to repentance and save her from being vomited out of his mouth. God has a tailored training programme for each one of us too, and we should submit to his rebuke and discipline cheerfully and obediently.

Although verse 20 has been much used as a Gospel verse for non-Christians, Jesus speaks it primarily to Christians. *"Here I am! I stand at the door and knock. If anyone hears my voice and*

---

[8] Just for starters, I am very grateful for the direction of verses like Proverbs 13:24; 19:18; 22:15; 23:13–14; 29:15, 17. These verses need some unpacking, and Christians disagree about what the word *"rod"* justifies in our culture. This thorny question is tackled in my book *Straight to the Heart of Solomon*.

[9] Acts 20:28 is one of the scariest verses for church leaders in the whole Bible. The church is God's flock, so any shepherd he appoints within it must lead it his way or not at all.

[10] Revelation 3:21.

opens the door, I will come in and eat with him, and he with me." Jesus is beating on the door of our lives with his rod of discipline. We must not complain about the banging, but recognize it as a fatherly knock on the door of our hearts. If we welcome his discipline and yield to his knock, we will feed our souls on the instruction he brings. We will find ourselves ready to reign with him forever.

The Vision of Heaven

Twenty-Four Plus Four (4:1–11)

Surrounding the throne were twenty-four other thrones, and seated on them were twenty-four elders. They were dressed in white and had crowns of gold on their heads... Around the throne were four living creatures.

(Revelation 4:4, 6)

Even apostles get lost for words sometimes. It happens quite a lot to John in the book of Revelation. When he recalled his vision of Jesus in chapter 1, he told us that he turned to *see* his voice.[1] Now words fail him even more in chapters 4 and 5 as he describes his vision of heaven. There is a *green rainbow* around God's Throne. There is a group of elders who are seated on thrones yet constantly bowing down on their faces, and who wear gold crowns on their heads yet are continually throwing them at God's feet.[2] Confused yet? John will make sure you are by the end of the vision, when he tells us that there is half an hour of silence in a room where noisy worship never ceases.[3] John is not trying to help religious artists to paint these scenes. He is trying to convey feelings rather than sights, and to stir our hearts to prepare us for the rest of Revelation.

Jesus has already given us one overview of AD history in chapters 2 and 3, but there are five more to come, and they

---

[1] Revelation 1:12.

[2] Revelation 4:3, 4, 10.

[3] Try reconciling Revelation 4:8 with 8:1. I think John had a lot of fun trying to describe what he saw.

will strike terror in our hearts.[4] A new believer came to me two weeks ago in a state of shock and horror because he had started reading the Bible. For some reason, he had started with Revelation, and he was so terrified that he had to stop reading. Jesus is about to show us the history which *"must take place after this"*,[5] but before he can do so, he knows that we need to see a vision of heaven to add to our vision of him in 1:12–18. We need to see God sitting on a Throne so unshakeable that the moat around it is as calm as glass and as pure as crystal. We need to see God holding the Book of World History, unlocking its events one by one through the blood of his Son. We need to hear resounding songs of glory, praise and worship to the Ruler of History. Only if we have seen God's throne-room will we be ready for all that is to come.

Around God's Throne are twenty-four elders ruling with him. They are seated on thrones and have crowns on their heads, but they are completely submitted to the great Throne of God. There were twelve tribes of Israel and twelve disciples of Jesus, so we are meant to recognize the twenty-four elders as the People of God in both BC and AD history.[6] This will be stated more explicitly when heaven descends to earth in 21:12–14, with the twelve tribes of Israel and the twelve apostles of Christ forming its gates and foundations, but it is important that we grasp it here. It's also important that we grasp that this represents what is happening now in heaven and not just in the future (otherwise 5:1–5 makes no sense whatsoever), and that the twenty-four elders include us as well as our apostles (otherwise Moses, Aaron, and rest of the Levites are excluded from Christ's rule, since Levi was not one of the twelve tribal territories of Israel). This symbolism prepares us for five more horrific overviews of

---

[4] The five remaining overviews of AD history are in chapters 6–7, 8–11, 12–14, 15–16, and 17–20.

[5] Revelation 4:1.

[6] See also Jesus' words in Matthew 19:28. This symbolism of *12 + 12 = 24* becomes *12 × 12 × 1000 = 144,000* when describing the People of God in 7:4.

AD history by giving us an important fact to sustain us in it. God is on the Throne, and we are on thrones ruling with him.[7]

Alongside the twenty-four elders are four living creatures. We are meant to match their descriptions immediately to those of the four cherubim-angels which Ezekiel saw in his vision of heaven in 593 BC,[8] and we are meant to recognize their song as that of the seraphim-angels which Isaiah saw in 740 BC.[9] So angels lead the worship choruses of heaven, and when God's People hear them sing, they fall down on their faces and worship him too.

The vision of heaven reminds us that God's Throne is the control room of history. There are only twenty-five verses in chapters 4 and 5, but the Greek word *thronos,* or *throne,* occurs a massive nineteen times. Like those who saw God in the Old Testament, John tells us very little about the appearance of God himself, but conveys his indescribable glory by describing the immeasurable magnificence of all those who surround him.[10] The elders and living creatures worship him as the eternal God, who not only made the world but sustains it too. We need not fear. God is on the Throne.

The vision also reminds us of who we are in heaven. We live on earth, but we have also been *"seated in the heavenly realms in Christ Jesus"*.[11] The world may sneer at the Gospel and ravage the Church, but we rule with Christ and we will prevail.

---

[7] Another clue that these events are happening now is the Greek word *ekporeuontai* in 4:5. This is a present tense, which means that lightning *is coming forth* from the throne. It's present tense because it's happening in the present.

[8] See Ezekiel 1:4–14, where four similar living creatures are also covered with eyes. The main difference is that each of John's four living creatures have the face of either a man, a lion, an ox or an eagle, while each of Ezekiel's four living creatures have all four faces.

[9] See Isaiah 6:1–6 where those angels also have six wings and sing the song *"Holy, holy, holy is the Lord God Almighty."* This phrase, *"holy, holy, holy"*, appears nowhere in Scripture except for Isaiah 6 and Revelation 4.

[10] Compare this with Exodus 24:9–10 and Ezekiel 1:26–28, where the writers also try to communicate the indescribable majesty of God by describing the brilliant glory of the lesser objects that surround him.

[11] Ephesians 2:6.

Finally, the vision also reminds us of how we are to live on earth. Christians pray *"Your kingdom come, your will be done on earth as it is in heaven"*,[12] and part of the answer to that prayer is in our own hands. We must be *worshippers*, in the good times and the bad, because God's praise deserves our every breath, and to give less than he deserves is to steal from the One Who Sits On the Throne. We are encouraged in our worship by the knowledge that our songs are fused together with those of the angels as sweet perfume to him.[13]

We must be *humble*, recognizing that our victory crowns make us more, and not less, indebted to God. Every soul we ever led to Christ, every church we ever planted, every victory we ever won for the Kingdom of God, is simply another object to lay at his feet in worship.[14] He not only stooped to save us, but stooped again to use us, so he is worthy of even more praise! We must let this vision rebuke and silence all our petty pride.

We must be *confident*, knowing that we reign with Christ and that none of Satan's schemes can defeat us. Armies assert great efforts before a battle to ensure that they possess the high ground from which to wield an advantage. Jesus shows us that we already have the highest ground of all, reigning in heaven as we battle on earth. That's why we must not rush into the overviews of earthly history without first feasting our eyes on the vision of heaven. We will get wounded and may even die in the fight, but we have already won the victory.

We have seen the control room of heaven. God is there and so are we. We are prepared for all that life has in store for us.

---

[12] Matthew 6:10.

[13] Revelation 5:8.

[14] *Stephanos* is the word used by the Greeks for the *victory wreaths* they presented to the winners of their sporting contests. It is used for the crowns worn by the elders in Revelation 4, and also in Revelation 2:10; 3:11; 1 Corinthians 9:25; 2 Timothy 4:8; James 1:12; 1 Peter 5:4. All our victories belong to God.

The Scroll of History (5:1)

Then I saw in the right hand of him who sat on the throne a scroll with writing on both sides and sealed with seven seals.

(Revelation 5:1)

Two of my friends are Iraqis living in England, and earlier this month they planned the holiday of a lifetime. They loaded their suitcases and drove to meet the cruise liner at Southampton docks, discussing excitedly the sights they would see from Barcelona round to Cyprus. They handed their passports and visas to the travel rep, passed her their £6,000 non-refundable tickets, and then listened in horror as she broke the bad news to them. Iraqi citizens need visas to cruise around Europe, and some of their visas were missing. They protested, pleaded and begged her to let them travel anyway, but they finally reloaded their car and drove silently home. They both cried. A lot.

I wonder what makes you cry? Would this have brought you to tears too? If we multiply what my Iraqi friends felt several times over, we will come close to what John felt halfway through his vision of heaven.

In the midst of the loud worship of chapter 4, John caught sight of a scroll in God's right hand, and he recognized it as the Book of History, which was mentioned by the *One Like a Son of Man* in Daniel 10:21.[1] This book had predicted the rise and fall of empires in chapter 11, from Alexander the Great's victory

---

[1] Jesus refers to it in Daniel 10:21 as *"the Book of Truth"* or *"the True [Royal] Edict"*. This is *not* the same scroll as the Lamb's *Book of Life*, which appears in Daniel 12:1 and in Revelation 3:5; 13:8; 17:8; 20:12, 15; 21:27. That book records the names of those who will be saved throughout history, whereas the

over Persia in 331 BC to the Roman conquest of Palestine in 63 BC.[2] God now held the same book in his hand, but this time it was sealed firmly shut.

John saw writing on both sides of the Scroll of History, as a sign that God's plans for human history are complete and detailed.[3] They include judgments as listed in chapter 6, and God's great salvation story as described in chapter 7. John already knew some of the contents from his years as a disciple of Jesus,[4] but he craved much more revelation. Like my Iraqi friends, beaming with expectation, he awaited the grand unveiling of world history which would carry on where Daniel 11 left off. A mighty angel cried out *"Who is worthy to break the seals and open the scroll?"* Then heaven fell ominously silent. With horror many times greater than the scene at Southampton docks, John was suddenly granted a vision of what world history would be like if it were not for Christ.

We live in an age where anything is tolerated except intolerance, and where every faith is relative except for the belief that every faith is relative. John's vision shows us just how foolish such thinking is. Among those who had died by the time John saw this vision were Mary the Mother of Jesus and most of the apostles of the Early Church, and yet none of these was worthy to break the seals on the Book of History to unfold God's plans for judgment and salvation. Abraham, Moses, David, Elijah and all the other heroes of Judaism were also there, but none of them was worthy to break the seals either. As for other

Book of Truth records the events and judgments which take place throughout history.

[2] David also mentions the Book on a more personal level in Psalm 139:16.

[3] This Book of History, filled with God's judgments, also appears in Ezekiel 2:9–10 and Zechariah 5:1–3. Both times it is pictured as complete and detailed. Ezekiel's scroll flouted convention by being written on both sides. Zechariah's scroll measured a massive thirty feet long by fifteen feet wide!

[4] Jesus prophesied frequently about the events which would take place between his Ascension and his Second Coming. See Matthew 24 for a good example.

religions, the Buddha had already died of dysentery in India and passed into the afterlife, but he was found unworthy too.[5] John's vision silences our philosophical debate over the question *"do all religions save?"* and records God's own definitive answer. When John saw the Scroll of History in God's hand, and grasped that *"no religion saves"*, he broke down and wept.

We should not be surprised that no other religious figure was found worthy to unleash God's judgments and his plan of salvation. No sinner could ever do so, and even the best of men and women are men and women at best. In the New Testament, Mary confesses her need for a Saviour, and Paul calls himself *"the worst of sinners"*.[6] In the Qur'an, Muhammad admits that he is a sinner,[7] and other religious teachers must do so too.

If John's vision of heaven demonstrates anything, it is that no amount of religious ritual, ceremony or devotion can ever truly satisfy the living God. Like a man who hopes to pay off his £5,000 credit card bill with repayments of £1 a month, the sights of chapter 8 destroy any last vestige of hope that even the most devout religious leader people could ever be worthy to unleash God's salvation. Muhammad admits this in the Qur'an when he confesses that *"I am nothing new among the prophets; I do not know what will happen to me and to my followers; I am only a plain warner"*.[8] The early apostles confessed this more explicitly when the writer to the Hebrews says that *"without the shedding*

[5] Some Buddhists feel that it detracts from the Buddha's greatness if he succumbed to sickness, so they argue that he died in c. 483 BC of a gastric problem linked to old age rather than of dysentery. At least we can agree on three facts: he ate some kind of pork or mushroom, he died of gastric difficulty, and he stayed dead. No one claims that he rose from the dead. The best Buddhists can offer is a temple in Sri Lanka devoted to a relic of one of his teeth.

[6] Luke 1:47; 1 Timothy 1:15.

[7] The Qur'an 48:2. Many Muslims are surprised by this verse since they are taught that the prophets did not sin. They grasp instinctively that they need a perfect, sinless Saviour, but their own scriptures show them that they are looking towards the wrong man.

[8] The Qur'an 46:9.

of blood there is no forgiveness", and when Peter confesses about Jesus that *"Salvation is found in no one else, for there is no other name under heaven given to men by which we must be saved."*[9]

We need to grasp what John saw because it is the basis upon which we can answer the religious pluralism of our own day. John's vision passed a definitive verdict upon the Roman gods and the Eastern mysticism of the first century, and on Islam, Buddhism, Judaism, and the other religions of our own day. John did not see in Christianity a religion better than all the rest; he saw in Christ the only true Saviour. John saw that no one was worthy except for the *"Lamb, looking as if it had been slain, standing in the centre of the throne"*.

Jesus was in the centre of the Throne because he is not a mere man working his way to God from earth, but is as much God as the Father who sits on the Throne in 4:2 and as the Holy Spirit who blazes before the Throne in 4:5.[10] He does not just bridge the gap between human beings and God because he is the best of men, but because he is both man and God. He was not just found worthy because he lived a better life than the pretenders, but because *"you were slain, and with your blood you purchased men for God"*.[11] He is the only one who has offered an acceptable sacrifice for our sins. He is not simply top of the league, but a league unto himself.

This scene is the foundation of the Gospel. It is only when we pass through the weeping of 5:1–4 that we can enjoy the sweet rejoicing of 5:5–14. It is only when we understand that there is no Saviour but Jesus that we can truly rejoice in Jesus the Saviour.

The glory of the Gospel is that God has wept with John and has turned tragedy into triumph. He has done as he promised in

---

[9] Hebrews 9:22; Acts 4:12.

[10] Apocalyptic literature in the Bible uses the number *seven* to refer to *completeness* or *perfection*. Therefore the *seven spirits of God* is probably a symbolic way of referring to the *Holy Spirit of God*.

[11] Revelation 5:9.

Isaiah 59:16: *"He saw that there was no one, he was appalled that there was no one to intervene; so his own arm worked salvation for him, and his own righteousness sustained him."*

This message of salvation is so glorious that in verse 11 a hundred million angels rejoice over it. If you've truly understood the implications of what John saw here, you will want to worship with them too.

The Lion of the Tribe of Judah (5:5)

Then one of the elders said to me, "Do not weep! See, the Lion of the tribe of Judah, the Root of David, has triumphed. He is able to open the scroll and its seven seals.

(Revelation 5:5)

My children love to play the game *Guess Who?* If you've never played it, it's very easy to learn. Each player chooses a card with one of twenty-four faces, and then they take it in turns to ask simple questions to guess which face is on their opponent's card. *"Does your person have blue eyes?"* asks the first child, before flipping over tiles to eliminate any faces with brown eyes on his board. *"Is your person wearing glasses?"* asks the other, before flipping over several tiles on her own board. Eventually, one player has a single tile face remaining. He asks *"Is your person Theo?"* before emitting loud shrieks of glee when he discovers that he has won.

It's a great game, and even God likes to play it. He doesn't use a board, though, he uses the Bible. And he hasn't pulled a card at random. He reveals the identity of his Messiah, slowly but surely, throughout the Old Testament. Join me for the game so that we can celebrate together the wonderful meaning of Revelation 5:5.

In Genesis 3:15, God simply reveals that there is a Messiah. He calls him *"the seed of Eve"*, barely narrowing down his identity at all, but to Adam and Eve who had just sinned and fallen, this was a sweet promise of salvation. Later in Genesis, he revealed that this Messiah would be a descendant of Abraham, an idolater from Ur of the Chaldees.[1] Later still, that this descendant would come through Abraham's son Isaac and his grandson Jacob, rather than through their elder brothers.[2] All this to the sound of tiles being flipped over on the Messianic *Guess Who?* board.

Then, at the end of the book of Genesis, something surprising happens. It is no surprise that Jacob's favourite son Joseph is chosen to receive the double inheritance of a firstborn, but it is very unexpected when Jacob proclaims from his deathbed that it would be through *Judah*, not Joseph, that the Messiah would come into the world. Judah's brothers would all bow down to him, the Gentile nations would submit to his rule, and his tribe would steward the royal sceptre until the appearance of *the One to Whom it Belongs.*[3] Still reeling from this unexpected honour, Judah hears his father liken his tribe to a lion, a lioness, and a lion's cub. The kings of Israel would come from his tribe, and he would be the ancestor of the great Lion, the Messianic King.

Over 800 years passed before God's next great clue. Laying hold of the prophet Samuel, he narrowed down the field to only one family in Judah by telling him that *"I am sending you to Jesse of Bethlehem. I have chosen one of his sons to be king."*[4] What follows is Samuel's quick-fire round of *Guess Who?*, which eliminates each of Jesse's sons until only the youngest son, David, is left. Sure enough, within several years he is made king of all Israel and founds a great royal dynasty. God has yet another surprise in store when he tells David that his oldest son will not succeed him as heir. His young son Solomon is to be the next king and the ancestor of the Messiah.[5]

The house of David ruled in Jerusalem for 400 years, and

---

[1] Genesis 22:18; Galatians 3:16; Joshua 24:2–3.

[2] Genesis 21:12; 25:21–23.

[3] Genesis 49:8–12. See also Genesis 48; 1 Chronicles 5:1–2.

[4] 1 Samuel 16:1.

[5] 1 Chronicles 28:5–7.

for much of the time they were so wicked that it looks like we've flipped over the wrong tiles. Yet the Old Testament prophets who rebuke them for their sin also promise that a greater King is coming to David's house who will rule in justice and righteousness. He will bring God's promised salvation to people from every nation. Isaiah prophesies that the Messiah will shoot up as *"the Root of Jesse"* from *"the stump of Jesse"* and that he will *"reign on David's throne"* forever.[6] Micah adds that he will be born in David's home town of Bethlehem,[7] and Jeremiah and Ezekiel also speak of him as a *"Branch"* who will come from David's line and rule forever on his throne.[8] Unless we understand this background to the New Testament, we simply won't grasp the cry of delight in its first verse when Matthew announces the coming of *"Jesus Christ the Son of David"*,[9] or the reason why the gospels refer sixteen times to Jesus as *"the Son of David"*.

The first verse of the New Testament is where God ends his game of Messianic *Guess Who?* by revealing the face on his card. Revelation 5:5 is a cry of delight at what that means for us. Jesus is *"the Lion of the tribe of Judah"* in Jacob's deathbed prophecy. Jesus is *"the Root of David"* promised by the prophets.[10] Jesus is the one who has conquered sin and death, and whose revealed identity now wipes every tear from our eyes.[11]

It's not just that Jesus has a face which matches God's clues – he has the only face. Of the babies who were born to the tribe of Judah in Bethlehem,[12] only he went on to fulfil the other

---

[6] Isaiah 9:7; 11:1, 10. See also Isaiah 16:5.

[7] Micah 5:2. Note that even the chief priests and teachers of the law understood this clue in Matthew 2:1–6.

[8] Jeremiah 23:5; 33:15; Ezekiel 37:24–25.

[9] Matthew 1:1.

[10] Jesus expands on this title in Revelation 22:16 and says that he is in fact *"the Root and Offspring of David"*.

[11] Revelation 5:5; 7:17.

[12] The genealogies in Matthew 1:1–17 and Luke 3:23–38 are there in such detail to demonstrate Jesus' pure lineage from Judah on both Mary and Joseph's sides. They are his biological and his legal genealogies. Bethlehem was a small

300 predictions about the Messiah. Only he was brought up in Egypt and Nazareth before riding into Jerusalem on a donkey to be crucified, buried, and then raised to life.[13] Furthermore, God has packed up his *Guess Who?* game and put it back in the box, because all of the genealogical records were lost when Jerusalem was destroyed in AD 70. No Jew since then has ever been able to demonstrate convincingly which tribe he is from. God makes it very clear to them and to us that it's *game over*. It's no use waiting, because the Messiah has already come. The face on the card belongs to Jesus of Nazareth.

This is why God's game of *Guess Who?* is more than just child's play. When one of the elders tells John that Jesus is *"the Lion of the tribe of Judah"*, he is proclaiming that Jesus is God's Saviour and Deliverer who was promised in the Old Testament and revealed in the New. He is explaining that, within hours of Adam and Eve's sin, the reason God could promise Jesus' coming was that he had planned it before the creation of the world.[14] He is proclaiming that God is so sovereign that Satan's attempts to thwart his plan have not only failed but played into his hands. He is telling us that the Lord of BC history can also be trusted in the dark hours of AD history.

Satan has a throne, but God's Throne is far greater.[15] Nothing can stop the seed of Eve, the seed of Abraham, the Son of David, the Lion of the tribe of Judah – whatever name we use for him – from crushing Satan's head. *"Do not weep! See, the Lion of the tribe of Judah, the Root of David, has triumphed."*

---

town, yet Luke 2:4–11 confirms that Jesus was born there in fulfilment of Micah 5:2.

[13] Hosea 11:1; Judges 13:5; Zechariah 9:9; 12:10 fulfilled in Matthew 2:15, 22–23; 21:6–9; John 19:34–37.

[14] Genesis 3:15. See also 1 Peter 1:19–20; 2 Timothy 1:9–10; Ephesians 1:4; Titus 1:2–3; Revelation 13:8.

[15] Revelation 2:13; 13:2; 16:10.

Kings and Priests (5:10)

You have made them to be a kingdom and priests to serve our God, and they will reign on the earth.

(Revelation 5:10)

The kings of Israel were expressly forbidden from acting as priests. King Saul ignored this and it cost him his kingdom. King Uzziah did the same and was struck down with leprosy.[1] God chose his kings from the tribe of Judah and his priests from the tribe of Levi. It was the ancient Israelite "separation of powers".

But it had not always been this way. Deep in the recesses of patriarchal history, a king named Melchizedek ruled in Jerusalem, serving the Lord as both king and priest. David later used him in Psalm 110 as a picture of the coming Messiah, and the writer to the Hebrews does so in great detail.[2] The Messiah would receive the kingship and the priesthood, uniting both elements of the hope of Israel in one person. There would be no more "separation of powers" when the Messiah came, because he could be entrusted with all power and authority. He would be the supreme and eternal Priest and King.

We can read more about this in Hebrews, and it stirs our hearts to worship, but it's only half the story. God shared the other half at Mount Sinai when he told Israel that his plan was also to make them into *"a kingdom of priests and a holy nation"*. Peter talks about it further when he quotes those words in one of his letters and applies them to the Church.[3]

Scripture phrases this concept in different ways, but they

---

[1] 1 Samuel 13:8–14; 2 Chronicles 26:16–21.

[2] Genesis 14:18–20; Hebrews 5:1–10; 6:20–10:22.

[3] Exodus 19:6; 1 Peter 2:9.

all amount to the same thing. In Exodus it is *"a kingdom of priests"*, in 1 Peter it is *"a royal priesthood"*, in Revelation 1:6 and 5:10 it is *"a kingdom and priests"*. Some Greek manuscripts of Revelation 5:10 actually phrase it most simply of all, as *"kings and priests"*.[4] Having told us in 2:26–27 that the Messianic promises of the Old Testament also belong to us, Jesus now gets specific and tells us that this one does too. The role of King and Priest are not simply united in him. He also wants to unite them in us as we serve him as *kings and priests* every day.

Old Testament priests and kings were meant to pray for the people. The priest did this as he offered incense before the Lord both day and night,[5] bearing the names of the twelve tribes of Israel on his breastplate and on his shoulders.[6] The king did so too, both in the good times and in the bad.[7]

The priests were to emerge from God's presence as his mouthpiece to speak his instructions, commands, blessings, and curses to the world with the authority which comes from having stood before his Throne.[8] The kings were to rule as custodians of that Throne, bringing God's justice to evildoers and raising an army to lead into battle.[9] God's plan was that his priests and kings would reflect his glory and cause both Israel and the Gentiles to serve the Lord. It was a plan which worked brilliantly under godly priests like Aaron, Phinehas and Jehoiada, and under godly kings like David, Solomon, Hezekiah

---

[4] Most modern English translations follow the Nestle-Aland text which reads *"a kingdom and priests"*, but the Byzantine and Textus Receptus manuscripts read *basileis kai hiereis*, which simply means *"kings and priests"*.

[5] Exodus 30:7–8. See the chapter on "Incense" for more on this.

[6] Exodus 28:9–21.

[7] Solomon prayed in the good times in 1 Kings 8:54. Hezekiah prayed in the bad times in 2 Kings 19:14–20.

[8] Leviticus 10:8–11; Numbers 6:22–27; Deuteronomy 31:9–13.

[9] 1 Kings 8:55–60; 1 Chronicles 29:23; 1 Samuel 8:20.

and Josiah.[10] But, generally, the priests and kings of Israel and Judah failed to rise to their calling.

The issue was self-centredness, or sin. The kings acted as consumers, as if the world revolved around them and they had no responsibility from the Lord towards their subjects.[11] The priests, in turn, also acted as consumers, abusing the priesthood for personal gain and daring to tamper with the message God told them to speak to the world.[12] By the time the Messiah came, the priests despised their divine calling to such a degree[13] that they led the people to reject and crucify the Son of God.[14]

This is where we can slip up too. God's plan is to unite the kingship and the priesthood in Jesus the Messiah, and then to recruit an army of *"kings and priests"*, ready not just to be the People of God but also to pray, preach, teach, proclaim, bless, curse, fight and protect. He wants an army of missionaries, starting on our knees, crying out to him for the needs of the world and for more of his Spirit, and then rising from our knees to bring salvation and justice from the Church to the world. We should not be so foolish as to think we are immune to the failings of the kings and priests of Israel. Christian consumerism is a spiritual cancer in the Church too. In the words of songwriter Keith Green:

Do you see? Do you see all the people sinking down?
Don't you care? Don't you care? Are you gonna let them drown?
How can you be so numb, not to care if they come?

[10] Even Solomon, who presided over the "golden age of Israel", was only godly for the first half of his reign.

[11] See Jeremiah 21:1–23:8, and especially the description of their consumerism in 22:13–17. This passage culminates in the revelation of the coming Messiah as the great King who would rule justly.

[12] 1 Samuel 2:12–17; Malachi 2:7–8; Ezekiel 22:26.

[13] See Matthew 27:3–10 for an example of their hypocrisy. Luke 10:31 also shows their prevalent attitude.

[14] John 19:6, 15.

You close your eyes and pretend the job's done.

Bless me Lord, bless me Lord. You know, it's all I ever hear.
No one aches, no one hurts, no one even sheds one tear,
But he cries, he weeps, he bleeds, and he cares for your needs,
And you just lay back and keep soaking it in.

Can't you see it's such a sin?
The world is sleeping in the dark that the church just can't fight
'Cause it's asleep in the light.
How can you be so dead, when you've been so well fed?
Don't close your eyes and pretend the job's done.[15]

Jesus Christ is the great King and Priest, but he has also made us into a whole nation of kings and priests under him. The picture of the twenty-four elders on thrones reminds us this that is true. The question for our generation is whether we will sleep in the light or rise up to fulfil our royal priestly calling. If we do then, like the Israelite kings and priests at their best, we will *turn many back from sin*. If we do not, we will repeat their sins at their worst, and we will *turn people from the way and into sin.*[16] God has deliberately tied the fate of the nations to the faithfulness of his People.

Let's be those who lay hold of our calling, like Paul who described his passion in Romans 15:16 as *"to be a minister of Christ Jesus to the Gentiles with the priestly duty of proclaiming the gospel of God, so that the Gentiles might become an offering acceptable to God, sanctified by the Holy Spirit"*.

---

[15] Keith Green "Asleep in the Light" (Sparrow Records, 1979).

[16] Malachi 2:6, 8.

The Lamb Who Was Slain (5:12)

Worthy is the Lamb, who was slain, to receive power and wealth and wisdom and strength and honour and glory and praise!

(Revelation 5:12)

People in every culture share a common instinct when they become conscious of sin. They offer a sacrifice to appease their god's anger before they draw his wrath. Romans and Russians, Aztecs and Australians, Indians and Israelis, Babylonians and Britons, all have this in common. They offer gifts to the one they worship in order to appease his wrath and secure his blessing.

There may seem to be a world of difference between the Greek king Agamemnon sacrificing his daughter to the goddess Artemis, the Hindu king Ravana amputating parts of his body to appease the god Shiva,[1] a Pakistani Muslim fasting at Ramadan or making a pilgrimage to Mecca, and a secular Westerner telling herself that *"I'm a good person"* and *"if there is a God then I'm sure he'll forgive me"*, but there isn't really. They are all doing the same thing in the clothing of their own culture. They are all offering their god the sacrificial gift which they think he requires from them – whether blood sacrifice, self-mutilation, religion, or good works.

It's no surprise, then, that the Bible is full of instruction about what kind of sacrifice the real God, Yahweh, wants from people, and which kinds he does not. On the first day that Adam

---

[1] These two events occur in Homer's *Iliad* and the Sanskrit epic *The Ramayana* respectively.

and Eve sinned, they tried to guess the right sacrifice to bring. They covered their nakedness with garments of fig leaves, and tried to hide their sin with the work of their own hands. God taught them two lessons that evening. First, he rejected their man-made clothes and gave them fur clothing of his own, bought at the price of killing an animal for the first time in Eden. Second, despite the fact that they had accumulated many good deeds during their sinless lives in the Garden of Eden, they were banished from Paradise on the basis of one sinful deed.[2] Act One of God's great drama left them in no doubt that there is only one sacrifice that pleases him. It's not good deeds and it's not man-made religion. It's the blood of an innocent sacrifice.

The book of Genesis continues this important theme, as God shows each generation the sacrifice he requires. When Cain offers crops and Abel sacrifices a lamb, the Lord expects Cain to know why his offering is rejected. He asks him *"Why are you angry? Why is your face downcast? If you do what is right, will you not be accepted?"*[3] God told Cain that blood must be shed for the forgiveness of sin, and he seems to have taught Noah this lesson too.[4] Abraham's many altars show that he understood this as well, and God explained it most clearly to him when he provided a sheep to die in the place of his son Isaac.[5]

The Lord taught the Hebrews this lesson in more detail when he gave them the Law at Mount Sinai. The book of Leviticus is not for the faint-hearted, with more bloodshed and slaughter than a Quentin Tarantino movie. God tells the Israelites to slaughter goats, rams, ewes, lambs, bulls and even pigeons to atone for sin and to receive his blessing. He instructs them to offer blood sacrifices on big feast days like Passover and

[2] Genesis 3:7, 21.

[3] Genesis 4:3–7.

[4] Genesis 8:20–22. Noah took extra animals on the ark because he knew the Lord wanted blood sacrifices.

[5] Genesis 12:7–8; 13:4, 18; 22:9–13. The Hebrew word for altar in all of these verses is *mizbēach*, which means specifically an *altar of blood sacrifice*.

the Day of Atonement, and to do so at sunrise and sundown on the other days too.[6] He explains that *"the life of a creature is in the blood, and I have given it to you to make atonement for yourselves on the altar"*.[7] Reliance upon blood sacrifice, not on good works, therefore stood at the heart of the Hebrew religion, celebrated in both Tabernacle and Temple for 1,500 years of Jewish history.

Hold on a minute, we might complain. *How can killing an innocent lamb or goat atone for my sin?* The prophet David's shocking answer is that it can't – at least not by itself. He argues in Psalm 40:6–8 that even though the Lord told people to sacrifice goats and bulls at his altar, they were only effective because they pointed to the true atoning Sacrifice, which would come in the future.[8] The prophet Isaiah links this to the Messiah and tells us that he would atone for sin by being *"led like a lamb to the slaughter"*.[9]

That's why when John the Baptist proclaimed in 27 AD that Jesus of Nazareth was *"the Lamb of God, who takes away the sin of the world"*, those who heard him concluded that this might be the Messiah.[10] It's what Paul means when he refers to *"Christ, our Passover lamb"* and what Peter means when he speaks of *"the precious blood of Christ, a lamb without blemish or defect"*.[11] It's also what John means here when he speaks of *"the Lamb who was slain"*, and it's why he uses the Greek word for *Lamb* twenty-nine times in Revelation as a name for Jesus.

He is telling us that the ultimate proof that God is not satisfied with good works, man-made religion, self-mutilation, and even the sacrifice of animals is that he gave his Son to die as the *Lamb*

---

6 Exodus 12:1–14; Leviticus 16:1–34; Numbers 28:1–8.

7 Leviticus 17:11.

8 When the New Testament quotes this verse in Hebrews 10:4–7, it uses a variant reading of the Greek Septuagint to emphasize that David was speaking words on behalf of Jesus the Messiah, and that the sacrifice they pointed to was the *body* of Jesus.

9 Isaiah 53:5–7.

10 John 1:29, 36, 41, 45.

11 1 Corinthians 5:7; 1 Peter 1:19.

of God to atone for our sins. He is telling us that Jesus was the only reason why the Jewish sacrifices were ever effective, and that there is no sacrifice left on earth through which people can be forgiven except for the once-for-all sacrifice which Jesus made on the cross.[12] He is telling us that Jesus' sacrifice guarantees forgiveness to the rankest and most habitual of sinners.

Many non-Christians struggle to believe that God could truly forgive them, and many Christians struggle to believe that he has truly done so. Nine times out of ten, this is because they have not grasped the truth of this verse. If forgiveness came from *religious activity*, they would indeed be right. Their works would be totally insufficient to secure their forgiveness, and no amount of discipline would change that. If forgiveness came from *good works*, they would also be right. If Adam and Eve had not accrued enough good deeds in Eden, we can be pretty sure that we will not either, no matter how hard we try to pull our socks up. But if forgiveness comes through the shed blood of Jesus, God's perfect blood sacrifice, our hope is entirely different.

The reason why Christians and non-Christians who are convicted of their sin struggle to accept God's offer of complete forgiveness is that deep down they know that what they have done is too sinful to be swept under the carpet. The fact that Jesus is the Lamb means it hasn't been. Our confidence is based not on the fact that God has ignored our sin, but that he has carried our sin. The elders and the angels sing that *"you were slain, and **with your blood you purchased** people for God"*.[13]

Jesus Christ is not a robber, seeking to steal people unfairly away from God's wrath and judgment. He is *the Lamb* who has purchased his People by bearing God's wrath and judgment in our place. This is the message which answers the need of every nation and every culture, but first we need to grasp it ourselves. We are forgiven, completely, forever, because we have been purchased by the blood of the Lamb.

---

[12] Hebrews 7:27; 9:12, 26; 10:10; 1 Peter 3:18.

[13] Revelation 5:9.

The Second Overview of AD History

The Seven Seals: Why Does God Allow Suffering? (6:1–8:1)

> *I watched as the Lamb opened the first of the seven seals. Then I heard one of the four living creatures say in a voice like thunder, "Come!"*
>
> (Revelation 6:1)

This is the point where some people stop reading the book of Revelation. It's not that the first five chapters are easy, but there is something more straightforward about a vision of Jesus, letters to seven churches, and a vision of heaven. From chapter 6 onwards, we need more help to keep up with the unfolding story of Revelation. Seven seals, seven trumpets, seven bowls, two beasts, two witnesses, Babylon and Jerusalem, a prostitute and a bride: all this needs much more of an explanation. So some people give up, and others simply skim-read the middle of the book until they reach chapter 21.

My hope and prayer is that, helped by this book, you will resist the urge to leave three-quarters of Revelation to somebody else, and that you will dig deep into the middle chapters to grasp Jesus' message in five more overviews of AD history. One of the reasons he tells the story six times in six different ways is precisely because the message is so important. Each time, Jesus addresses a slightly different question posed by Christians in every generation, and with the Seven Seals he tackles the question *"Why does God allow suffering?"*

The breaking of the Seven Seals depicts the unfolding

of AD history. They will be echoed in the Seven Trumpets and Seven Bowls, which come later on in Revelation, but it is also important that we notice that they closely parallel Jesus' account of AD history in Matthew 24 and Mark 13. Compare the two accounts:

The Seven Seals	Mark 13
Wars and conquest	Wars
International strife and carnage	International strife
Famine	Earthquakes
Death	Famine
Persecution	Persecution
Earthquakes, eclipses, and shaken heavens	Eclipses and shaken heavens
Divine judgment	Divine judgment

In my experience, most of the mistakes we make in interpreting Revelation stem from our failure to make this link back to Mark 13. We assume that the Seven Seals must follow one after another, and that the Bowls must follow the Trumpets, which must follow the Seals. As a result, many of us force-fit history into our misunderstanding of what Scripture really says. In contrast, when we notice the link with Mark 13, it is like putting the right key in a door, turning the lock, and swinging it open. Mark 13 stops us from viewing the Seven Seals as seven consecutive waves of judgment, since Jesus speaks clearly in Mark about these things happening all together.[1] It also stops us from assuming that the Seven Seals just focus on the years immediately before the Second Coming, because Jesus says clearly in Mark that *"such things must happen, but the* ***end is still***

[1] Since the Seventh Seal speaks of the Second Coming itself, the Sixth Seal may well indicate that the troubles will get worse just before the end.

***to come**... These are the **beginning** of birth pains."*[2] The Seven Seals in 6:1 – 8:1 therefore depict the whole of AD history and God's judgments throughout that period.

So, back to our question of *"Why does God allow suffering?"* This is easily the number one question posed by both Christians and non-Christians. The premise goes something like this: either God is *good but not strong enough* to be able to prevent suffering in the world, or he is *strong but not good enough* to want to prevent suffering in the world. Either way, he is less than worthy of our trust and praise. Jesus answers this charge head on through his description of the Seven Seals.

First, God is both *good* and *strong*. His strength is seen by the way in which the four horsemen only ride out when Jesus breaks each seal,[3] and by the very clear limits which he sets on the authority of Death and Hades.[4] His goodness is seen by the way he marks and protects those who follow him,[5] and by the way that he judges the world with silence and sobriety, rather than with pleasure.[6] Jesus makes no attempt to shift the blame onto Satan, pretending that suffering has nothing to do with him. He takes full responsibility for what is happening on Planet Earth, and reveals that he has a bigger agenda than our knee-jerk demands for it to stop.

He points out that there are actually two questions behind the complaint *"Why does God allow suffering?"* We are not merely asking *"Why do bad things happen to good people?"* We are also asking *"Why do good things happen to bad people?"* In the Clint Eastwood movie *Pale Rider*, Clint plays the fourth of these horsemen – a heroic gun-toting preacher who comes in

[2] Mark 13:7–8.

[3] Revelation 6:1, 3, 5, 7. Some people assume from 19:11–16 that the rider of the white horse must be Jesus, but it is a mistake to see him playing such a minor role. He has the lead role in this scene, as the Lamb breaking the seals.

[4] Revelation 6:8, which makes sense since he holds their key in 1:18. See also his restraint in 7:1.

[5] Revelation 7:1–8.

[6] Revelation 8:1.

response to a little girl's prayer in order to wreak vengeance on a prospector who is oppressing her village.[7] Even Hollywood recognizes that the innocent should be protected and wrong-doers should be judged, so we should not be surprised that God is doing something about it. The four seals see him harness the sin of wicked people – whether *greed* in 6:2, *selfish ambition* in 6:4 or *injustice* in 6:6[8] – and use it to judge the rebellious nations. Then, with the sixth seal in 6:15–17, he appears in person to judge wicked people, so that he can usher in his new creation.[9] Judgment is the natural response to human sin, and Jesus expects us to praise him for it.

But what about the innocents who are caught up in the judgments? Jesus addresses this with the opening of the fifth seal. John sees those martyred for the Christian faith crying out to God to bring vengeance on the earth. Note that their prayer is actually for more judgment to come, not for it to stop, and that God gives them his answer. He will indeed judge the whole earth and sweep away life as we know it, but he tells his People to be patient like him as he waits for the complete number of non-Christians to be saved, and for the complete number of Christians to lay down their lives for the Gospel.[10]

God is not only *good* enough to care about suffering, and strong enough to prevent it, but he is also *wise* enough to see the fruit yielded through suffering. If God is strong enough to blame for our suffering, he must also be big enough to trust in the midst of it. We can't have it both ways. God promises to

---

[7] *Pale Rider* (Warner Brothers, 1985). Clint Eastwood, the rider on the white horse, is the hero of the movie. We instinctively agree with God that sin needs to be judged and the oppressed need to be delivered.

[8] Note that *oil* and *wine*, the luxuries of the rich, are unaffected while the price of staple foods rocket.

[9] God explains this strategy most clearly in Habakkuk 1–2, where he explains that he will use the violent Babylonians to judge the earth, before judging the Babylonians in turn for their violence.

[10] We understand why it is worth the wait in 6:9–11 when we feast our eyes on what it accomplishes in 7:1–17.

protect his People in the midst of the judgment,[11] but he is also frank that we will experience pain and suffering in the midst of it.[12] Christians will not be mere spectators of suffering, but then nor is he. The one who opens these seals is the *Lamb*, the one who suffered more than anyone else in human history. He does not try to get himself "off the hook" when it comes to suffering. He placed himself firmly "on the hook" of suffering at Calvary in order to ensure that when he eliminates sin from the world at his Second Coming (6:15–17) he will be able to lead those who receive him as Lord to a place where suffering will be no more (7:15–17).

Sin causes suffering. The world suffers, and Christians suffer too. But Jesus Christ has suffered for the world to make an end to sin and suffering in his glorious new Kingdom.

[11] Revelation 7:1–3.

[12] Revelation 6:9–11. John is not speaking mere theory here. His brother was martyred in 43 AD in Acts 12:1–2.

The Wrath of the Lamb (6:16)

Fall on us and hide us from the face of him who is seated on the throne, and from the wrath of the Lamb.

(Revelation 6:16)

The word *arachnophobia* means the fear of spiders. *Spheksophobia* means fear of wasps, *selachophobia* means fear of sharks, *ophidiophobia* means fear of snakes, *chiroptophobia* means fear of bats and *ailurophobia* means fear of cats. In fact, there are nearly 300 words in the English language to describe different kinds of phobia.

Interestingly, however, there is no word to describe the fear of lambs. That may not surprise you, because lambs tend to be scared of us rather than the other way around. We like them on our dinner plate covered in mint sauce and served with roast potatoes. It would make sense for lambs to fear us, but not for us to fear woolly, gambolling and bleating lambs.

So Revelation is delivering a deliberate oxymoron when it speaks about *"the wrath of the Lamb"*.[1] The sixth seal describes the Second Coming of Jesus and the seventh seal his Final Judgment,[2] and Jesus wants us to gasp in surprise and horror at what is in store for the unrepentant. A day is coming, he says,

---

[1] An *oxymoron* is a phrase which seems to contradict itself. For example, *crash-landing*, *smart-casual, bitter-sweet* and *vegetarian meatballs.*

[2] This is clear from the parallel passage in Mark 13:24–26 and from the link which is made back to the destruction of the northern kingdom of Israel in Hosea 10:8.

when he will finish breaking open the seals of history and will return to wrap up this present age. At that point every eye will see him for who he really is, just as John saw him as he really is in chapter 1, and they will tremble and cry out before *"the wrath of the Lamb"*. Not just the weak ones, the irrational ones, or the ones we might normally expect to find at a phobia clinic. It will be kings, the great politicians, the generals, the rich, the strong and those hardened by manual labour. All of them will quiver and shake with fear when they see Jesus the Lamb of God. They will try to hide, but will find that nothing can hide them from his wrath.[3]

That's why we need to read the Revelation of Jesus Christ and let it shape our picture of Jesus as much as the four gospels. Otherwise, we are in grave danger of mistaking Jesus' *meekness* for *weakness*, and treating him as someone far less than he really is.

Many people have made this mistake throughout history. King Herod felt sure he could dispatch the baby Jesus by slaughtering the defenceless toddlers of Bethlehem, but within weeks he was struck dead by an excruciating case of kidney disease and genital gangrene.[4] The men of Nazareth thought that they could easily throw him off a cliff, but they were powerless to stop him from shrugging them off and going on his way.[5] Judas Iscariot thought he could betray him to death for pieces of silver, but it cost him his own life.[6] Even Satan hoped that he could destroy Jesus, but merely played into his hands. Thousands of Christ's enemies have made the same mistake ever since.

We must never forget that Jesus is only the *Lamb* because he gave himself over to death by his own free choice, in spite of the fact that he had over 72,000 warrior-angels on standby to

---

[3] See Job 34:22; Psalm 139:11–12; Amos 9:2–3.

[4] This is how medical experts understand Josephus' description of Herod's final illness in *Antiquities* (17.6.5).

[5] Luke 4:29–30.

[6] Acts 1:15–19.

rush to his aid.[7] As Paul reminded the stubborn and rebellious church at Corinth, Jesus died in weakness but he did not die because he was weak. He died in weakness because he is strong, and because he chose to bear the wrath of God in our place, before being raised by the power of God to the highest of heights.[8] The one who is the *Lamb of God* is also the fierce and unconquerable *Lion of the tribe of Judah*.[9]

These verses are for you if you are reading this book but you are not a Christian. Revelation is a fascinating read, but Jesus doesn't want you to miss your own role within it. Unless you repent and hand over your life to him, you have just read a description of your own future. Don't be a fool and convince yourself that God will not judge you for your sin. He gives you the truth here, right between the eyes, and warns you to repent before it is too late. Either he's lying, or you need to do as he commands.

These verses are also for you if you are a Christian. Too many churches and too many Christians focus uniquely on Jesus of Nazareth, the meek and suffering sacrifice, and forget that he is also full of wrath, power and might. The result is the kind of half-hearted Christianity described in chapters 2 and 3. Don't play around with following Jesus. This Lamb is not safe.

Whoever we are, there is hope for us all as we wait for this sixth seal to be opened. Paul tells us that *"God demonstrates his own love for us in this: While we were still sinners, Christ died for us. Since we have now been justified by his blood, how much more shall we be saved from God's wrath through him!"*[10] He tells you that you can meet Jesus today on your knees as the Lamb who averts the wrath of God towards your sin, or that you can wait to meet him at the end as the Lamb who brings the wrath of God upon your sin. The choice is yours.

---

[7] Matthew 26:53.

[8] 2 Corinthians 13:1–4.

[9] Revelation 5:5.

[10] Romans 5:8–9.

144,000 (7:4–8)

Then I heard the number of those who were sealed: 144,000 from all the tribes of Israel.

(Revelation 7:4)

Cults and sects love the book of Revelation. It is cryptic enough, and sufficiently misunderstood by Christians, for them to claim it as their own and use its verses as proof texts for all manner of strange religious theories.

Take, for example, the *144,000* who appear in 7:4–8 and 14:1–5. A nineteenth-century Russian cult known as the *"Skoptsy"* (the "castrated ones") seized upon these verses to teach that the Messiah would return to earth as soon as they reached 144,000 in number. They never managed to do so, probably because they taught that testicles and breasts were implants of the forbidden fruit of Eden, and that people needed to be castrated or given mastectomies at conversion. They were a weird and tragic reminder that if we as Christians do not understand the book of Revelation, other people will interpret it for us.

Or take, more famously, the Jehovah's Witnesses who number over 7 million people worldwide. They base one of their core beliefs on these verses, and teach that 144,000 of them will inherit "the heavenly hope" of reigning with Christ forever in heaven, while the other Jehovah's Witnesses inherit "the earthly hope" of living in a renewed paradise on earth. It must be disappointing for Jehovah's Witnesses from India to hear that there is therefore still a "ruling caste" and a "servant class" even in the age to come, and it is presumably even more disappointing when they hear that they will almost certainly not make it into the 144,000. One Jehovah's Witness website states that there are currently 9,986 members of the 144,000 still alive today, although it does not reveal their identities.

Sadly, even mainstream Christian denominations seem confused as to the meaning of the 144,000. Some argue that since 7:4 tells us that they are *"from all the tribes of Israel"*, they must therefore be 144,000 ethnic Jews who are equally spread across the twelve tribes of Israel.[1] At the other extreme, some argue that the Church has "replaced" ethnic Israel and that this is just a spiritual way of referring to Christians.[2] The majority of Christians are too confused to comment either way, and most decide that it doesn't really matter too much and they would be better off reading a gospel, a psalm, or another easier part of Scripture. That's a real shame, because Jesus is telling us something important here, and he really wants us to listen.

The first thing we need to note is that this cannot refer simply to a group of ethnic Jews. Jesus has shown this through two clues in the passage, although if we are skim-reading through these chapters, we will probably miss them. One clue is that the tribe of *Ephraim* has been replaced by the tribe of *Joseph*. Now Joseph was Ephraim's father, so this could simply be a poetic name for Ephraim, but he was also Manasseh's father and Manasseh is mentioned here by his own name. The second clue is that the tribe of *Dan* is missing from the list and it has been replaced by *Levi*, which was never counted among the twelve territorial tribes of Israel since they were the priests who were scattered throughout Israel. I have read all sorts of

[1] Those who believe this must also believe in a "pre-tribulation rapture". This is a complicated name for a simple theory, which we will assess in the later chapter on "The Millennium".

[2] I briefly examined "replacement theology" earlier on in the chapter on "True Jews". Romans 11 tells us that the Church has not *replaced* Israel, but has been grafted into Abraham's Jewish tree through faith in Christ. In the same way, it also tells us that Jews can be broken off from Abraham's tree by rejecting Christ.

explanations for why *Dan* might be missing from the twelve tribes of Israel, but none of them seems at all convincing.[3] Everyone knows that if you are assembling flat-pack from Ikea and you need to twist and force the parts to fit them together, you've probably gone wrong somewhere with the instructions. The same is true with Scripture.

Nor can the *144,000* refer to a literal number of believers. The way that they are split into twelve perfectly even groups of 12,000 is meant to alert us to the fact they are symbolic. We have already seen in an earlier chapter that the book of Revelation uses the number *twelve* to symbolize the People of God,[4] and so here it uses the number *12 × 12 × 1,000* to symbolize the vast multitude of the People of God.

The key to unlocking this passage is found in Ezekiel 9, where God gave his prophet an out-of-body vision of Jerusalem in 592 BC, six years before the destruction of the city by the Babylonian army. The Lord told Ezekiel that he was about to destroy Jerusalem, but before he carried out his judgment he commanded one of seven angels to place a mark on the foreheads of all the faithful believers in the city.[5] Those who received the mark on their foreheads were spared from the death and slaughter which was to come. Now, in the same way that 6:16 referred back to Hosea 10:8 and likened the Final Judgment to the destruction of Old Testament Israel, this passage refers back to Ezekiel to liken it to the destruction of Jerusalem. So what does Jesus want us to grasp from this sight of the 144,000?

---

[3] The best argument I have seen is that Dan's tribe was "the tribe of the Antichrist" since Jacob prophesied that he would be a snake to his brothers in Genesis 49:16–17. But if this is true, it begs the question why there is no explicit reference to it anywhere else in Scripture.

[4] See the chapter on "Twenty-Four Plus Four", based particularly on Revelation 21:12–14 and Matthew 19:28. In chapter 4 John saw *12 + 12 = 24*. Here he sees *12 × 12 × 1,000 = 144,000*.

[5] I agree with those commentators who link the seven angels of judgment in Ezekiel 9 to the seven angels who blow the Seven Trumpets in Revelation 8–11.

First, that however bad the trials of AD history may be, he has clearly marked those he has redeemed and has placed them under his secure hand of protection. We may need to lay down our lives for the Gospel,[6] but Satan and even death itself cannot snatch us out of his hand.[7]

Second, he will save all those that the Father has given him and will not fail to save a single one who turns to him. These symbolic numbers are perfect, round numbers because not one of us is missing.

Third, the number of those who will be saved is going to be large. The number is not merely twelve times two, but twelve squared times a thousand. Better still, we discover in Revelation 14 that these simply represent the *first-fruits* of God's People, and that there are many, many more still to be saved.[8] Perhaps these are the *"great multitude that no one could count"* in 7:9.

Satan would be overjoyed if he could use passages like this to distract people into cults or to convince them that God's great plan for them is to airlift them from Planet Earth and leave a remnant of Jews to evangelize the "post-rapture" earth for them. That is the exact opposite of what Jesus is saying here. He is telling us that he has marked us to dwell in the midst of this age as his agents scattered throughout the earth to worship him, to suffer for him, to preach the Gospel and to win the great multitude from every nation, tribe, people group, and language which is revealed in 7:9.

We need to make sure that we understand the identity of the 144,000, because Jesus did not give John this vision for the sake of Jehovah's Witnesses or self-mutilating Russians. Jesus gave it him for us, to encourage us to press on in the battle for the souls of humankind.

---

[6] Revelation 6:9–11.

[7] John 10:28–29; Revelation 1:18.

[8] Revelation 14:4. The *first-fruits* were the early crops, which the Israelites offered to the Lord in anticipation of a much larger harvest to come later in the summer. See Leviticus 23:9–14.

From Every Nation (7:9)

> *After this I looked and there before me was a great multitude that no one could count, from every nation, tribe, people and language, standing before the throne and in front of the Lamb. They were wearing white robes and were holding palm branches in their hands.*
>
> (Revelation 7:9)

"I have a dream", declared Martin Luther King on 28th August 1963.

> *I have a dream that one day on the red hills of Georgia the sons of former slaves and the sons of former slave-owners will be able to sit down together at a table of brotherhood... I have a dream that my four children will one day live in a nation where they will not be judged by the colour of their skin but by the content of their character. I have a dream today.*

It was a dream which consumed his life and which led to his premature death five years later from an assassin's bullet.

Jesus of Nazareth had a dream which consumed him and which led to his death on the cross at the age of thirty-three. The writer to the Hebrews tells us that *"for the joy that was set before him he endured the cross, scorning its shame"*.[1] He is not specific over whether that joy was the people he would save or the glory he would receive, but Jesus himself sheds light on this verse in

---

[1] Hebrews 12:2.

John 12:20–33. A number of Greeks had come to see Jesus, and this triggered him to speak of his great dream for the future. It was a bigger dream than for blacks and whites to eat together on the red hills of Georgia. It was the dream we see realized in Revelation 7:9. *"Unless a grain of wheat falls to the ground and dies", he declared, "it remains only a single seed. But if it dies, it produces many seeds... I, when I am lifted up from the earth, will draw all men to myself."*

It's easy to assume that the joy that was set before Jesus was simply his own glory or his Father's pleasure, but verses like John 3:16 and these ones from John 12 refuse to let us narrow the angle of our lens. That's why it's so exciting to read the verses of Revelation 7 and to see the crowd of believers from every nation, tribe, people group and language worshipping the Lord together. This isn't a pleasant side-effect of Jesus' death and resurrection. This is the dream which gripped his heart and which should grip ours too.

It was the dream which gripped Paul's heart as he poured out his life *"leading the Gentiles to obey God"* because *"it has always been my ambition to preach the gospel where Christ was not known"*.[2] He was not simply passionate to see many people saved, but specifically that *"through the church, the manifold wisdom of God should be made known to the rulers and authorities in the heavenly realms"* because *"through the gospel the Gentiles are heirs together with Israel, members together of one body, and sharers together in the promise in Christ Jesus"*.[3] He grasped the same thing which Jesus talked about when the Greeks came to see him in John 12 – that God's great dream is to draw all people to himself so that he might be glorified by an international church made up of people from every nation.[4] It

---

[2] Romans 15:18, 20.

[3] Ephesians 3:6, 10.

[4] Jesus is the fulfilment of the promises God made to Jacob that he would turn him into a *community of nations* in Genesis 28:3 and 35:11.

was a dream which could not be quenched even by beatings, floggings, imprisonment, danger or exhaustion.[5]

It was the dream which laid hold of a young shoemaker from Northamptonshire named William Carey and turned him into "the father of modern missions". It caused him to sail with his family to India in 1793, never to see Britain again, and to endure seven years of fruitless preaching before he saw his first Indian convert. It kept him steady in his task when his five-year-old son died of a tropical disease and his wife had a nervous breakdown and went mad. It spurred him on in his work so that by the time he died there were half a million Protestant Christians in his part of India.

It was the dream which stirred the young Jim Elliot to venture with the Gospel to the Auca Indians of Ecuador and to be murdered and mutilated at their hands in January 1956. It was what gripped his mind as he wrote in his journal that *"He is no fool who gives what he cannot keep to gain that which he cannot lose."* It was what enabled his widow Elisabeth to live for two years among those same Aucas, and to lead many of them to faith in Christ through her practical demonstration of God's forgiveness.

It is the dream which Jesus wants to stir in your heart today so that it grips you for the rest of your life. It's not just that God is glorified by being worshipped by lots of people. It's specifically that he is more glorified when he is worshipped by a multiracial crowd of people from every nation, tribe, and tongue.[6] Last Sunday evening, with the news talking once again about tensions between Pakistan and India, I watched a Pakistani pastor embrace a group of Indian pastors and worship the Lord together. That glorifies Jesus. A few years ago, on the day of the 7th July terrorist bombings in London, I was at a conference with several thousand church leaders. One of them was an Iraqi who

[5] 2 Corinthians 11:23–28.

[6] In fulfilment of the prophecy about the *One Like a Son of Man* in Daniel 7:13–14.

had been involved with terrorist cells before his conversion. As he shared and led us in prayer for the nations of the Middle East, that glorified Jesus too. When those who are divided by race, colour, history, and culture are united around the Throne of Jesus in worship, he is truly exalted and the peoples display his glory.

This vision stops us from talking about *"the Muslim world"* or *"hard-to-reach people groups"*. The whole world belongs to Christ, and he has determined that every nation, tribe, and language will yield to his rule. This vision stirs many of us to leave the comforts of our own home in order to plant Jesus-glorifying churches in other nations. It should at the very least stir each one of us to reach the nations in our own backyard. The make-up of Western cities is changing, and within the distance I can throw a tennis ball from my house I have neighbours from England, Wales, France, Germany, Italy, America, Colombia, Pakistan and Brunei. I wish I could include Poland in that list too, but seven months ago I knocked on my neighbour's door and discovered that he had died. I am excited that one neighbour has received Christ and taken her place in the great multitude, but I am heart-broken that for my Polish neighbour it is now too late.

Time is running out for the people of the world, but they have hope because millions of Christians dream Jesus' great dream. One of the church leaders who tried to discourage William Carey told him that *"If the Lord wants to convert the heathen, he can do it without your help"*, but the shoemaker refused to adopt that apathetic creed. Because Carey caught the dream and refused to be silenced, new nations were brought into this great throng.

This vision is an encouragement and a promise to us, but it's also an invitation. Go in faith, because you have already seen that Jesus' dream will come true.

The Lamb Who Shepherds Us (7:17)

For the Lamb at the centre of the throne will be their shepherd; he will lead them to springs of living water.
(Revelation 7:17)

Revelation is full of oxymorons and apparent contradictions. Here is another one. Jesus is not only the *Lamb*, but the *Lamb who shepherds God's People*. Jesus is able to be our *Lamb* and our *Shepherd* at one and the same time.

Jesus is the Shepherd who *loves us*. That was the main thrust of Jesus' Parable of the Lost Sheep. If you or I went to the bank with a hundred £10 notes and discovered that one of them was missing, we would not leave ninety-nine on the counter to look for the missing one. It would be madness to risk £990 for the sake of finding £10, so we would just cut our losses and move on. Jesus tells us that parable to show us he is madly in love with each one of us. He died as our Lamb because his love does not count the cost, and he now lives as our Shepherd motivated by that same love.[1]

Jesus is also the Shepherd who leads us and feeds us. In this verse he leads us *"to springs of living water"*,[2] but he also leads us to all the other places that we need to go. Psalm 23 says that he leads us to green pastures, beside quiet waters, in paths of righteousness, through the valley of the shadow of death, to a table of blessing and to intimate fellowship together in his

[1] John 10:28–29.

[2] John 4:10–14 shows us that this is a reference to the *Holy Spirit*. We will pick up on this later in the chapter on "The River of God".

house. He died as our Lamb so that we might feed on his flesh and blood, but he lives as our Shepherd to make sure that we do.[3] That's why this passage promises that we will never hunger or thirst because of our Great Shepherd.

Finally, Jesus is also the Shepherd who protects us – not just from the scorching sun but from every other danger too. David was able to boast to King Saul that *"When a lion or a bear came and carried off a sheep from the flock, I went after it, struck it and rescued the sheep from its mouth. When it turned on me, I seized it by its mane, struck it and killed it."*[4] I can't even begin to imagine how a teenaged shepherd-boy managed to grab a lion by the mane and kill it, but I can see why it attracted God's attention.[5] Even so, Jesus went one further: *"I am the good shepherd... I lay down my life for the sheep."*[6] It's not simply that Jesus is both our Lamb and our Shepherd. He is the Good Shepherd because he was willing to become the Lamb of God who delivers us from Satan's mouth.

So there we have it. Jesus is not only our *Lamb* but also our *Shepherd*. He *loves* us, *leads* us, *feeds* us, and *protects* us, and his shepherding will reach its fullness in the glories of the age to come. This should be enough to stir our hearts to worship him and to follow him gladly as his willing sheep, but there is one more thing he wants to say to us for our worship to be complete: he told Peter three times in John 21:15–17 that those who love him should show it by shepherding his sheep. It is good to love and worship Jesus the Shepherd. It is even better to pour out our lives in his service as his deputy shepherds on earth.[7]

---

[3] John 6:53–57.

[4] 1 Samuel 17:34–35.

[5] Psalm 78:70–71; Acts 13:22.

[6] John 10:11–15.

[7] Peter picks up on this teaching in 1 Peter 5:1–4 when he tells elders to shepherd their churches as deputy shepherds who serve the *Chief Shepherd*. I firmly believe that this also has wider application to anyone who has spiritual leadership in their home group, their family or simply as a Christian among non-Christians.

Jesus wants you to shepherd the people around you by loving them as he loves you. He told the Parable of the Lost Sheep twice in the gospels: once to stress his love for Christians and once to stress his love for non-Christians.[8] We glorify *the Lamb who is our Shepherd* by laying down our lives for Christians and non-Christians, just as he laid down his life for us. That was the point of the Parable of the Good Samaritan. The priest and the Levite were too religious or too busy to help someone in need, but the Samaritan crossed cultural barriers to pour himself out to shepherd the man in his need.[9] What would it mean for you to leave behind "ninety-nine" and to pour out your life seeking the "lost sheep'? Do that, and you will truly glorify Jesus the Shepherd.

Jesus also wants you to shepherd those around you by *leading* and *feeding* them as he does you. Turn on the TV and you'll see what most non-Christians feed themselves on. Spend time with many Christians and you may find it not much different. Jesus is sick of Christians tutting at other people and complaining about their lives, and he calls us to take responsibility for leading them to him so that they can eat what is good. Some time ago I discovered my one-year-old son cramming his mouth full of pebbles. Of course I made him spit them all out, but I also took the hint that he was hungry and gave him some proper food to eat! Hungry people eat whatever is at hand, so let's lead people to God's Word, to his Spirit and to his Gospel. It only takes a conversation, a book or an audio file to change a person's diet, and changing a person's diet can change their destiny.

Finally, Jesus wants you to shepherd those around you by *protecting* them as he protects you. Satan is prowling around like a lion to devour the Christians and non-Christians around

---

[8] He told it in Galilee in Matthew 18:10–14 to speak of his love for every single Christian, but he told it again on the east side of the Jordan in Luke 15:4–7 to speak of his love for non-Christians.

[9] Luke 10:25–37.

us,[10] so we must not be too scared to confront sin and to bring God's Word tactfully, specifically and lovingly. David grabbed lions by the mane, and Jesus took on Satan himself. He loves it when his People follow his lead and protect those around them with his Word. That's real worship.

John wants us to grasp that Jesus is *the Lamb who shepherds us* and to fall down in worship. But he also recounted Jesus' conversation with Peter because he wants our worship to include imitating the great Shepherd-Lamb by being his shepherds to those around us. Like Jesus, we get to pour out our own lives on behalf of God's sheep.

If Jesus has called you to be his sheep, he will also empower you by his Spirit to be one of his shepherds. In the age to come you will *"serve him day and night in his temple"*.[11] Praise God that by his grace you can begin doing so today.

[10] 1 Peter 5:8–9.

[11] Revelation 7:15.

The Third Overview of AD History

The Seven Trumpets: Why Does the Church Look So Weak? (8:2–11:19)

And I saw the seven angels who stand before God, and to them were given seven trumpets.

(Revelation 8:2)

When Jesus says something, we need to listen. When he says the same thing twice or even three times, we need to sit up and take note of something very important. That's the case here. The Seven Trumpets summarize AD history in the same way that the Seven Churches and the Seven Seals did before them.[1] Part of this is simply for emphasis, but it is also because this time Jesus wants to address another question we are bound to ask: *"If God is on the Throne, why does his Church look so weak?"*

Note the similarities between the Seven Trumpets and the Seven Seals. Both recount God's judgments upon the whole earth, and both contain a reassuring interlude to encourage the Church before the seventh judgment. The first four seals release *four horsemen* and the last three trumpets mirror this by the way they release *three woes*.

But note the differences too. The Seven Seals parallel Jesus' words in Mark 13, but the Seven Trumpets reflect the Ten

---

[1] We can see this from the way in which the sun is snuffed out with the sixth seal but is still shining in full strength when the fourth trumpet darkens it by a third. It is also clear from the fact that there is no gap in Mark 13:26–27 between Jesus' Second Coming (the sixth seal) and the Final Judgment. The Seven Trumpets must therefore be a restatement of what was described by the Seven Seals.

Plagues which fell on Egypt under Moses: four disasters on the land, sea, rivers and heavens, followed by a woe which brings pain but not death, and another woe which does bring death. The seventh seal brought silence to heaven, but the seventh trumpet brings great noise to heaven.[2] So what are we to make of all this?

First, God has firmly decided that these judgments will take place throughout history. Joseph warned in Genesis that *"The reason the dream was given to Pharaoh in two forms is that the matter has been firmly decided by God, and God will do it soon."*[3] Far from praying that these judgments should not take place, Jesus actually expects our prayers to play a key role in making them happen.[4]

Second, these judgments are the only right and fair response of the one true God to the self-seeking idolatry of humanity. Since God is on the Throne of heaven, with all creation at his feet, it is completely abhorrent that people on earth should be giving themselves to *"worshipping demons, and idols of gold, silver, bronze, stone and wood – idols that cannot see or hear or walk"*.[5] Although we see sinful symptoms all around us in the form of violence, theft, magic, superstition and sexual immorality,[6] Jesus is clear that idolatry is the root cause, and that these judgments are his gracious call for the world to repent before they share the fate of their demon-idols. This is why the Seven Trumpets echo the Ten Plagues through which God exposed the false idols of Egypt and drew many Egyptians to repentance and faith in him.[7] The *hail*, the *darkness*, the *locusts* and the *water turned to blood* all remind us that God took on the false gods of Egypt and

---

[2] Revelation 8:1; 11:15–19.

[3] Genesis 41:32.

[4] We will explore this together in the next chapter, on "Incense".

[5] Revelation 10:20.

[6] Revelation 10:21.

[7] Exodus 9:14; 12:12; Numbers 33:4. We are told about numbers of Egyptians who joined the People of God because of the plagues in Exodus 12:37–38.

won, and that he will do so again with the twenty-first-century idols of our own age.

Finally, God will work this victory over the false gods of the earth *in spite of the fact that his Church will look weak*. He will allow those who serve idols to look as though they have the upper hand, despising Christians as much as the Egyptians despised their Hebrew slaves, and oppressing the Church so badly that at times she will look as though she is defeated and will never rise again.[8] God's plan to save the nations involved his Son suffering, dying and looking defeated as part of heaven's master strategy, and it involves the Church walking that same road. As the Church bares her weakness to the world, God will suddenly rush to her aid and display his strength, so that through miracles and great revivals he can draw more people to salvation than would ever have been saved had the Church looked strong and problem-free.[9]

So how should we react in the midst of the trials and judgments of AD history? We should be *confident*, knowing that God has counted his People and committed to protect them.[10] He knows the exact names of those who will be destroyed in his judgments, and he promises to preserve those he has sealed as his own.[11] We should trust God, knowing that he has set exactly the right hour, day, month and year for his judgments to take place,[12] and exactly the right length of time for each judgment to last.[13] He has placed precise limits on the scope of his judgments,[14] and even Satan himself dares not trespass

---

[8] Revelation 11:7–10.

[9] The miracles of 11:5–6 and the revival of 11:11–13, which causes unbelievers to give glory to the true God.

[10] Revelation 11:1. As we saw in the chapter on the "144,000", when God counts people it serves as a promise that not one of them will go missing.

[11] Revelation 11:13 tells us literally that *"seven thousand **names** of men were killed in the earthquake"*.

[12] Revelation 9:15.

[13] Revelation 11:2, 3, 9, 11.

[14] A *third* in 8:7–12 and in 9:15, 18. A tenth in 11:13.

the God-given parameters of his authority.[15] Furthermore, by prophesying ahead of time that these things will happen, Jesus has made it very clear that they are his sovereign judgments upon the idolatry of the nations. Suffering is not a sign that he is weak, but that he is strong.[16]

Above all, we should *preach the Gospel* in the midst of our troubled age, knowing that people will repent when God's judgment is followed up by our faithful witness to his Name.[17] We should *praise* God for his righteous judgment upon sin and idolatry, and for the fact that his justice means that the wicked will not go unpunished.[18] And we should *pray*, bringing our requests as sweet perfume before God's Throne so that we can play our role in his severe but gloriously effective plan for Planet Earth.[19]

That's what we're going to look at in our next chapter.

---

[15] Revelation 9:1, 3–5, 10, 14–15, 19. The Greek word used here for *power* is *exousia* which actually means *delegated authority*.

[16] Revelation 10:7, which picks up on what God says in the Old Testament in Isaiah 43:9–13 and Amos 3:7.

[17] Revelation 10:11; 11:7, 11–13.

[18] Revelation 11:18.

[19] Revelation 8:3–5.

Incense (8:3–5)

The smoke of the incense, together with the prayers of the saints, went up before God from the angel's hand.

(Revelation 8:4)

The most expensive perfume of all time belongs to the British designer Clive Christian. 500ml retails at an eye-popping $215,000. Special bottles of "Imperial Majesty" were first put on sale in London and New York in 2007, and they are even decorated with a five-carat diamond on their lid.[1]

Perfume has definitely come a long way since it was invented by the ancient Egyptians before the Exodus. Back then, the first perfumes were known as *incense*, and were a mixture of gum resin, frankincense, myrrh and other spices, and they were burned together as a sweet fragrance in Pharaoh's palace or in the temples of his gods. The word *incense* simply comes from the Latin word *incendere*, which means to *burn*, and the word *perfume* comes from the Latin words *per fume*, which mean *through smoke*. Incense was therefore the perfume of the ancient world and it has always been part of worship, from the temples of ancient Egypt and Babylon, right up to modern Buddhist, Hindu, Taoist and Shinto temples in Asia, or Catholic and Orthodox churches in Europe.

Yahweh told the Israelites at Mount Sinai that he wanted his Tabernacle to be full of the smell of incense, and he even gave them his own exclusive recipe. He told the priests to offer it day and night at the golden altar of incense in the Holy Place,

---

[1] See *The Guinness Book of World Records*.

and they were never to let its fires go out.[2] He showed David that this was a picture of fervent prayer,[3] and he repeats that lesson through John in Revelation 5:8. The incense we read about here is therefore a picture of the prayers which are offered by Christians throughout history.[4]

Jesus wants us to understand this so that we can grasp that *God loves it when we pray*. Think about it. Of all the things in the ancient world which God might have chosen to serve as a picture of prayer, he chose one of the choicest, sweetest, most fragrant objects known to the human race. He really loves it when we pray, and it really grieves him when we don't. In fact, the prophet Samuel, who had grown up in the Tabernacle from a very early age, understood this so well that he told the Israelites: *"Far be it from me that I should* ***sin against the Lord*** *by failing to pray for you."*[5]

But note that the picture of incense reminds us that God only loves it *when we pray in his way*. God was extraordinarily precise in Exodus 30:34–38 about the exact mixture of incense he wanted, and this reminds us that we are to pray in his way and not our own. Jesus told us to come to *"Our Father in heaven"*, full of confidence as sons and daughters, and not with brow-beating or self-condemnation. Have a listen to yourself next time you pray and check that you are doing this. Many Christians have developed a rut in which they always start prayer by telling God how bad they have been, yet Jesus expressly tells us to start by telling God how great he is! There is definitely a place for honest confession of sin in prayer, but Jesus instructs us to leave it until much later on.[6] We are to begin with our eyes fixed

---

[2] Exodus 30:1–10, 34–38.

[3] Psalm 141:1–2.

[4] Don't be confused by the word *"saints"*, even though some church traditions use it to refer only to Christian heroes. The New Testament is very clear that *all* Christians are saints. See Romans 1:7; Philippians 1:1.

[5] 1 Samuel 12:23.

[6] Matthew 6:9–13.

on God's greatness, not our own shortcomings, because this is the kind of prayer which smells sweet to God. *"Enter his gates with thanksgiving and his courts with praise."*[7] That's the royal protocol.

Jesus also wants us to grasp this link between incense and prayer because we must learn that *prayer is a gift of grace* and not a work of man. I have to confess that I spent my early years as a Christian rejoicing that I had been saved by grace but striving to win things in prayer through my own hard work. God gave explicit instructions to the priests that they should only burn incense using the fire from the bronze altar of blood sacrifice, fire which the Lord himself had placed on the altar,[8] and when two of the priests sinfully tried to burn incense using *"unauthorized fire"* of their own, they paid for it with their lives.[9] Jesus wants to make sure that we do not treat prayer as a work of the flesh, trying to win something from God through our own efforts and self-exertions. The prayer God requires is a supplication made by grace, relying on the fire of the Holy Spirit to apply the blood of Jesus to our situation.[10]

If we pray this way, Jesus promises us that *our prayers will be answered*. Make sure you don't miss this and start complaining about the severity of God's judgments through the Seven Trumpets. These judgments come upon the earth because Christians pray! Before the seven angels are ready to blow their trumpets, the prayers of the saints must reach God's nostrils as sweet incense, and he must instruct his angel to throw them to the earth mixed with fire from his altar. The thunder, lightning and earthquake which come from the prayers of the saints serve as a starting pistol for the seven angels to sound their trumpets. When we pray *"hallowed be your name"*, we are asking the

[7] Psalm 100:4.

[8] Leviticus 9:24; 16:12.

[9] Leviticus 10:1–2.

[10] See also 1 Peter 2:5, where we are told that our prayers are only *"acceptable to God through Jesus Christ"*.

Lord to judge the idols of the nations and to vindicate himself before the world. When we pray *"your kingdom come on earth as it is in heaven"*, we are asking him to flex his royal muscles and remind the nations that he is on the Throne. We must not complain about the judgments of chapters 8 to 11 any more than the miracles and revivals of 11:5–6 and 11–13. These are all glorious answers to our prayers, as our own cries to heaven play their part in the unfolding of AD history.

You may not feel as though God answers your prayers very much. It may feel very distant when you hear great stories of how the British church prayed and the Nazis were defeated, or how European churches prayed and the Soviet Union collapsed. You may even feel as though God ignores your simple prayers about very mundane issues. But there is one final encouragement which Jesus gives us through this picture of incense, and it's for you. He shows us in 5:8 that the prayers of Christians have been gathered up in *golden bowls*, each one lovingly and carefully stockpiled ready for the right moment in time. God reserves the right to say *no* or *not yet* to our prayers – and these chapters certainly show us that we can trust the master-strategist to know best – but he really loves to say *yes*. Unlike ours, his resources will never run out. He is the great Giver, and he is more glorified by giving than receiving.

So let's pray. Let's pray with confidence. Let's pray laying hold of God's grace towards us in Jesus Christ. And let's keep praying, persisting through the trials of this present age, knowing that *"more things are wrought by prayer than this world dreams of"*.[11]

[11] King Arthur in Alfred Lord Tennyson's poem *Le Morte d'Arthur*, published in 1842.

The Star that Fell to Earth (9:1–19)

The fifth angel sounded his trumpet, and I saw a star that had fallen from the sky to the earth. The star was given the key to the shaft of the Abyss.

(Revelation 9:1)

We have heard about him and seen his work, but now it is time to meet him. The Devil has already been mentioned by name six times so far,[1] but at last it is time for Jesus to reveal our great enemy up close so that we can assess his tactics and the threat that he poses. Although he is not named as *the Devil* or *Satan* in this chapter, there are good reasons for assuming that *the star that fell to earth* is Satan himself.

First, he rules over the *Abyss*. This word simply means *bottomless* in Greek, but it is the word which Jesus uses in Luke 8:31 to refer to the bottomless pit of hell. Second, he is called *Abaddon* and *Apollyon* in verse 11. These are the Hebrew and Greek words for *Destruction*, *Place of Destruction*, or the *Destroyer*, which is why the word *Abaddon* is used several times in the Old Testament to refer to *Hell*.[2] Third, he is referred to

[1] He is called *the Devil* once in 2:10, and *Satan* five times in the four verses 2:9, 13, 24 and 3:9.

[2] See Job 26:6; 28:22; 31:12; Proverbs 15:11; 27:20. It possibly also refers to hell in Psalm 88:11. Some commentators argue that *Abaddon* in Revelation 9:11 is one of Satan's lieutenants rather than Satan himself, but he is called the *king* of the demon armies, not just their *prince*.

as a *star*, which ties in with the account of the fall of Satan in Revelation 12:4 and in an Old Testament prophecy in Isaiah.[3]

Interestingly, Scripture never speaks plainly about the origins of Satan. Like the book of Revelation, it is far more interested in talking about the glorious Creator-God than it is about his mere creature Satan. However, Christians have generally understood Isaiah 14:12–17 to speak about the fall of Satan from heaven. This is why people refer to Satan as *Lucifer*, since that is the Latin word for the *morning star* in 14:12. The Isaiah passage addresses the king of the Assyrian Empire and condemns his pride, but since he is (rather confusingly) referred to as the *king of Babylon*,[4] and it matches a similar passage about the king of Tyre in Ezekiel 28:11–19, most commentators assume that God is addressing the spiritual force behind the wicked earthly throne.

Isaiah and Ezekiel tell us that Satan was once a beautiful angel in heaven, but that he became proud on account of his beauty and tried to make himself a rival to God. With sin threatening to contaminate heaven itself, God threw him outside and cast him down to *"the depths of the pit"*. Jesus confirmed this when he told his disciples that *"I saw Satan fall like lightning from heaven"*,[5] and he goes on to reveal it in more detail in Revelation 12:7–12. The key point in all of these passages is

[3] Commentators disagree over whether or not the *falling star* of Revelation 8:10–11 is the same as the *falling star* Satan in 9:1. I personally think that those verses could be read either way. Interestingly, after the nuclear disaster in April 1986 at Chernobyl in Ukraine, many Christians heard that *Chernobyl* is the Ukrainian word for *Wormwood* and pointed to that disaster as the sounding of the third trumpet in Revelation 8. In fact, this may well be a mistranslation, and the fall-out of the disaster has certainly not affected a third of the waters, even in Europe. This is a helpful example of what happens when Christians fail to grasp the big picture of Revelation, and instead use its verses as proof texts to demonize whatever is on CNN this week.

[4] Babylon was one of the greatest cities in the Assyrian Empire, and the Assyrian kings spent part of their year there. It only became confusing a century later when the city threw off Assyrian rule and formed its own Babylonian Empire.

[5] Luke 10:18.

that Satan is down and out, excluded and defeated. He is not a powerful rival who opposes God, but a broken and battered has-been, desperately clawing to keep his hold over human hearts before the Second Coming of Jesus consigns him and his demons to their inevitable doom.[6]

And this is exactly what Jesus shows us in Revelation 9. It is very important that we see beyond the initial picture of victorious Satan at the head of his destructive armies throughout AD history. Yes, it is true that his *locust army* released by the fifth trumpet and his *cavalry army* released by the sixth trumpet – both demonic armies – are fearsome and terrifying. But note what is also true. Like a bulldog on a leash, they are restricted to the exact limits which God has set for them, and when he calls time on their party they will be snuffed out as quickly as they arose.

Satan rules over the Abyss, but only because he receives the key to it from the Lord Jesus.[7] His locust-soldiers have savage teeth and scorpion stings in their tails, but only because God grants them delegated authority to arm themselves in that way. Similarly, the 200 million riders have fire-breathing horses with venomous bites in their tails, but only because God permits them to do so.[8] He sets the exact moment when they can begin their work, and he binds them as his powerless captives until he is ready.[9] He sets the exact length of their work,[10] tells them

---

[6] See Matthew 25:41 or the pathetic pleading of the demons in Matthew 8:29 and Luke 8:31. Isaiah 14:16 hints that those who see Satan as he really is are amazed by his puny brokenness, not by his colossal power.

[7] Revelation 11:1. See also Revelation 1:18.

[8] The Greek word *exousia* in Revelation 9:3, 10, 19 does not so much mean *power* as *delegated authority*. I don't obey a policewoman's instructions because she is stronger than me; she isn't! I obey because she has delegated power from the government, and they are much stronger than me. Therefore even as Satan's armies do their worst, they tacitly admit that God is on the Throne.

[9] Revelation 9:13–15. The Euphrates is mentioned here symbolically because the Assyrians and Babylonians who destroyed Israel and Judah in 722 BC and 586 BC both came from the other side of the Euphrates.

[10] Revelation 9:5, 10.

who they can and can't harm,[11] and dictates exactly how much they are permitted to injure their victims.[12] Jesus wants us to be struck first that Satan appears in control, and then second that he isn't really. That is how things will appear throughout AD history, and he wants us to be those who see beyond the first impressions.

This should not lead to an unhealthy Christian triumphalism. Satan is defeated, but he has fallen from mighty heights and should not be trifled with. Make no mistake, he will ravage the nations of Planet Earth with venom and spite until Jesus comes again. But we must never forget that he is a mere creature,[13] fighting a battle he cannot win against the mighty Creator, whose vastly superior wisdom makes each one of Satan's weapons a rod to discipline idolaters with the aim of bringing them to repentance. The message of Revelation 9 is that, despite appearances, the star that fell from heaven can never withstand the force of heaven.

Even in the darkest points in AD history, God is on the Throne.

---

[11] Revelation 9:4.

[12] Revelation 5:15.

[13] Ezekiel 28:13.

Idols and Demons (9:20)

The rest of mankind that were not killed by these plagues still did not repent of the work of their hands; they did not stop worshipping demons, and idols of gold, silver, bronze, stone and wood – idols that cannot see or hear or walk.

(Revelation 9:20)

Satan did not fall alone. A whole army of rebels fell with him. They are called angels in verses 14 and 15, and depicted as locusts and cavalrymen elsewhere, but in verse 20 John finally names them for what they are: demons. We have just examined the work of Satan in the world, but now John invites us also to consider the very active work of his foot soldiers.[1]

Satan's sin was to plot that *"I will make myself like the Most High"*,[2] and his followers still march to the beat of that same drum. They utterly failed to satisfy their lust to be worshipped in heaven, but still they hope to win the worship of humans on earth. John therefore warns us, just like the rest of the Bible, that we must not think that the idols and false gods of this world are merely foolish human inventions.[3] He warns us that

---

[1] Revelation 12:3–4, 7–9 tells us that roughly a *third* of the angels joined Satan's rebellion and were cast out of heaven with him. A *third* means a large number, but nowhere near enough to defy the angels of heaven.

[2] Isaiah 14:14.

[3] Deuteronomy 32:17 and Psalm 106:37–38 both talk clearly about idolatry, telling us that *"they sacrificed to demons, which are not God – gods they had not known, gods that recently appeared"*, and that *"they sacrificed their sons and their daughters to demons… they sacrificed to the idols of Canaan"*. Paul confirms this in 1 Corinthians 10:20 when he states that *"the sacrifices of pagans are offered to demons"*.

demons are at work behind every idol, deceiving the nations into worshipping them instead of the true God. In a world where all the praise belongs to God alone, they try to make themselves like him to steal a share of his worship.

This was a pretty offensive message in the first century. The early Christians tended to preach *for* Jesus rather than *against* the Roman gods,[4] but inevitably this teaching provoked a reaction. The Ephesians rioted because Paul *"says that man-made gods are no gods at all"*, and because they were afraid that their patron-goddess Artemis would be *"robbed of her divine majesty"*.[5] Many believers were executed in the first 300 years of AD history on the charge that they were "atheists" who defamed the gods of Rome (the greatest of whom was Caesar himself). Readers from India, China or Tibet might feel the same offence at the suggestion that demons are behind the grotesque idols of their own culture, but generally Westerners are unfazed by this teaching. After all, idolatry doesn't really feature much in secular Western society. Right?

Wrong – and Jesus uses some strange language in Matthew 6:24 to tell us so. There he personifies money as *Mammon*, the Aramaic word for *Wealth*, in order to help us grasp that idols dress in secular clothes as easily as religious ones.[6] Demons are smart and unscrupulous, and they don't mind how they steal people's affections away from God, just so long as they do. This is where Westerners begin to get offended because, according to Jesus' definition, our own culture is riddled with demonic idolatry.

Scripture tells us that the first and greatest commandment is for us to *"Love the Lord your God with all your heart and with all your soul and with all your mind."*[7] Money can be a good thing, but demons are expert at taking a good thing and turning it into

---

[4] Acts 19:37.

[5] Acts 19:26–27.

[6] Jesus does this again in Luke 16:13.

[7] Jesus says this in Matthew 22:37 as a quotation from Deuteronomy 6:5.

a god thing. As soon as money becomes our goal, our security, or the driving factor in our decision-making, it has become the false god Mammon to us, and we have fallen for the oldest trick in the demons' book. We may not look as though we are worshipping *"idols of gold, silver, bronze, stone and wood – idols that cannot see or hear or walk"*, but demons are just as happy to receive worship as idols of bricks and mortar, steel and rubber, and the numbers on a bank statement.

I often wonder what idols we might see in our culture if we could see it with the same hindsight as we see the cultures of the past. It seems so obvious now that a demon was behind the Canaanite god Molech, who demanded that his worshippers throw some of their children onto a bonfire while priests played loud instruments to drown out their dying cries. They offered this child sacrifice because Molech promised them blessing, prosperity and advancement, and so I wonder how it might appear to a later generation to read that millions of children were aborted in the early years of the twenty-first century because their birth would have meant too much damage to reputation, career or finances.[8] I wonder how it might appear for them to read about our worship of celebrities, as we watch *Pop Idol* and *American Idol* before gathering at great sporting cathedral-stadiums to sing worship songs to our national gods. I wonder what they might think if they heard the radio songs which celebrate that our girlfriend or boyfriend can be *"The First, The Last, My Everything"*.[9] They may well consider them thinly disguised idols indeed.

I am not seeking to demonize our culture, but simply to

---

[8] There are around 1,250,000 abortions each year in the US and just under 200,000 each year in the UK. This is by no means the only motive behind those abortions, but it is a common motive and one not a million miles away from what motivated the worshippers of Molech.

[9] I am not particularly picking on Barry White, "the Walrus of Love", for his 1974 hit "*You're The First, The Last, My Everything*". However, its worship-chorus is so similar to the description of Jesus in Revelation 1:17; 2:8; 22:13 that, for me, it epitomizes the idolatry of romantic love in Western culture.

point out that demons are as busy in the West as they are in Hindu India. I'm simply unpacking what Jesus tells us, both in Matthew 6:24 and in Revelation 9:20, so that we can make sure that all of our praise goes to him and not to the demon-idols of our own age. Paul defines Christian conversion as *"turning to God from idols"*,[10] and I want you to wake up to the idols in your own life.

True spiritual warfare is not shouting at demons and telling them that we have bound their work in the world. It is spotting demons at work in our own lives and binding their activity by kicking them out along with the idols they inspire. Every time we write a cheque that means genuine sacrifice and put it in the collection basket, we perform a powerful act of spiritual warfare against the demon-god Mammon. Every time we resist the temptation to visit a pornographic website, we win a spiritual battle with the demon-goddess Aphrodite. Every time we refuse to sacrifice our families, our rest and our worship on the altar of career advancement, we strike a mighty blow to the demon-god of Worldly Success. We have all been made to worship, and we will all worship someone or something. All we get to choose is *who* and *how much*.

Feed your mind on the descriptions of demons in Revelation 9, and remind yourself that it is because of demon-gods like these that God's judgment is falling on humankind. Get radical with Satan's foot soldiers, and choose to love the Lord your God with all your heart, all your mind, all your soul and all your strength.

[10] 1 Thessalonians 1:9.

John's Bitter-Sweet Supper (10:10)

I took the little scroll from the angel's hand and ate it. It tasted as sweet as honey in my mouth, but when I had eaten it, my stomach turned sour.

(Revelation 10:10)

What is the strangest thing that you have ever eaten? During a three-week visit to China, I ate chickens' feet, duck's brain, field rat, sheep's lung, scorpion, shark, and solidified mare's milk.[1] You may well have eaten stranger foods than these, but I bet you have never done what John did in this verse. He ate a book. That's just not normal.

Fortunately, Jesus hasn't left us second guessing why he asked him to do so. The Old Testament prophet Ezekiel tells us in his third chapter that the Lord asked him to do so too. As soon as he ate his scroll he was told to *"Go now to the house of Israel and speak my words to them"*, and as soon as John ate his own scroll he was told that *"You must prophesy again about many peoples, nations, languages and kings"*.[2] Therefore this little scroll is not the same as the great scroll of chapter 5. It represents the Gospel message which God's servants speak to their generation, and Jesus repeats this scene from Ezekiel to show us what that Gospel is and what it isn't.

Both Ezekiel and John found the Gospel very sweet. Sometimes as Christians we can forget that. We let the amazing

---

[1] In retrospect, my interpretation of Luke 10:8 may have been too literal. I had food-poisoning after the rat.

[2] Ezekiel 3:4; Revelation 10:11.

transforming power of God's Word become so familiar that we forget it is *"sweeter than honey, than honey from the comb"*.[3] The Gospel proclaims that Jesus is King of kings and that he has conquered sin, death, Satan and sickness. It promises us new relationship with God, new purpose in God and new partnership with God, both now and beyond the grave. We must never lose our wide-eyed wonder at the Good News of Jesus Christ. The Gospel is sweet. Deliciously sweet.

Ezekiel and John also found that it had a bitter aftertaste.[4] Sometimes we forget that too. The message that Jesus is King of kings means life to those who accept it, but it also means *death* to them too. The Gospel is not God's timid offer to help humankind, much less an invitation for people to negotiate terms with him. It is a bold command to fall into line with the reality that he is Lord of the universe, and to surrender to him freely before he comes back to enforce his rule.[5] It is not simply the offer of a better life, but a call to die to our old life. Jesus insists that *"If anyone comes to me and does not hate... his own life, he cannot be my disciple"*,[6] which is why those who proclaim the Gospel in 11:3 do so dressed in sackcloth. The Gospel is free but it is not cheap. Jesus gives us a twenty-five verse interlude between the sixth and seventh trumpets because he wants to settle this matter once and for all.[7]

If the Church forgets that the Gospel is both bitter and sweet, she will never win her neighbours to Christ, let alone the nations. Christians tell unbelievers that Jesus is King because they genuinely believe that they will live a far sweeter life if they surrender to him. Christians who fail to share the message

---

[3] Psalm 19:9–10; 119:102–103.

[4] Although Ezekiel talks mainly about its sweetness, he adds in verse 14 that it gave him *bitterness of spirit*.

[5] See Revelation 14:6–7 and its summary of *"the eternal Gospel"*.

[6] Luke 14:26.

[7] Revelation 10:1–11:14 concentrates on the Church's evangelistic mission throughout AD history. There is a similar interlude between the sixth and seventh seals in chapter 7 which concentrates on her security.

assume that some unbelievers "have no need of God", and they forget that people will either submit to Jesus as King gladly in this life, or with bitter regret in the next.

If Christians tone down the bitterness of the Gospel, they will never see the kind of converts that the Lord is seeking. They will offer people life without death, and redemption without true repentance. Like a motorboat moored to the riverbank, they will find that no amount of teaching classes, worship celebrations, or charismatic experiences can ever cause their converts to power through the water. The moorings must be loosed before any progress can be made. People must die to their old life before they can step into the power of the new.

If Christians forget that the Gospel is bitter as well as sweet, they will falter in the face of hatred, offence, contempt and persecution. They will back-pedal and try to please their hearers, mistaking their rejection for failure. Christians who grasp that the Gospel is bitter can cope in 11:10 when their words irritate and torment their hearers. They are willing to stand alongside John who was exiled to Patmos *"because of the word of God and the testimony of Jesus"*.[8] The message that the Allies had defeated Nazi Germany caused the world to rejoice in 1945, but it was actually terrible news for those who were Nazi Germans. Similarly, the sweet message of Jesus' victory is bitter news to anyone who sides with Satan and his broken empire. We must not be surprised at their venom and persecution. The Gospel announces their doom.

Surprisingly, these verses tell us that persecution and opposition are the soil in which the Gospel flourishes. When Christians modify and doctor the Gospel to avoid making people *mad*, they find that they rob it of its power to make them *glad* too. But when they preach the glories of the bitter-sweet Gospel, the true Gospel of Christ's Kingdom, they find that they are fruitful in the midst of persecution. The interlude of 10:1 –

[8] Revelation 1:9.

11:14 promises us that even when the Church is attacked and killed for the message she bears, her bitter-sweet Gospel will always have the final say.

So chew on the bitter pill of the Gospel. Chew on it in your own life, tasting the sting of its death sentence so that you may experience the fullness of its sweet new life. Then proclaim its bitter-sweet message to the world around you, obeying the words which the Lord spoke to Ezekiel as he ate his scroll: *"Do not be afraid, though briers and thorns are all around you and you live among scorpions. Do not be afraid of what they say or terrified by them, though they are a rebellious house. You must speak my words to them, whether they listen or fail to listen"*.[9]

Do not sugar-coat the bitter-sweet challenge of the Gospel. This is the message which Christ has given us, and it is the message which overcomes the world.

[9] Ezekiel 2:6.

The Two Witnesses (11:1–14)

These men have power to shut up the sky so that it will not rain during the time they are prophesying; and they have power to turn the waters into blood and to strike the earth with every kind of plague as often as they want.

(Revelation 11:6)

The God of the Bible performs miracles. Hopefully there's nothing too controversial for you in that statement. The Bible is the story of one divine miracle after another, from Creation to the Exodus, from Elijah to Daniel, from Jesus to the Early Church. The Christian God is the God of miracles, and to make him anything less is to describe someone other than the God of the Bible.

But that's not all that Jesus is telling us in this passage. He is revealing something far more challenging as he finishes off his third overview of AD history. He is telling us that the Christian God *still* performs miracles today, that he will continue to do so throughout Church history, and that any church which expects less from him is in danger of worshipping a shadow of his real self.

This is where Christians start disagreeing with each other, and often misunderstanding each other too. Those at one end of the spectrum criticize "cessationists" for not believing in modern-day miracles, when actually they do believe in miracles – they just believe that the miraculous *charismatic gifts* died out after the first century of Church history.[1] Those at the other end of the spectrum criticize "charismatics" for relying too much on experience and not enough on Scripture, when frankly their experience seems to match up with Scripture far better than the non-experience of their critics.

Jesus answers this debate by presenting *"two witnesses"* as a picture of the Church[2] throughout AD history.[3] He wants us to grasp that – labels aside – we should expect him to work miracles, both inside the Church and in the wider community through the Church, right up until the end of time. He warns us that we if we tone down our expectations of his activity, we will become something less than his witnesses and will testify to someone less than the real God. Having read his warnings against idolatry in chapter 9, we need to take this message very seriously, and Jesus deliberately makes it hard for us to ignore it.

First, he tells us that the two witnesses – those who are part of the Church – will perform great miracles. We are meant to be familiar enough with the Old Testament to recognize the list in verses 5 and 6 as some of Moses and Elijah's "greatest

---

[1] Specifically the "gifts of the Spirit" listed in 1 Corinthians 12:7–11, 28–31; Romans 12:6–8; Ephesians 4:11.

[2] Jesus wants us to remember the apocalyptic vision which God gave over 600 years earlier in Zechariah 4, where he showed a lampstand shining brightly from the oil of two Olive Trees. Jesus has already used the picture of a *lampstand* to represent the Church in 1:20, and now he calls those in the Church *two lampstands* and *two olive trees*. The reason that there are two of them is probably that the Mosaic Law demanded two witnesses in Deuteronomy 19:15 for testimony to be considered credible.

[3] *"Forty-two months"* (v. 2) and *"1,260 days"* (v. 3) are both the same length of time, approximately *3½ years*. This is the same period of time given in 12:6; 13:5 and which is referred to in 12:14 as *"a time, times and half a time"*. It's all a reference to the rough period of time which the Lord used in Daniel 7:25; 8:14; 12:7; 12:11–12 as a symbol of the complete span of AD history. We are not meant to get out our calculators, but simply to grasp that the Lord has predetermined the exact length of AD history according to his master plan.

hits".[4] Jesus is very clear that performing miracles through the Holy Spirit is an essential part of the Gospel message. As Paul puts it in his letter to the Romans, if he had not preached and performed miracles in his travels, he would not have *"fully proclaimed the Gospel of Christ"*.[5]

Second, Jesus treats these miracles as an essential demonstration that the Kingdom of God has come. He told his critics that *"If I drive out demons by the Spirit of God, then the kingdom of God has come upon you"*,[6] and when John the Baptist asked him for reassurance that he was truly the promised Messianic King, he gave him the simple proof that *"The blind receive sight, the lame walk, those who have leprosy are cured, the deaf hear, the dead are raised."*[7] Without proof of the Kingdom, many people refuse to accept the truth of the Kingdom, which is why Satan has worked so hard to restrict supernatural Christianity to the realm of private devotions and predictable public meetings.

Third, Jesus tells us that these miracles are the irresistible weapon through which the Church advances with the Gospel and wins the world for Christ. The two witnesses confound their enemies by performing miracles, and they even rise from the ashes of defeat through a great and unexpected miracle. Armies advance not by debating their weapons but by using them, and the Church advances when Christians stop debating divine miracles and start performing them.

I saw this for the first time a few years ago on a Sunday

---

[4] Elijah brought fire down from heaven in 2 Kings 1:9–10 and stopped it raining for over three years in 1 Kings 17:2. Moses turned water into blood and struck Egypt with a succession of plagues in Exodus 7–11. They so much epitomized the BC people of God that they were the two men who met Jesus at his Transfiguration in Matthew 17:3–4, and so they are used here to tell us that the AD Church will have power in at least the same measure as the greatest heroes of the Old Testament.

[5] Romans 15:19.

[6] Matthew 12:28.

[7] Matthew 11:5.

morning which revolutionized my own life and ministry. I had agreed to preach the Gospel at a guest service in another town, and a friend and mentor had encouraged me to pray for the sick to be healed before I preached. His logic was that Paul attributed his success in Gospel preaching *"from Jerusalem all the way round to Illyricum"* to the fact that he came with *"the power of signs and miracles"*,[8] and that if this was his method, it ought to be mine as well.[9] His logic was too impeccable for me to ignore, but I still have to confess that the church had more confidence than me that God would heal anyone that Sunday morning. I can truly say that I was more surprised than anyone when God healed people in response to my prayers in Jesus' name. All I know is that God healed people so clearly, despite my having no previous track history as a "healing evangelist", that when I made an appeal at the end of my Gospel presentation I saw more people respond for salvation than in the whole previous year put together.

I know we don't always see as many miracles as we would like to, and that not every step of faith seems to be met with the power that Jesus promises here. I often feel like Gideon who complained to God *"where are all the wonders that our fathers told us about?!"*[10] John Calvin gives us his own answer in his commentary on 1 Corinthians, where he tells us that *"We now see our leanness, nay, our poverty; but in this we have a just punishment, sent to requite our ingratitude. For neither are the riches of God exhausted, nor is His benignity lessened; but we are neither deserving of his bounty, nor capable of receiving his liberality"*.[11] I actually think we have more reason to expect miracles from God than Calvin implies. My confidence is based

---

[8] Romans 15:19.

[9] This friend was Lex Loizides, who is one of the leaders of Jubilee Church in Cape Town, South Africa.

[10] Judges 6:13.

[11] John Calvin's *Commentary on 1 Corinthians*, commenting on 1 Corinthians 12:32.

partly on Jesus' description of the two witnesses, and partly on the famous words which accompany that picture of the lampstand and olive trees in Zechariah 4. It's a verse which urges us to pray and step out in miracles of healing, miracles of prophetic revelation and miracles of judgment as the great missing weapon for advancing the Gospel in our generation.

It says, *"'Not by might nor by power, but by my Spirit,' says the Lord Almighty. 'What are you, O mighty mountain? Before Zerubbabel you will become level ground!'"*[12]

[12] Zechariah 4:6–7.

A Tale of Two Cities (11:8)

Their bodies will lie in the street of the great city, which is figuratively called Sodom and Egypt, where also their Lord was crucified.

(Revelation 11:8)

The Bible is a tale of two cities: Babylon and Jerusalem. The early chapters of Genesis record the first attempt to build the city of Babylon, and the last two chapters of Revelation focus on the new city of Jerusalem. Jesus wants us to grasp that spiritual forces were behind these two earthly cities, and to do so he takes the phrase *"the great city"* (a phrase which he will use several times in the second half of Revelation to refer to Babylon),[1] and he tells us that *"the great city"* was figuratively at work in the town of Sodom, the nation of Egypt, and even the first-century city of Jerusalem.[2] Jesus expects us to see "Babylon" and "Jerusalem" as two spiritual cities at war over Planet Earth, and we need to grasp this concept here or else we will struggle to understand the rest of Revelation.

Nearly 4,000 years ago, in Genesis 11, the people of the earth gathered to build the city of Babylon. Most people refer to this story as the *"**Tower** of Babel"*, but note that they plotted *"Come, let us build for ourselves a **city**, with a tower that reaches*

---

[1] Revelation 16:19; 17:5, 18; 18:10, 16, 18, 19, 21.

[2] The city of *Sodom* speaks of sin and depravity (Jeremiah 23:14; Jude 7), the nation of *Egypt* speaks of Satanic oppression and slavery (Micah 6:4), and *Jerusalem* was the city of rebellion where Jesus was crucified. I think that Jesus deliberately groups the earthly city of Jerusalem with Babylon, Sodom and Egypt so that we will grasp that both Babylon and Jerusalem are spiritual rather than earthly cities.

to the heavens, so that we may make a name for ourselves and not be scattered over the face of the whole earth." The tower was only part of a bigger building project, one which aimed to defy the Lord and to exalt humankind. It took place on the *"plain of Shinar"*, the site of the great city of Babylon,[3] and the city was named *"Babel"*, which is the Hebrew word for Babylon.[4] Here we have the Spirit of Babylon, stirring humankind with lust for their own fame, urging them to climb up to God's Throne and defy his command to scatter throughout the earth.[5] God was unimpressed. He quickly scattered the builders and *"they stopped building the city"*.

Babylon was down but not out. Some time later a man named Nimrod succeeded in building the city,[6] and it became one of the greatest cities in the world. It was so powerful that the Assyrian Empire is simply referred to in Isaiah 13:1 as *"Babylon"*,[7] and it was not long before the city threw off Assyrian rule and became a superpower in its own right from 626 to 539 BC. It was Babylon which conquered the world, dashing out the brains of babies, raping women and even little girls, and killing or enslaving the men.[8] They even did this to the kingdom of Judah in 586 BC and exiled to Babylon the minority which they did not kill. It therefore comes as no surprise when the Old

---

[3] Genesis 11:1; Daniel 1:2.

[4] The Hebrew word *babel* is translated once as *"Babel"* in Genesis 11:9, and 261 times to mean *"Babylon"* in the rest of the Bible. It is unfortunate that English translations use the name *"Babel"* in Genesis 11:9, because the original Hebrew readers of Genesis would have grasped straight away that this city was Babylon, the city famed for its high ziggurat towers.

[5] Genesis 1:28; 9:1.

[6] Nimrod's building work is described in the middle of a genealogy in Genesis 10:8–12, although he actually lived after the events described in Genesis 11:1–9.

[7] Isaiah 13–14 prophesies against the Assyrian Empire, calling it *"Babylon"*. It's quite confusing unless you know a little about the role of Babylon within the Assyrian Empire. It makes a good advert for Study Bibles.

[8] Isaiah 13:16; Lamentations 5:11.

Testament prophets identify Satan at work behind Babylon[9] and its constant desire to increase its power, make a name for itself, and steal the worship which belongs to God.[10] Nor is it a surprise that God prophesies its destruction and that he carried out his threat in 539 and 516 BC.[11]

History lesson over. Now for the present. Jesus tells us that although the city of Babylon has long since been destroyed, the Spirit of Babylon is still very active in the world. Even while Babylon stood on the Plain of Shinar, the Spirit of Babylon was also at work in Sodom and ancient Egypt, and even after the city fell it continued its work in Jerusalem as Jesus was crucified. Jesus warns us that *"the great city"* is at work in any human culture which refuses to accept Jesus as Lord, and he outlines its rise and its fall in human history.

In chapter 17, he will portray Babylon as *"the Great Prostitute"*, the sexy and alluring madam who tries to rival Jerusalem, *"the Bride of Christ"*.[12] Her rise will be meteoric, offering money, sex, power, fame and religion – all without the commitment demanded by Jerusalem, the Bride.[13] She will dominate the governments of the earth,[14] seducing them with her ravishing looks and her sweet promises, for she is quite literally "drop-dead gorgeous" and "dressed to kill".[15] She is a liar who is after people's blood, determined to entice them away from the New Jerusalem, and to get them drunk on her pleasures or dead with her spite.[16] Jesus lays all this out for us in chapters 11 to 19 in order to prepare us for his call to give our lives to the New Jerusalem.

---

[9] Isaiah 14:12–15. We saw in the chapter on "The Star That Fell to Earth" that this refers to Satan as the power behind Babylon.

[10] Isaiah 13:19; Habakkuk 1:7, 11; 2:5.

[11] The best examples are in Jeremiah 50–51 and Habakkuk 2.

[12] Contrast Revelation 17:1–5 with 21:2, 9.

[13] Revelation 14:8; 18:9, 10, 14, 23; 19:2.

[14] Revelation 17:18.

[15] Revelation 17:4.

[16] Revelation 14:8; 17:6; 18:3, 24; 19:2.

When the southern half of the United States seceded to form the Confederate States of America in 1861, there was one great question on the lips of Americans: *"Which side are you on?"* Trains ran north to south and south to north as citizens fled the wrong side of the divide and threw their swords in with the Union or Confederate causes. Whole states declared themselves for the North or for the South, and battle lines were drawn for the war that ensued. Jesus wants us to understand that the whole of AD history is just such a time for the citizens of Planet Earth. "Babylon" and "Jerusalem" are at war, with one declaring for Satan and his Antichrist, and the other declaring for God and his Christ. There are no neutrals in the fight, because failure to declare for God is to declare for the God-hating war aims of Babylon. *"Come out and be separate!"* is the battle cry of Jerusalem, and it's God's call to you at this stage in Revelation.[17]

Babylon is smart, sexy, alluring and attractive. Her packaging sells products, movies, politics and ideas much more successfully than the packaging of Jerusalem. But here's the thing: she is doomed to destruction. Ancient Babylon destroyed ancient Jerusalem, but at the end of Revelation it is Babylon which is destroyed and the New Jerusalem which stands forever.[18] This "tale of two cities" will only end one way, and we all need to decide which side we are on.

Babylon will offer us fame, power, sex, money and a life free from the commands of God. Jerusalem offers you sacrifice, discipleship, hardship and persecution, joyfully submitting to King Jesus and to his Plan of History. The Queen of Babylon's voice may sound sweeter, but she is ultimately after your blood, and wants to drag you down to hell with her. Meanwhile Jesus,

---

[17] Revelation 18:4; 2 Corinthians 6:17; Isaiah 48:20; 52:11; Jeremiah 50:8; 51:6, 45.

[18] Revelation 18; 21–22.

the Great King of Jerusalem, has shed his own blood for you to raise you up to heaven with him.[19]

It's a pretty simple choice, really, when we grasp what Jesus sets out on the pages of Revelation. Yet too many Christians fool themselves that they can have Jesus *and* all that Babylon has to offer. Jesus is going to tell us again and again in the rest of Revelation that war has been declared and there is no dual citizenship on offer. *"Come out from her and be separate"*. Your life depends on it.

[19] Contrast the differing mission statements of Satan and Jesus in John 10:10–11.

The Second Coming of Jesus Christ (11:15–19)

The seventh angel sounded his trumpet, and there were loud voices in heaven, which said: "The kingdom of the world has become the kingdom of our Lord and of his Christ, and he will reign for ever and ever".

(Revelation 11:15)

The elderly servant pushed gingerly on his master's door. He had been working feverishly for the past two weeks on his latest masterpiece, but the music from his room had stopped and the house was now filled with an eerie silence. Concerned, the servant nudged open the door and tiptoed inside. There was his master, the great composer Handel, sitting in a chair with his freshly written score of "The Hallelujah Chorus" laid out in front of him. He had just completed one of the most famous and most rousing classical pieces of all time, and there were tears pouring down his cheeks. The composer turned and whispered to his servant in reverent awe: *"I did think I did see all Heaven before me, and the great God himself."*[1]

I find "The Hallelujah Chorus" from Handel's *Messiah* very moving. The words are simply a quotation from this verse and two others in chapter 19, and they seek to convey the pomp, power, and excitement of the Second Coming of Jesus Christ.[2]

---

[1] This story spread all over Britain when *Messiah* was first performed in 1742. Some historians consider it legendary rather than historical, but no one knows for sure.

[2] In addition to Revelation 11:15, the Chorus also quotes from 19:6, 16.

Whether classical music moves you or not, Jesus wants you to be stirred by this passage and by the great promise that he is coming back.

Jesus has masterfully whetted our appetites in the run-up to these verses. He began Revelation with a promise that *"the end is near"* and a command to *"look, he is coming with the clouds and every eye will see him"*.[3] He ended each of his letters to the Seven Churches with a promise about his Second Coming. The Seven Seals echo with the cry *"how long?!"* and the promise *"wait a little longer"*.[4] Finally, he sends an angel in between the sounding of the sixth and seventh trumpets to give a teaser-trailer that, when the trumpet sounds, *"the mystery of God will be accomplished"*.[5] We are meant to feel excited and impatient to read about the great Christian hope in 11:15–19.

Jesus is coming back. He came the first time to live within history, but he will come a second time to end history. When he returns, he will no longer be praised as *"the one who is, and who was, and who is to come"*, but simply as *"the one who was and who is"*. We will stop singing about the future age and will start to enjoy the future age instead.[6] He came the first time to proclaim his Kingdom, but he will come a second time to enforce his Kingdom. Note the past tenses which we will use when we praise him on that day: *"the kingdom of the world* ***has become*** *the kingdom of our Lord... you* ***have begun*** *to reign"*.[7] He came the first time to call people to follow him, but he will come a second time to vindicate and reward those who chose to do so, and to judge those who refused his call. He came the first

[3] Revelation 1:3, 7.

[4] Revelation 6:9–11.

[5] Revelation 10:6–7.

[6] Contrast Revelation 11:17 with 1:4, 8. The Textus Receptus Greek manuscript assumes that this is an error and "corrects" it, but the more reliable manuscripts leave the words as they stand. Jesus wants us to understand that his Second Coming will end this age and begin the age which is to come.

[7] Revelation 11:15, 17. These are aorist past tenses in Greek and fulfil the Gospel promise of Matthew 3:2; 4:17; 10:7.

time to bear the wrath of the nations and ultimately the wrath of God for our sin, but he will come a second time to pour out his own wrath on the wicked.[8] He came the first time largely unannounced, ignored by the innkeepers of Bethlehem, and crucified by the Jews and Romans. He will come a second time with great fanfare so that in the words of 1:7, *"Every eye will see him, even those who pierced him; and all the peoples of the earth will mourn because of him."*

Put simply, Jesus' Second Coming will blow the whistle on AD history and will reveal once and for all which side each person is on. We will all cry tears – either tears of joy and delight like Handel, or tears of mourning and bitter regret like those in 1:7. It will be the last and defining Day of world history, and Jesus tells us about it here so that we can live with it constantly in mind.

At the end of the second *Lord of the Rings* movie, the heroes are under siege in the fortress of Helm's Deep, fighting for their lives against an innumerable army of evil orcs. Things look bleak, and they finally accept that the fortress cannot hold out any longer. They will die. Suddenly they look up and see a white figure coming over the brow of a hill. Their faces brighten. It's Gandalf, riding at the head of a great army of horsemen, leading reinforcements who can lift the siege. He had promised to do so earlier in the film, but it was so long ago that we had almost forgotten he was coming. His sudden appearance is unexpected, and it brings deliverance, vindication and victory for our heroes, along with doom, death and defeat for the orcs. It's a wonderful picture of how people will feel when Jesus returns. No matter how weak and defeated the Church may appear, the fortunes of the battle will change in an instant. How terrible it will be for those who only discover that they are on the wrong side when Jesus appears and it is too late to change!

---

[8] The words for *were angry* and *wrath* in Revelation 11:18 both come from the same root word in Greek.

The promise of the Second Coming of Jesus should transform your life if you are not yet a wholehearted follower of Jesus Christ. When the seventh trumpet sounds, you will have no opportunity left to switch sides. You will weep bitter tears of regret as you reap your reward for a lifetime of resisting your Creator. But today you still have a chance to kneel before him and submit to his rule.

The promise should also transform your life if you have surrendered to Christ. Since we know that this is how the story ends, we pour out all our time, our money and our energy for his sake alone. We laugh at the cost, for we know what it stores up for us for that great Day. This vision excites and sustains us as we wait for the last trumpet to sound. Then we will suddenly see with our own bewildered eyes what Handel glimpsed at his music, and we will sing the "Hallelujah Chorus" as it has never been sung before.

The Fourth Overview of AD History

Vantage Point on World History (12:1–14:20)

A great and wondrous sign appeared in heaven: a woman clothed with the sun... And I saw a beast coming out of the sea... Then I looked, and there before me was the Lamb, standing on Mount Zion.

(Revelation 12:1; 13:1; 14:1)

One of cleverest thrillers of recent years is the Dennis Quaid movie *Vantage Point.*[1] After the opening scene in which the President of the United States is assassinated, we are shown the same fifteen-minute scene five times through the eyes of five different witnesses. It is only after we have seen all five perspectives that we suddenly grasp with surprise what really happened.

Jesus produces something very similar in Revelation chapters 12, 13 and 14. Rather than stick to the same motif of *Seven* Churches, *Seven* Seals, *Seven* Trumpets and *Seven* Bowls for his fourth overview of AD history, Jesus chooses to take a different approach and shows us history from three very different perspectives.[2] Chapter 12 shows us AD history from

---

[1] *Vantage Point* (Sony Pictures, 2008).

[2] Note that some commentators call these three chapters the *"Seven Pictures"* because a phrase such as *"then I saw"* or *"then there appeared"* begins 12:1–6, 7–12, 13–17; 13:1–10, 11–18; 14:1–5, 6–20. I personally think that this is more driven by a desire for neatness rather than by the text itself, particularly because those same phrases are also used in five other places within the "pictures". Revelation makes a clear reference to Seven Churches, Seven Seals, Seven Trumpets and Seven Bowls, but it makes no such clear reference here. Rather than force-fitting the number seven on to these three chapters, I

heaven's perspective, as Satan is defeated and hurled down to earth. Chapter 13 shows us *earth's* perspective, as the Beast deceives the human race. Chapter 14 gives us the *Church's* perspective, as God protects every single believer, grants them great success with the Gospel, and saves them from the Final Judgment. We need to grasp the message of all three perspectives if we are to have a complete understanding of the thrust of AD history.

Chapter 12, *heaven's* perspective, shows us that *Satan means business*. He tried to kill Jesus at the hands of King Herod from the very moment he was born into the Jewish nation.[3] Having failed, he then tried to attack the Church instead.[4] Having failed even to destroy the Church, he switches his target to individual Christians.[5] The message is clear: we must not underestimate Satan's determination to destroy us.

But chapter 12 also shows us that *Satan will ultimately fail*. At times we will have cause to doubt this. He will look as fierce as a dragon, sporting seven powerful crowns and followed by a large army of demons.[6] His fury will be intense, and it will claim the lives of many Christians through deception, persecution and martyrdom.[7] Yet if we look a little more closely, we will see that it is indeed true. He was outgunned by the archangel Michael and his army, and only came to earth at all in the wake of being

---

think it does much more justice to the actual text to see Jesus giving us *Three Perspectives* on AD history.

[3] Revelation 12:1–5. Since Joseph saw Jacob, his step-mother and his brothers as the *sun, moon and stars* in Genesis 37:9–10, we are probably meant to understand this woman as *the People of God* rather than as *Mary*. Beware the surprisingly widespread speculation that *twelve stars* must be a reference the European Union and its twelve-starred flag. This simply makes no sense within the wider context of the woman giving birth to Jesus!

[4] Revelation 12:13–16. *"1,260 days"* and *"a time, times and half a time"* are references back to Daniel 7:25; 8:14; 12:7 and 12:11–12, where the Lord uses this as a symbol of the complete span of AD history.

[5] Revelation 12:17.

[6] Revelation 12:3–4.

[7] Revelation 12:11–12.

cast out of heaven.[8] His seven crowns are mere *diadēmata*, or *royal crowns*, but the People of God wear a *stephanos* or *victory crown* which he will never wear.[9] God is the one who sits on the Throne in this chapter, and Jesus is the one who holds the true royal sceptre. Therefore every single one of Satan's attacks will be frustrated.[10] He is not full of fury because he is winning, but because he knows he has lost.[11]

Chapter 14, the *Church's* perspective, shows us that *we will win in this age*. The Gospel will spread around the world, Babylon will fall, and the Beast will not be able to prevent it. Jesus fills this scene with urgency, reminding us that the Final Judgment is coming upon the people of the earth, and urging us to throw off passivity and step up as missionary churches to win the world for Christ. We must not retreat into *dispensationalism*, the view that Christians should hold on tight to be "raptured" away from the all-too-powerful challenges of Planet Earth. God has not consigned the rest of humanity to their horrible fate, but expects us to be the agents through whom he can save them.[12] We have seen the end of the story, and it involves a great multitude from every nation, tribe and language rejecting Satan and turning to Christ.

Chapter 13, the *earth's* perspective, shows us that *the fight will be fierce*. It is probably the gloomiest chapter in the whole of Revelation, with very little positive encouragement at all except for a call to display *"patient endurance and faithfulness"*. Jesus sandwiches this chapter between the other, more positive, chapters because he does not want us to fall prey to *triumphalism*

[8] Revelation 12:7–9.

[9] The woman wears a *stephanos* in Revelation 12:1, which is worth more than all seven of Satan's *diadēmata* put together. Romans 8:37 reminds us that the People of God are *more than conquerors in Christ*.

[10] Revelation 12:5 and 12:5, 16.

[11] Revelation 12:12.

[12] I will examine the idea of a "rapture" later on, in the chapter entitled "The Millennium". Sadly, this view actually promotes the exact kind of hold-on-to-the-end defeatism that these chapters tell us to avoid.

and fool ourselves that the battle will be easy. We will not simply be able to "name and claim" our way to an easy victory. There will even be short-term defeats along the way.[13]

The reason the movie *Vantage Point* is so clever is that each time we watch one of the five perspectives of the assassination, we think that we understand what really happened. It is only at the end of the movie that we suddenly see the truth as all five perspectives weave together into one coherent whole. This is what Jesus does with this fourth overview of AD history. If we grasp *heaven's* perspective and the *Church's* perspective without *earth's* perspective, we will slip into unhealthy *triumphalism*. If we grasp *earth's* perspective but not *heaven's* or the *Church's* perspectives, we will fall prey to *defeatism*. If we focus only on *heaven's* and *earth's* perspectives, we will slip into *dispensationalism*, battening down the hatches and praying to be "raptured" from Planet Earth. We will have forgotten the here-and-now victories of the *Church's* perspective, and God's urgent call to make disciples of all nations and win all cultures for Christ.

Jesus gives us a unique vantage point from which to see history from three different perspectives. They should drive out naïvety, passivity, fear and defeatism, and they should spur us on to follow our victorious King.

If we weave together these three perspectives, we will see the events of AD history as they really are. We will be ready to brave the choppy waters of our own place in time.

---

[13] Revelation 13:7. We will examine this in more detail in the chapter entitled "The Church Defeated".

Deceiver and Accuser (12:9–10)

The great dragon was hurled down – that ancient serpent called the Devil or Satan, who leads the whole world astray.

(Revelation 12:9)

The outcome of the American Civil War was changed by a single stupid mistake. General Robert E. Lee, possibly the greatest general of his day, had led the Confederate Army to several surprising victories in the first year of the war. He had invaded the North, and many feared that he was poised for victory. Until one morning in September 1862, that is.

Part of the Union Army had slept the night in a former Confederate campground in Maryland, anxiously listening for the sound of guns. In the morning, one Corporal Barton Mitchell noticed three cigars wrapped in paper and lying in the long grass. He eagerly retrieved them as the spoils of war, but when he looked at the paper wrapped around them, he could scarcely believe his eyes. That paper was "Special Order 191", which had been issued by General Lee to his senior officers and which gave the exact movements of all of his troops over the next few days. When the paper was passed to General McClellan of the Union Army, he exclaimed, *"Now I know what to do! Here is a paper with which, if I cannot whip Bobby Lee, I will be willing to go home!"* Sure enough, armed with that paper, McClellan was able to outmanoeuvre Lee, win the Battle of Antietam, and force the Confederates to abandon their invasion plans. One piece of paper changed the course of a whole war.[1]

In Revelation 12:9, John hands you the equivalent of Satan's "Special Order 191". It is vital information about your enemy's tactics, and John expects you to make full use of it. He is not merely naming your enemy in this verse, but names him in order to describe his tactics and to help you outmanoeuvre him in the fight.

First, John calls him the *dragon* and the *ancient serpent*. He is the *ancient* serpent because he is the one who appeared as a snake in the Garden of Eden. Dragons lurk in caves and breathe fire at their foes. Snakes hide in the shadows and sink venomous fangs into their unsuspecting victims. We need to understand that Satan is low-down and dirty, and that anyone who plays around with sin makes a fatal mistake.

Second, John calls him *the Devil*. The Greek word *diabolos* simply means *liar* or *deceiver*.[2] Jesus warned in John 8:44 that *"When he lies, he speaks his native language"*, and we can see from other Scriptures that this is his primary tactic. If possible, he will persuade people that he doesn't really exist, as he did with the Sadducees, so that he is free to work other, follow-up deceptions. He has done a very good job of this in Western culture, and many readers of Revelation prefer to assume that its talk of the Devil and his demons is mere symbolism. It isn't, and such assumptions merely reflect his accomplishment as a liar.

Where Satan cannot convince people that he doesn't exist, he still has plenty more lies to try. With Eve he used the line,

[1] This is known to southerners as the Battle of Sharpsburg. General McClellan probably failed to exploit this intelligence to the full and could have won a greater victory, but even what he did was enough to put the invasion army into retreat and give President Lincoln the confidence to issue his Emancipation Proclamation.

[2] Paul uses this same word in an everyday sense in 1 Timothy 3:11 to mean a *slanderer* or *malicious talker.*

"Did God really say...?" and convinced her to believe his own word over the Lord's.[3] He has been doing this for centuries and is very good at sounding convincing. We hear the same question *"Did God really say...?"* when considering the Gospel, church government, marriage, parenting, same-sex marriages, promiscuity, drunkenness, creation, the authority of Scripture, salvation through Christ alone, and so on. We need to get smart, reading John's "Special Order 191" and training ourselves to spot the Deceiver while he is still afar off. Following consensus or majority opinion, even within the Church, is no safeguard against his lies. His agenda is to *"lead the whole world astray"*, and he has no problem twisting Scripture to do so.[4] We need to be clear about what God has said in Scripture, and not debate it with the Devil.

John's third name for him is *Satan*, which is the Hebrew word for *The Accuser* or *The Adversary*. It is the word which was used in court for the barrister for the prosecution, and he is forever accusing us at the dock of God's Judgment. Zechariah had a graphic vision of this in Zechariah 3:1–5, when he saw Satan attacking the High Priest Joshua – one of the godliest believers of his day – and pointing out the filth which polluted his clothes. The Lord showed Zechariah that our only hope against Satan's accusations is to admit our guilt and shame but ensure that they drive us to Christ instead of away from him. I love the way that the Lord silences Satan and strips Joshua of his filthy clothes, dressing him in his own spotless clothes of righteousness instead. Satan may be the barrister for the prosecution, but we also have a defence barrister in the blood of Christ, and that always makes it an open-and-shut case in our favour.[5] I love the old hymn which teaches us what to do to defeat the Accuser:

[3] Genesis 3:1–6.

[4] Matthew 4:1–11.

[5] Hebrews 12:24.

When Satan tempts me to despair and tells me of the guilt within,
Upward I look and see him there who made an end to all my sin.
Because the sinless Saviour died, my sinful soul is counted free,
For God, the Just, is satisfied to look on him and pardon me.[6]

You have received your "Special Order 191" from John, and it contains vital intelligence to turn the tide of your fortunes in the spiritual battle. Make no mistake; this compendium of names reveals that Satan is your bitter enemy and that he longs to devour you.[7] Don't ignore him, don't give ground to him, and don't play games with sin. Instead, let faith be your shield to deflect his deceptions. Let the Gospel help you to reject his accusations, and get ready to take the fight into his own territory.

This verse does not just give us three descriptions of Satan. It also tells us three times that he has been *thrown down* in defeat.[8] You've got your hands on Satan's "Special Order 191". Use that intelligence to remind him that he is a defeated foe.

[6] Charity L. Bancroft wrote this in 1863. The title of the hymn is "Before the Throne of God Above".

[7] 1 Peter 5:8.

[8] The NIV only translates it twice in this verse, but many other English translations reflect that it says it three times in the Greek text.

The Road to Victory (12:11)

They overcame him by the blood of the Lamb and by the word of their testimony; they did not love their lives so much as to shrink from death.

(Revelation 12:11)

Every day hundreds of Christians are martyred for their faith. It's impossible to know exactly how many, but some reports suggest that it may even be as many as 500 a day. Proclaiming that Jesus Christ is the King of kings is one of the most dangerous things a person can do in some parts of the world. This may surprise you if you live in the West, but it has always been the case throughout Church history.

The deacon Stephen was the first Christian to be martyred for his faith, only three years after the Day of Pentecost.[1] John's brother James was martyred ten years later, and nearly all of the other disciples followed suit. Thousands of rank-and-file Christians lost their lives in the first 300 years of Christianity – burned, beheaded, branded, boiled, crucified, flayed or fed to wild animals as part of the Roman games. The Gospel message that *"Jesus is Lord"* was deeply offensive to the Romans, and they would stop at nothing to silence it.

But here's the amazing thing: they couldn't. They might silence the Christians who were martyred, but they couldn't silence their message. In fact, so many were converted through their courageous deaths that the Early Church leader Tertullian famously argued that *"the blood of the martyrs is the seed of the*

---

[1] Acts 6:8 – 7:60; 12:1–2. Stephen and James were probably martyred in 33 AD and 43 AD respectively.

Church". Jesus gave his Revelation to John in the midst of fierce persecution, and he expects his words in 12:11 to spur on every generation of Christians in the midst of their own trials.

Note that Jesus does not tell us to pray *for* persecution, as if this might be a solution for apathy and compromise within the Church. He is very clear that it is a *woe* which comes from Satan, and that we are very blessed if we live in peaceful times.[2] Nor does he tell us that persecution will inevitably backfire on Satan. It can often be very successful in the short term and can leave the Church looking down, dead and defeated.[3] Jesus simply promises that if we truly follow him, we are bound to meet some form of persecution along the way,[4] but that he has given us three great weapons through which we can always overcome in the end.

First, we need to meet it with *"the blood of the Lamb"*. The Gospel means that Jesus has utterly defeated Satan through his death and resurrection,[5] and this is the only fact which will keep us hanging on to our faith as the cost soars ever higher. This is what enables us to look our persecutors in the eye and keep on following Jesus.

Second, we must meet persecution with *"the word of our testimony"*. The world needs to hear the Gospel and to see a demonstration of its truth in the lives of believers. Persecution aims to silence the Gospel, but we will overcome it if we keep on speaking.

Third, we must meet persecution by *"not loving our lives so much as to shrink from death"*. There is great power in the Gospel message itself, but it is even more convincing when its messengers are willing to die because they really believe it is true.

Church history shows us that persecution cannot survive against these three weapons. When Jan Hus of Prague preached

---

[2] Revelation 3:10.

[3] Revelation 11:7; 12:10; 13:7.

[4] See also 2 Timothy 3:12.

[5] Colossians 2:15.

salvation through Jesus' cross rather than by works at the start of the fifteenth century, he saw so many converts that he was told that he would be burned at the stake unless he recanted his message. His fearless death provoked a 100-year revival in his native Bohemia, and this profoundly affected Martin Luther. When Luther proclaimed that same Gospel message at the start of the sixteenth century, he was also threatened with death. He replied that *"If I had a thousand heads I would rather have them all cut off than revoke"*, and *"My conscience is taken captive by God's Word. I cannot and will not recant anything, for to act against conscience is neither safe for us, nor open to us. On this I take my stand. I can do no other."* So began the great Reformation revival in Europe, which in turn influenced the bishops of England. When two of them were about to be burned at the stake in Oxford in 1555, Bishop Latimer turned to Bishop Ridley and told him to *"Be of good comfort, master Ridley, and play the man: we shall this day light such a candle, by God's grace, in England, as I trust shall never be put out."* Sure enough, their sacrifice spawned a church of zealous missionaries who took the Gospel to the ends of the earth in the nineteenth century.

I have highlighted this one particular strand of history because I happen to come from the land of Latimer and Ridley, but I could just as easily have chosen the story of the Gospel in Africa, South America, India, China, Burma or Korea. Wherever people hold on to the blood of the Lamb, preach the Gospel and their own experience of it, and are willing to shed their own blood for its sake, persecution is overcome and the Kingdom of God advances. The challenge for most of us is simply whether those three weapons are present in our own spiritual battles.

Have you noticed that there is a daily battle, even within the Church, to hold on to *"the blood of the Lamb"*? It is attacked doctrinally by the rise of religious pluralism and a desire to appear "tolerant" in a multifaith society. It is attacked experientially by legalism and formalism, which seek to push the cross of Christ away from its central position in our Faith. There is a similar battle to hold on to *"the word of our testimony"*, as churches become introverted subcultures instead of missionaries to their culture. Above all, there is a battle to play it safe, and to make Christianity something individual, private and unthreatening in case the message *"Jesus is Lord"* offends, provokes and even leads to persecution.

We are not to look for persecution, but neither are we to buy peace by sacrificing the three things through which it can be overcome. There may come a day when we are called to give our lives for our faith, but today's challenge is simply to hold on to it, to proclaim it and to sacrifice anything necessary to keep on speaking it. It's a simple plan, a painful one, and a very, very effective one.

When I was first converted to Christ, I was deeply affected by a tract which someone gave me on what it truly meant to follow Jesus. I quote part of it here, with a prayer that we will each live this way in the trials of our own generation:

> *The die has been cast. The decision has been made. I have stepped over the line. I won't look back, let up, slow down, back away or be still... I no longer need pre-eminence, prosperity, position, promotions, plaudits or popularity. I don't have to be right, first, top, recognized, praised, regarded or rewarded... My face is set, my gait is fast, my goal is heaven, my road is narrow, my way is rough, my companions are few, my Guide is reliable, and my vision is clear. I cannot be bought, compromised, detoured, lured away, turned back, deluded or delayed. I will not flinch in the face of sacrifice, hesitate in the presence of adversity, negotiate at the table of the enemy, ponder at the pool of popularity or meander in the maze of mediocrity. I won't give up, shut up, let up or slow up until I have stayed up, stored up, prayed up, paid up and spoken up for the cause of Christ. I am a disciple of Jesus.*[6]

[6] This anonymous creed is sometimes referred to as "The Fellowship of the Unashamed".

The Antichrist (13:1–18)

And I saw a beast coming out of the sea. He had ten horns and seven heads, with ten crowns on his horns, and on each head a blasphemous name.

(Revelation 13:1)

I find this the darkest chapter in the whole of Revelation. It is difficult to understand and also quite difficult to endure, because it is the one chapter of Revelation where hope and encouragement are very thinly spread. Many other people feel the same, so I want to examine the exact message of Revelation 13. My hope is that by the end of this chapter you will be able to stare these eighteen verses in the face, to heed their warning, and to see hope in the midst of their terror.

The first thing to establish is that the Leopard-Beast which emerges from the sea is the one to whom John refers in his letters as *the Spirit of the Antichrist.*[1] In English the prefix *anti-* means *"opposed to"* (as in anti-ageing, anti-aircraft, anti-clockwise, and anti-social), but in Greek the prefix *anti-* also means *"instead of"*.[2] Therefore the Leopard-Beast represents the Spirit of the Antichrist because it tries to take the place of Christ. It parodies his death and resurrection,[3] it parodies his seal on the redeemed,[4] and it even parodies the Trinity with an unholy threesome of Dragon, Leopard-Beast and Lamb-Beast. It

---

[1] 1 John 4:3.

[2] One good example of the Greek word *anti* being used in this way is in Matthew 20:28.

[3] Revelation 13:3, 12, 14; 17:8.

[4] Revelation 13:16–17; 14:9–11; 16:2; 19:20; 20:4. Christ's seal in 7:3–8 brings protection, but the Beast's seal brings judgment and hell.

makes a blasphemous bid for the worship of the nations,[5] and it operates by the power of Satan's throne to fulfil Satan's plan and lead the whole world astray.[6]

This leads on to the second thing that we need to establish. There is a difference between saying that the Leopard-Beast is *the Spirit of the Antichrist* and saying that it is *the Antichrist* himself. We will see in the chapter entitled "666" that Christians have speculated for the past 2,000 years over who *the Antichrist* may be, and so we need to grasp that Revelation 13 describes the spirit who is at work behind the Antichrist, and not just the Antichrist himself. Since chapters 12, 13 and 14 are three different perspectives upon the whole of AD history, we must remember that this chapter cannot simply describe the coming of one man or woman towards the end of history. It must speak of what will happen in the whole of AD history, which is why we are told that the Beast's reign will last for *forty-two months.*[7] John tells us more clearly in his letters that *"the spirit of the antichrist... is already in the world"*, and that *"the antichrist is coming, even now many antichrists have come"*.[8] Since John tells us that anyone can become *"an antichrist"* by following the lead of the Spirit of the Antichrist,[9] we must see the Leopard-Beast as a strong demon at work in the world, who will work through a long succession of individuals and eventually through one great Antichrist.

A final thing to establish is that, although the Spirit of the Antichrist is able to work through governments and societies, it is primarily active through key individuals throughout history.[10] Paul speaks of the Antichrist as *"the man of lawlessness... the*

[5] Revelation 13:1,4–8.

[6] Revelation 12:9; 13:2, 4.

[7] We already saw in the chapter on "The Two Witnesses" that this symbolizes the complete span of AD history.

[8] 1 John 2:18; 4:3.

[9] 1 John 2:22; 2 John 7.

[10] We saw in the chapter "A Tale of Two Cities" that the great city of Babylon represents human societies which oppose the Lord. Babylon rides on the

man doomed to destruction", and he refers to him as *"he"* rather than as *"it"*.[11] So we are to expect *the Spirit of the Antichrist* to be working throughout history in the lives of key individuals who are *antichrists*, and then at the end of time through one person who is so mighty that he can be described as *the Antichrist*, with a capital "A". So what does Jesus want us to do in response?

He calls us to *persevere*. Jesus is clear in verse 10 that we will need to show faith and endurance before the Spirit of the Antichrist. It will be very successful and will be worshipped by many people as the demon-idol with a thousand disguises.[12] Jesus warns us about its work so that we will not be surprised when we see it, and so that a realistic "earthly perspective" on history will prepare us for the great trials which lie ahead.

He calls us to be *on our guard*. Although political leaders like Emperor Nero and Adolf Hitler may well have been empowered by the Spirit of the Antichrist, the main thrust of Revelation 13 is that the Antichrist wears religious clothes and is very difficult to spot. He rises to power on the shoulders of the Lamb-Beast, which is later called the *"False Prophet"*,[13] and he relies on counterfeit miracles and man-made religion to deceive the people of the earth.[14] John is very clear in his letters that the antichrists of his own day were operating *within* the Church as apparent believers and had only belatedly revealed their true colours as antichrists.[15] I find it very off-putting when Christians attack a president, a pop artist or a fiction writer as "the Antichrist", when the message of this chapter is that he will be very hard to spot. We are far more likely to find antichrists at

---

Beast's power in Revelation 17:3, but she is not the Beast itself, for the Beast will ultimately turn on her and destroy her in Revelation 17:16.

[11] 2 Thessalonians 2:3–10. Paul majors in that passage on the one ultimate Antichrist, but he also warns that *"the secret power of lawlessness is already at work"* through many antichrists.

[12] Revelation 13:7, 8.

[13] Revelation 16:13; 19:20; 20:10.

[14] Revelation 13:13–15; 16:13–14; 19:20.

[15] 1 John 2:18–19.

work in the Church than we are to see their undisguised faces on the evening news.

Most importantly of all, Jesus wants us to *be confident.* Although the "earthly perspective" of Revelation 13 reads as though the Beast is in control, the rest of the Bible tells us there is more to this scene than meets the eye. Paul tells us that when Jesus returns he will merely need to blow on the Antichrist to destroy him.[16] The end of Revelation tells us that he will capture both the Leopard-Beast and the Lamb-Beast, and will throw them into hell along with Satan.[17] The Spirit of the Antichrist will look strong and invincible while we live on the earth, but Jesus tells us that the days of his rule have been numbered and will soon come to an end.[18]

The Spirit of the Antichrist relies on the throne of Satan, but we have seen time and time again in Revelation that God's Throne is the only one that matters. The Beast may parody Christ, but in the end it will be exposed as an absolute phoney. There is no one who can compare with the Lord Jesus. We have been promised this ahead of time.

---

[16] 2 Thessalonians 2:8.

[17] Revelation 19:19–21; 20:10.

[18] This is the significance of him only being given authority in v. 5 to rule for the *forty-two months* which symbolize AD history.

The Church Defeated (13:7)

He was given power to make war against the saints and to conquer them.

(Revelation 13:8)

One of the most famous telegrams of all time was sent by the great American novelist Mark Twain. Hearing in 1897 that *New York Journal* had mistakenly published his obituary, he cabled across the Atlantic from London with the short statement that *"Reports of my death are greatly exaggerated."*

Revelation tells us that this will also be true for the Church again and again throughout history. Although she will be victorious in the end, Jesus warns us several times that her path to victory will include defeat, setback and decline. He tells us plainly in 11:7 and 13:7 that she will be overcome, conquered and crushed.[1] She will seem to have died, but reports of her death will be greatly exaggerated. We need to take this message to heart, or else we will lose faith in God's power at the very moments when we most need to be strong.

Isaiah promised that the Lord is the *"source of strength to those who turn back the battle at the gate"*.[2] God has often empowered bold men and women to revive the Church at the precise moment that she appeared defeated. When the medieval Church grew corrupted by wealth and respectability, and appeared spiritually dead, the Lord raised up John Wycliffe and the Lollards in England. They stared the defeat of the Church in

---

[1] The Greek word which is used for the Beast *conquering* the Church in 13:7 is the same word as is used for the Church conquering the devil in 12:11 and the Beast in 15:2.

[2] Isaiah 28:6.

the face, then translated the Bible into English and travelled the country to preach what it said. Within several years the nation was so revived that one observer claimed that *"You cannot travel anywhere in England but of every two men you meet one will be a Lollard."*

Or take 1710, when the English writer Thomas Woolston looked at the Church and predicted that Christianity would be wiped out by the year 1900. Within a generation of him making his prediction, John Wesley and George Whitefield pioneered a massive revival across the entire English-speaking world. Hundreds of thousands of people were converted, and thousands of new churches were planted.

Towards the end of the eighteenth century, the French thinker Voltaire predicted that Christianity would crumble and die within fifty years. In fact, the nineteenth and twentieth centuries saw the explosion of Christianity around the world, and yielded more converts to Christ than the previous eighteen centuries combined. Again and again, the Church has looked beaten and in terminal decline. Again and again, reports of her death have been greatly exaggerated.

It is crucial that we grasp this fact biblically and historically because we live at another such time for the Church in the West. In 1966 the front cover of *Time* magazine asked the stark question *"Is God Dead?"* and predicted the decline of Western Christianity in the decades to come.[3] Much of the warning has been fulfilled, and such predictions are now commonplace. In 2000 a headline in *The Independent* screamed that the "Church Will Be Dead In Forty Years' Time".[4] A few years later, in 2009, an article in *The Daily Telegraph* quoted the confession of an Anglican bishop that *"At this rate it is hard to see the church*

---

[3] *Time* Magazine, 8th April 1966.

[4] *The Independent* newspaper is based in London, UK. This headline ran on Easter Sunday 16th April 2000.

surviving for more than 30 years."[5] The haemorrhage of the Church in the West is so evident that even her leaders confess it openly in the daily papers.

Some Christians prefer to ignore these realities and pretend that the Church is not declining. This is a particular danger for churches or denominations which are doing well and growing, because their own local experiences mask the dire national picture. Jesus warns us very clearly in 11:7 and 13:7 that the Church will see times of decline and defeat, and that we must not ignore them when they come.

Other Christians slide into despair and finger-pointing, blaming any number of factors for their seemingly irreversible losses. The people blame their leaders, while the leaders blame their people. The young blame the old for their stuffiness and tradition, while the old blame the young for neglecting the values which once made the Church strong. Evangelists blame the Church for not witnessing, while preachers blame the Church for not listening. Fingers are pointed, blame is apportioned, and in the meantime the decline continues.

Another group of Christians cope with disappointment by reinterpreting Christ's promises of a victorious Church, arguing that those promises apply to the age to come and not the here-and-now. They explain that their nation is "hard to the Gospel" and look longingly for the day when Jesus will return to whisk them away from this dark world. At first it sounds virtuous, withdrawing from the world and praying for Jesus' return, but beneath the veneer is an attitude at odds with Christ's own. They hold hands and long to leave the world behind, like panicking crowds running from a burning building. They can't wait to leave the world to burn and get into the fresh air of heaven, but the Jesus they look to is the same Servant who was willing to leave heaven to come into the world. Their disappointment has

---

[5] *The Daily Telegraph* newspaper is also based in London, UK. This article ran on 27th June 2009.

blinded their eyes to the Word made flesh. They play the game of religion while the world around them burns.

But there is another way. It's the Jesus Christ way. It's the Revelation 13:10 and 14:12 way. In those two verses God repeats a single phrase, which is his message to the Church Defeated. It simply reminds us that *"This calls for patient endurance and faithfulness on the part of the saints."* It's a more courageous creed than burying our heads in the sand, it's more challenging for us than finger-pointing, and it's more gritty and demanding than indulging in escapism. Yet it is the path through which the Church Defeated becomes the Church Victorious.

It calls us to meet together, to pray, to worship, to give, to proclaim the Gospel, to disciple, to fellowship and to pastor, day in day out, through the bad times and the good. It calls us to follow Jesus when his face seems hidden, when his arm seems slack, when his Spirit seems absent and when his victory seems distant. Then, as we persevere and remain faithful, suddenly and inexplicably we feel the breath of God blowing on us to revive us.[6] The path wasn't showy, it wasn't pretty and it wasn't always easy, but it was true Christian maturity. It was the character which perseveres through defeat and turns it into victory.

We do not grieve when the tide goes out on the beach, nor do we assume that its waves are gone for good. We trust God that when the tide is lowest, it is just about to turn. We trust that when the night is darkest, day is just about to dawn. Similarly, in the Church, we trust that God will use our patient endurance and faithfulness so that in the end we will indeed *"turn back the battle at the gate"*.

---

[6] Revelation 11:11.

Before the Foundation of the World (13:8)

All inhabitants of the earth will worship the beast – all whose names have not been written in the book of life belonging to the Lamb that was slain from the creation of the world.

(Revelation 13:8)

Let me ask you a question: *When did Jesus Christ die?*

If you like history, you will probably answer that it was at Passover 30 AD. If you know Paul's letters, you will probably say that it was *"at just the right time"*.[1] But there is another, deeper answer to the question, which serves as a beacon of hope in the middle of this chapter of gloom. John tells us that Jesus *"was slain from the creation of the world"*.

Think about what that means. Before God ever spoke *"Let there be light!"* and called the world into being, Jesus was already crucified.[2] Before Adam and Eve ever sinned by eating the forbidden fruit, Jesus had already died to redeem what they would lose. When Job despaired *"If only there were someone… to remove God's rod from me"*, Jesus had already given himself up as the answer to his prayer.[3] When King Herod tried to kill the baby Jesus in Bethlehem, he was utterly destined to fail because Jesus had already become the murder victim of one of his successors.

---

[1] Romans 5:6; Galatians 4:4.

[2] Jesus' death on the cross was already eternal reality, and would inevitably be played out in earthly history.

[3] Job 9:33–34.

This should make you want to worship. The mathematician Claude Shannon calculated that there are 64,000,000 different ways in which two players can make just their first three moves in a game of chess. There are 10^{120} different ways in which they could go on to play a whole game of chess – compared to only about 10^{81} atoms in the observable universe![4] If a simple game with thirty-two pieces contains such a vast number of variables, what complex sums lie behind the decisions of billions of people across thousands of years of world history? No wonder Paul concludes three chapters of examining God's sovereign plan for humankind by exclaiming, *"Oh, the depth of the riches of the wisdom and knowledge of God! How unsearchable his judgments, and his paths beyond tracing out! 'Who has known the mind of the Lord? Or who has been his counsellor?'"*[5]

Jesus wants this thought to encourage us in the darkest moments of our lives. He wants us to know that the world fell under the curse *"not by its own choice, but by the will of the one who subjected it"*,[6] and that Jesus was delivered over to death *"by God's set purpose and foreknowledge"*.[7] I can't ballroom dance even when my wife is leading me, let alone when she expects me to lead her, but Jesus tells us that God leads history firmly by the hand. He not only manages to respond to the way history moves, but he leads it, twists it, waltzes it and tangos it in any which way he wants.

This verse tells us another amazing thing too. The Greek text could mean either that *the Lamb* has been slain since the foundation of the world or that *the names of believers* have been written in his Book of Life since the foundation of the world. Since both readings are confirmed by other passages

---

[4] Claude Shannon, "Programming a Computer for Playing Chess" (*Philosophical* Magazine, March 1950). That's 1 followed by 120 zeroes compared to 1 followed by 81 zeroes.

[5] Romans 11:33–34.

[6] Romans 8:20.

[7] Acts 2:23.

of Scripture, John is probably being deliberately ambiguous because he wants us to understand that both are true.[8] Jesus tells us that even before the world was created, the Father had already written our names on his list of all those destined to become believers. This is the "Book of Life" which is mentioned in Revelation 3:5; 17:8; 20:12; 20:15; 21:17 and in several other places throughout the Bible.[9] Jesus promises us that the Father has not merely led world history firmly through the steps to crucify his Son, but that he has also bent the whole of history around his plan to save each individual Christian!

This promise that God has predestined every believer to salvation is meant to encourage us, but some people find it troubling. They feel genuine concern that this might make non-Christians feel excluded from the message of the Gospel, and that it might give Christians yet another excuse to not to share the Gospel with the lost. After all, if they are predestined, God will save them anyway, right? Wrong. Even in those passages where the Bible teaches most clearly about predestination, it also teaches very clearly that the Gospel invitation is for everyone, and that Christians need to make sure everyone hears it.[10] The Bible's teaching that God chooses people for salvation may tax the limits of our understanding, but it is nothing to be scared of.

Probably the biggest reason why some people struggle with this teaching is that it seems *unfair* for God to predestine some to salvation, because this seems to mean by implication

---

[8] The first interpretation is the main NIV reading and echoes 1 Peter 1:18–20, Titus 1:2, and 2 Timothy 1:9. The second interpretation is the NIV footnote and echoes Revelation 17:8 and Ephesians 1:4–5.

[9] Exodus 32:32–33; Psalm 69:28; 87:6; Daniel 12:1; Malachi 3:16; Luke 10:20; Philippians 4:3.

[10] For example, Jesus shows us clearly in John 6:37 that God's sovereign choosing does not bar anyone from the call to repent and be saved. Similarly, Acts 18:9–11 shows us that a true understanding of this teaching spurs us on to witness all the more, and that it is *misunderstanding* which leads to apathy and excuses.

that he predestines others to hell.[11] Note, that the main thrust of this verse and of 17:8 is not to talk about God predestining anyone to hell (that is a very different discussion), but to reassure us that even though everyone has sinned and deserves to go to hell, yet by God's grace he has filled his Book of Life with a written guarantee that he will protect and save his chosen ones. The Beast's deception is so strong that people are saved because God unblinds their eyes, not because they are smarter than anyone else. We have been saved by grace alone, which means we will be guarded by that same grace too.[12] Our security in the midst of the trials of chapter 13 is not based on our ability to hold on to God, but on his ability to hold on to us.

If you are a believer in Jesus Christ, God wants you to know that he will carry you, help you and preserve you through all the highs and lows of AD history. However dark your times may be, he will never let the darkness have the final say over your life.

But if you are a nominal Christian, masquerading as a believer, God wants you to know that you will never make it unless you turn to him in genuine repentance and surrender. You can choose to do so now, and if you do, you will look back one day and praise him in retrospect that he chose to open your eyes so that you could also choose him. You will look back and praise him that your name was written in the Lamb's Book of Life since before the foundation of the world.

---

[11] This is known as "double-predestination", and it goes beyond what this verse actually teaches.

[12] Philippians 1:6.

666 (13:18)

This calls for wisdom. If anyone has insight, let him calculate the number of the beast, for it is man's number. His number is 666.

(Revelation 13:18)

I whiled away many hours as a teenager watching *Countdown* with Carol Vorderman. It was one of the most popular TV game shows of its day, where contestants made words out of nine-letter anagrams and struggled to produce a large number from the small numbers they were given. I found the numbers round hardest, and could never understand how in only thirty seconds the contestants managed to produce the number 462 out of 55, 25, 8, 7, 6 and 3.[1] I was never very good at *Countdown*, but I was fascinated to watch people who were much better at it than me.

Many people assume that the Bible has its own version of *Countdown* in Revelation 13:18. They assume that since John gives us the number 666 and tells us to *"calculate the number of the beast"*, he must want to play the part of Carol Vorderman and challenge us to find the identity of the Antichrist. What is more, this is actually made possible through the Greek and Hebrew game of *gematria*.

I'm sure you are aware that the Romans did not have digits to express numbers when they wrote them down. They used "Roman numerals" instead, assigning numerical values to certain letters, so that the year 2010 is MMX, and the year 1888 is a very long-winded MDCCCLXXXVIII. The Greeks and Hebrews were similar,

---

[1] For fans of *Countdown* who can't resist this challenge, the correct answer is (55 + 25 – 3) × (8 – 7 × 6)!

but they assigned a value to every single letter in their alphabets. That's why the books of the Bible which we know as 1 John, 2 John and 3 John are actually known in the original Greek as John Alpha, John Beta and John Gamma, and how it is possible to hunt for a name whose letters add up to the elusive number 666.

The first-century game of *gematria* was a bit like *Countdown* and was particularly used for riddles and puzzles. The premise of the game was simple. You treated the letters in a name as if they were numbers, added them together, and challenged your friends to guess which name had been worth that total. Perhaps the most famous example of *gematria* was found in the excavated ruins of Pompeii, where one graffitist evidently taunted the public with the name of his secret lover, boasting that *"I love her whose name is in 545"*. Since I love my wife, Ruth Moore, I could use *gematria* to tell you that *"I love her whose name is in 794"*. But even she would think that was a bit geeky.

Many people in the past 1,900 years have tried to find a name which adds up to 666, especially when they discovered that in Greek the name *Jesus* adds up to 888.[2] The earliest contender was the wicked Emperor Nero, even though he died quarter of a century before John set foot on Patmos and the letters of his name didn't even add up to 666. There was a rumour doing the rounds in the late first century – Elvis Presley style – that he had faked his own death and was still alive and well in hiding, and 666 was oxygen to this conspiracy theory. By transliterating his Greek name into Hebrew, dropping its vowels, and then using Hebrew rather than Greek *gematria*, rumour-mongers found a way to make his name add up to 666.

In the Middle Ages it was the turn of the Muslim prophet Muhammad. Again, his name did not actually add up to 666, but someone discovered that *Maometis*, a lesser-used variant of his name, did. Cue mass medieval Islamophobia, and even the Crusades.

---

[2] It really does. The six letters IĒSOUS have the value of 10, 8, 200, 70, 400, and 200 respectively.

You're no doubt getting the hang of this now, so I'm sure it won't surprise you to know that the names of almost every bogeyman of the past thousand years have added up to 666, if tackled with the skill of Carol Vorderman. Candidates have included the Pope (so long as we use one of his most obscure titles), Martin Luther, John Wesley, Napoleon and Adolf Hitler. This afternoon, to prove that almost any name can add up to 666 with a little creativity, I even had a little go at *gematria* myself. So far I've managed to get my mother-in-law's name to add up to 691, and it's only a matter of time before I find the lateral thinking which will shave it down to 666.

The problem with all of this fancy *gematria* is not that it has yielded the wrong answers, but that it's asking entirely the wrong question. John is not encouraging us here to play *Bible Countdown* or *Scripture Sudoku* with the number 666. He tells us to calculate the number of the Beast, but then he gives us the answer by telling us that the number is 666 and that this number *"is the number of man"*. He is not telling us that the name of the Antichrist is hidden in the number 666. He is telling us that the Spirit of the Antichrist expresses itself through humans (the number of *man*), and that its attempts to be like God will always fall triply short of the mark (666 instead of 777).[3] I know that this is disarmingly simple, but don't let your love of *Countdown* make you miss it.

You can find out much more about *gematria* online, but most of it will be on the websites of Kabbalists, occultists and religious splinter-sects. Let's stop trying to make "Pope Benedict", "Barack Obama" or even "Phil Moore" add up to 666, and let's leave number games and proof texts to unbelievers such as these. We do not need to clutch at such superstitious straws. We have been given twenty-two whole chapters of the Revelation of Jesus Christ.

---

[3] *Seven* is a common motif in Revelation for the *perfection* of God. That is why the Holy Spirit is called the *seven spirits* of God in Revelation 1:4, 3:1, and 4:5, and why Revelation speaks of *Seven* Churches, *Seven* Seals, *Seven* Trumpets, *Seven* Bowls, and so on. If God is 777, the Beast's attempts to rival him through its antichrists will be forever found wanting.

Simply Church (14:1–20)

Then I looked, and there before me was the Lamb, standing on Mount Zion, and with him 144,000 who had his name and his Father's name written on their foreheads.

(Revelation 14:1)

Once, when I was swimming in the sea on holiday, a very powerful wave hit me and plunged me under water. I was too surprised and too winded to resist it, and I felt it push me deeper and deeper towards the seabed. I struggled frantically for what seemed like forever with my hands and my feet, clawing my way back to the surface as my empty lungs burned with pain. Finally, my efforts were rewarded and my head broke above the water. I have never gulped down such deep and grateful breaths of air.

I feel the same way when I emerge from the "earthly perspective" of Revelation 13 into the "Church's perspective" in Revelation 14. There is little original in this chapter – we can also find most of its contents in chapters 2, 3, 7, 17 and 19 – but Jesus provides us with this collection of references to other parts of Revelation in order to refresh us after the crashing waves of chapter 13. It showcases the Church, described here as *Mount Zion*,[1] and her mission and ministry throughout AD history. She is connected to the Father whose voice booms from heaven in verse 2, but this chapter focuses on her earthly activity. It outlines the Church's main priorities and calling, and we would be wise to pause and compare them with our own church life.

---

[1] Hebrews 12:22–23 tells us that the Church is the spiritual *Mount Zion*, the spiritual *Jerusalem*, and the spiritual *City of God*.

The Church that we see is wholeheartedly committed to Jesus the Lamb. While the rest of the world rushes eagerly after the Lamb-Beast of chapter 13, those in the Church *"follow the Lamb wherever he goes"*.[2] The Gospel message at its simplest is a call to follow Jesus,[3] and there is something deeply personal about the way in which these believers follow him here. Perhaps that is why no one can worship him like they do, with a new song which no unbeliever can sing. Their faith in Jesus is not mere sing-song. It is the deep worship which is only learned through a lifetime of following, shadowing, watching, listening, copying, obeying, and testing the Jesus who called them.

The Church that we see is a very different community to the world in which they live. While unbelievers drink the promiscuous wine of Babylon, the Church are as pure as virgins and completely undefiled by lies.[4] They are conscious that they were *"purchased from among men"* through the blood of Jesus, and that they have been offered to the Lord as living sacrifices to him.[5]

The Church that we see rejects the seal of the Beast, and her People are marked on their foreheads with the names of the Father and the Son. This links back to "God's Signature" in an earlier chapter, and it speaks of their ownership, authority, and authenticity. Because the 144,000 belong to the Lord, not one of their number has gone missing since chapter 7, despite six chapters of strife. Because they have authority, their active prayers are the incense which brings in God's harvest.[6] Because they are authentically Christ's, they bless the world with their

---

[2] Revelation 14:4.

[3] Matthew 4:19; 8:22; 9:9; 10:38; 16:24; 19:21; 19:27.

[4] There is a deliberate contrast between the sexual sin of v. 8 and the virginity of v. 4. This is a spiritual metaphor linked to the Church being the Bride of Christ. Hebrews 13:4 gives a positive view of sex within marriage.

[5] Revelation 14:4.

[6] The altar in Revelation 14:18 is specifically the *altar of incense* which we saw in 5:8 and 8:3–5. See the chapter entitled "Incense" for the link between our prayers and God's action.

labour and *good deeds*.[7] They are like Dorcas, the believer from Joppa, who was so diligent in helping the poor and needy that the Lord actually raised her to life so that her work would not stop.[8] In a world which is consumed by consumerism, the Church that we see takes responsibility for the needs all around her, and she pours out the same servant love as the God whose name she bears.

The Church that we see knows that her primary responsibility towards the world is to proclaim the Gospel, even though her People do so at the risk of their lives.[9] They treat it as *"the eternal Gospel"* and do not dare tamper with its message in the face of persecution. They declare boldly that Babylon's fall is certain, that God's great Judgment is coming, and that everyone needs to fear and worship him before it is too late.[10] They are even more passionate than the Beast to win the worship of *"every nation, tribe, language and people"*, but they direct that worship entirely towards the Lord rather than to themselves.[11] It therefore does not surprise us when we discover that the 144,000 are merely the *first-fruits* of the redeemed, and that the Church's faithful witness in the face of Satan and his Beast will be very, very successful.[12]

So, as *the One Like a Son of Man* appears at the end of the chapter to close off this fourth overview of AD history, he wants to make sure that we model our churches on this Church which he sets before us. Every local church has its individual flavour, emphases and sense of mission, but they must always reflect this clear vision of the Church as Christ wants her.

Is your church full of people who follow Jesus wherever he

[7] Revelation 14:13.

[8] Acts 9:36–42.

[9] Revelation 13:5.

[10] Revelation 14:7–11.

[11] There is a deliberate contrast between Revelation 14:6 and 13:7.

[12] This same Greek word *aparchē* or *first-fruits* in used in Romans 16:5 and 1 Corinthians 16:15 to speak of an early group of converts who will go on to see many more people saved as they pass on the Gospel to others.

goes, and who crave intimate relationship with him? Is it a church where people worship him through their songs and through their lives? Is it a church free from the "wine of Babylon", a pure and virginal Bride for the Lamb? Is it full of labour, good deeds and expressions of God's love? Is it consumed with its calling to proclaim the eternal Gospel, both locally and globally? Is that reflected in its prayer meetings, as believers throng together in faith that their fragrant prayers move the God of history? Jesus does not want us to be crushed by the shortcomings of our churches, but he does want to lift our eyes to see the Church as he wants her.

Unless you are a church leader, it may feel too big a task for you to change your whole church. Even if that is true, you can at least change yourself. Revelation 14 shows you the kind of believer that Jesus wants you to be, and he is with you all the way as you commit to walk his path. Others may follow Jesus half-heartedly and seek his presence sporadically, but you can be different. Others may neglect personal and private prayer, but you can choose to make up for their shortfall. Others may spoil their clothes with the filth of Babylon and may neglect the Gospel, the nations and the needy, but you can show them a different way. You can show them the Revelation 14 way. And as you do so, you will be amazed how many others follow your example.

How Can a God of Love Send People to Hell? (14:9–11)

He will be tormented with burning sulphur in the presence of the holy angels and of the Lamb. And the smoke of their torment rises for ever and ever. There is no rest day or night.

(Revelation 14:10b–11a)

Last January my Gran died. She was a generous person, lovely in a hundred different ways, but she did not follow Jesus. A few weeks before she sank into dementia, I wrote her a letter and urged her to respond to the Gospel she had heard so many times. She never replied, and soon it was too late for her. I'm telling you this now because it explains why I find it difficult to read verses like these. Revelation is packed with talk of hell, sulphur, fire, and smoke, and it upsets me. I think it's meant to.

Several years ago Pol Pot died. He was not a nice person. During his four short years of rule from 1975 to 1979, he slaughtered 1.5 million Cambodians, or a quarter of the population. Even when he fell from power, he survived in the jungle with the remnants of his Khmer Rouge army and was never brought to account for his crimes. When news broke of his death, *The Sun* newspaper was outraged by this injustice and printed a cartoon of him being poked by a trident-wielding

Devil in a cauldron of boiling water. The caption simply read: *"We hope that Pol Pot is now burning in hell"*.[1]

I find that very interesting. Because I love people, I shudder at the graphic pictures of hell in Revelation, but because I love justice, I agree with *The Sun* that they should be there. In preparation for a new preaching series, I recently asked church members to send me their toughest questions for God. In the same pile of questions was one complaining that God sends people to hell and another complaining that evil people live such happy lives. We seem to get upset with God for not punishing the wicked, but then get upset with him when he does. No wonder Jesus addresses this issue in Revelation.

Jesus uses phrases which refer to hell – such as *Hades*, the *Abyss*, *the lake of fire*, and *the Second Death* – a remarkable twenty-two times in Revelation's twenty-two chapters. He also uses the word *Gehenna* eleven times in the gospels. We may find this awkward, confusing and rather embarrassing in conversations with unbelievers, but Jesus clearly doesn't. In fact, he goes out of his way to make sure that we cannot deny it.

Simply consider the statements that he makes in these three verses of chapter 14. He will not let us reduce hell to a *metaphor*, because he says twice that it is very real *"torment"*. He will not let us talk of *annihilation*, because he tells us very clearly that *"the smoke of their torment goes up for ever and ever; there is no rest day or night"*. Nor will he let us view hell as something *passive* as God "excludes people from his presence", because he stresses that hell's torment will take place *"in the presence of the holy angels and the Lamb"*.[2] It is bizarre that while some Christian bishops and many Christian churches fail to grasp this,

[1] *The Sun* is Britain's best-selling newspaper. It ran this cartoon on Friday 17th April 1998.

[2] The idea that hell simply means exclusion from God's presence comes from 1 Thessalonians 1:9 and its statement that unbelievers will be *"shut out from the presence of the Lord"*. Revelation 14 helps us to see that this means that they will not be present in his heaven, not that he will not be present in their hell.

many non-Christians see it quite clearly. One prominent atheist argues that to deny the reality of hell *"would be to suppose that God or Jesus was either mistaken or misreported. But if Jesus was mistaken, he can't be divine. And if Jesus was misreported, the Bible can't be the true Word of God. The believer has no option, then, but to accept the doctrine of hellfire in all its obscenities."*[3] Even atheists can see what Jesus is saying here, so why is he not embarrassed to say it?

Jesus speaks frankly about hell because he has a perfect view of God's *holiness*. St Bernard wrote that *"Where all stink, no one smells"*, and we have spent too long in the stink of our generation to smell sin with Christ's perfect nose. We agree that monsters like Pol Pot and Adolf Hitler deserve to be sent to hell, but we fail to see the monster in anyone who fails to love God with all their heart, mind, soul and strength.[4] Unbelievers are not sent to hell primarily because they act meanly towards their neighbours, but because they are mere creatures who dare to revolt against their Creator-King. Hell was created in response to the treason of Satan and his demons, and Jesus knows that it is still the only fitting response to human treason against God.[5]

Jesus speaks frankly about hell because he has a perfect view of God's *justice*. The Bible is full of complaints that God appears to leave the wicked unpunished, but hell is God's perfect response.[6] Jesus does not hush up the reality of hell out of fear that it might cause us to view God as harsh, mean, and merciless. He actually parades hell as a reason for us to worship God because it shows that he is ***not*** harsh, mean and merciless.

[3] The atheist Dr Ray Bradley, professor of philosophy at Simon Fraser University in Vancouver, Canada, made this observation in 1994 in a debate on the question *"Can a God of Love Send people to Hell?"*

[4] Jesus tells us in Matthew 22:37–38 that this is *"the greatest commandment"* because it is the most basic demand that the Creator-God makes of his created humans. Breaking this greatest commandment is reason enough to receive the severest penalty.

[5] Matthew 25:41.

[6] We will tackle this complaint in much more detail in the next chapter.

Hell means that God hears the cry of the victims of sin, and that he will not rest until justice is done. Hell is not a reason to doubt God's character, but a reason to praise him for the full glory of his character.

Jesus also speaks frankly about hell because he has a perfect view of God's *love*. He knows that true love is never indifferent, but always stirs the heart of a lover to action. God's love means that he judges, but – praise God – it also means he makes a way so that he doesn't have to. These three verses in Revelation 14 drop large hints towards the great background story which makes Jesus the unrivalled expert on hell. They call Jesus "the Lamb" and they talk of the "cup of God's wrath", which reminds us that an anguished Jesus agreed to drink the cup of God's wrath in the Garden of Gethsemane. He drank the horror and punishment of sin when he died on the cross as our sacrifice for sin.[7] Jesus speaks frankly about hell because he has endured it in our place, so that none of us need endure it for ourselves.[8]

Jesus speaks frankly about hell precisely because he is the God of love and because he wants to save us and our neighbours from going there. He is the God who inspired Ezekiel to ask *"Do I take any pleasure in the death of the wicked? declares the Sovereign Lord. Rather, am I not pleased when they turn from their ways and live?... For I take no pleasure in the death of anyone, declares the Sovereign Lord. Repent and live!"*[9] He is the God who still asks this today.

We can shy away from Jesus' teaching about hell and leave it to atheists to rebuke our unbelief, or we can embrace it as a massive reason to praise him. Let's allow it to fuel our worship, to fuel our prayers, to fuel our evangelism, and to fuel our church planting. Let's allow it to make us like the Church of chapter 14.

---

[7] Matthew 26:39, 42.

[8] Acts 2:27; Revelation 1:18.

[9] Ezekiel 18:23, 32.

The Fifth Overview of AD History

The Seven Bowls: Where is the God of Justice? (15:1 – 16:21)

The judgments you have made are just, O Holy One… They are getting what they deserve!

(Revelation 16:5–6)[1]

The last chapter tackled a very Western question, and it gave a very Western answer. But it's not the question most people ask around the world, and it is not the question most people have asked throughout history. Although people who live in safety, luxury and peace complain that God should not send people to hell, those who live in war-torn or poverty-stricken lands generally do not. They tend to look heavenwards with eyes that have stared human wickedness in the face, and to cry out *"where is the God of justice?"* In chapters 15 and 16, the fifth overview of AD history, Jesus answers their cry.

Many of the Psalms were written in the face of injustice, and the writers plead with God passionately, forcefully and repeatedly that he might settle the score.[2] Habakkuk spends a whole book of the Old Testament doing so, asking *"How long, O Lord, must I call for help, but you do not listen?... Why do you make me look at injustice? Why do you tolerate wrong?... Justice never prevails. The wicked hem in the righteous, so that justice is perverted."*[3] I hope that you have not experienced such wickedness in your own life, but if you have, it is quite normal

---

[1] Good News Bible.

[2] For example, Psalm 35:17; 74:10–11; 82:2; 94:3.

[3] Habakkuk 1:2–4.

to cry out for God's vengeance. Even the Christian martyrs did so when the fifth seal was opened: *"How long, Sovereign Lord, holy and true, until you judge the inhabitants of the earth and avenge our blood?"*[4] Jesus gives us good news that his vengeance is indeed coming.

He promises that God will certainly judge *every* wicked person. Although the Seven Churches, Seven Seals, Seven Trumpets and Seven Bowls all describe the events of AD history, they each do so with a particular emphasis. Here, the Seven Bowls strongly echo the Seven Trumpets which in turn echoed the Plagues of Egypt,[5] but there is a crucial difference this time around. The Seven Seals struck a *quarter* of their targets and the Seven Trumpets struck a *third* of theirs, but the Seven Bowls strike *all* of the wicked. John assured us in 15:1 that the number *seven* refers to completeness, and we are meant to grasp that seven plagues from seven bowls in the hands of seven angels will bring God's justice to every single person who has acted wickedly on the earth.[6] Note the progression:

The Seven Trumpets	**The Seven Bowls**
Disaster on a *third* of the land	Disaster on *all* the land
Disaster on a *third* of the sea	Disaster on *all* the sea
Disaster on a *third* of the rivers	Disaster on *all* the rivers
Disaster on a *third* of the sun	Disaster from the sun on *all* people

[4] Revelation 6:10.

[5] The Lord also struck the Egyptians with boils, rivers of blood, darkness, frogs and hailstones. He made sure that they struck only the Egyptians and not the People of God, just as he does in 16:2. There is also a link in 15:3 with the song which Moses sang after the destruction of the Egyptian army at the Red Sea in Exodus 15.

[6] Some readers assume that John is telling us in 15:1 that the Seven Bowls end the account of God's Judgment. However, there are far too many judgments in Revelation 17–20 for this to be what he means.

Torment from Satan's kingdom	Torment from the *fall* of Satan's kingdom
A demonic army brings death	A demonic army brings *mass slaughter*
Noise in heaven	Noise in heaven proclaims *"It has happened!"*[7]

Jesus also promises that God's judgment will be *swift* and *unimpeded*. There is an urgency and intensity to the Seven Bowls which surpasses the previous four overviews of AD history. While there was time for an interlude before the seventh seal and seventh trumpet,[8] there is no time to pause here as we hurtle towards the climactic cry that *"It has happened!"* The Lord will even stop his People praying for mercy so that nothing can hinder the fullness of his justice.[9] He will judge every wicked person, both throughout history and at the end of history, and the fifty-kilogram hailstones of 16:21 show us that he really means business.

All this means that God's judgment will be *just* and *seen to be just*. As the wrath of God is poured out and the sea of glass turns fiery,[10] the only people complaining are the evildoers upon whom it is poured. The angels proclaim that *"you are just in your judgments"* and that the wicked are simply *"getting what they deserve"*. The martyrs under the altar also confess that their pleas have been answered and that *"true and just are your judgments"*.[11] Jesus promises that the question *"where is the God*

7 Green's Literal Translation.

8 Revelation 7:1–17; 10:1–11:14.

9 This is why he forces them away from his sanctuary in 15:8. For Old Testament examples of God deliberately stopping his People praying so that he can judge, see Jeremiah 7:16; 11:14; 14:11; 15:1.

10 The sea of glass was calm in Revelation 4:6. The fire shows us that God's unruffled rule has been angered.

11 Revelation 16:5–7.

of justice?" will be fully satisfied. God is here, God is just, and God will not be trifled with.

Jesus ends with one more fact which we must not ignore when God's justice seems slow and the wicked seem to prosper. Make sure that you don't miss the clue in the thunder and smoke of 16:17. John told us in John 19:30 that as Jesus died on the cross he shouted *tetelestai* or *"it is finished"*, but now he tells us that he will also cry out *gegonen* or *"it has happened"* when the Final Judgment takes place. We struggle with the slowness of God's justice because we live in the gap between the day that Jesus drank the cup of God's judgment on the cross and the Day when he will return and empty the last of the bowls of God's judgment.[12] He delays because he has many people still to clothe with robes of righteousness in 16:15, and he asks us to bear with this delay so that all of his People may come in. Then, and only then, will he cry out in jubilation that *"it has happened"*.

You may still want to complain to God that he should not send people to hell, and you can take it up with him if you still have to. But even if the last chapter on hell did not convince you, this one really should. If Jesus is tackling a question which you are not even asking, it is a warning that the thinking of your culture has drifted a long way from the truth. Jesus is coming back like an unexpected thief, and it is time for us to stop fighting him over his justice and to join in the worship song of the angels and martyrs.

Other readers live under the shadow of abuse, oppression, bullying and injustice, and they are far more in tune with the cry of these chapters. If that's you, receive the Seven Bowls as a Christ's sweet promise of hope to you. This fifth overview of history tells you that justice is coming, and that no oppressor can escape from the vengeance of God. A day is coming when God will lay bare his justice, while we look on and worship.

[12] John 18:11; Matthew 26:39.

The Harps of God (15:2)

> *They held harps given them by God and sang the song of Moses the servant of God and the song of the Lamb: "Great and marvellous are your deeds, Lord God Almighty. Just and true are your ways, King of the ages."*
>
> (Revelation 15:2b–3)

We are now about three-quarters of the way through Revelation, so you should be able to answer this quiz question: *What is the most frequent thing that people do in John's vision?* Have a good think, because the answer is very important. Have you got it? By far the most frequent thing that we find people doing in Revelation is *worshipping*.

John set the lead in the first chapter when he fell face down at the feet of Jesus, but we quickly find the twenty-four elders, the 144,000, the four living creatures, the angels in heaven and the nations of the earth all doing the same. At one point we even find *"every creature in heaven and on earth and under the earth and on the sea, and all that is in them, singing: 'To him who sits on the throne and to the Lamb be praise and honour and glory and power, for ever and ever!'"*[1] Chapter after chapter tells us that the Lord wants to be worshipped, and that Satan and his followers want to be worshipped instead.[2] Revelation speaks of the God who deserves to be worshipped, and of the evil spirits who lust to steal his worship from him.

Since God so strongly prizes our worship, it should not

---

[1] Revelation 5:13.

[2] Revelation 9:20; 13:4, 8, 12, 14–15; 14:11.

surprise us that he gives us clear instruction about how he wants it. Jesus taught that the Father is seeking *"true worshippers"* who *"worship in spirit and in truth"*,[3] and Revelation 15 is one of the clearest passages which shows us what he means. The chapter serves as a prelude to the outpouring of the Seven Bowls in chapter 16, and it is full of God's priorities for worship.

Perhaps the most obvious thing which God loves in worship, both here and throughout Revelation, is the *united* praise of his People. Although John alone falls at Jesus' feet in chapter 1, he does not see visions of individuals worshipping the Lord, but of large groups of people. There is not one elder, but twenty-four; not one redeemed person, but 144,000; not one Jew, one Greek or one Roman, but *"a great multitude that no one could count, from every nation, tribe, people and language"*.[4] God loves it when large crowds of diverse people gather together to express his praise with one united heart and voice.

That is why it is so foolish to develop a vision for a "Korean church" in England (or indeed an "English church" in Korea), or for a "church of professional twenty-somethings".[5]

God hates it when Christians only try to gather with people like themselves (or, worse still, not to gather at all), because he wants to receive worship from large, united crowds of disparate, dissimilar individuals. He hates it when we develop a vision for church which is too small, cosy and intimate. Some churches are small and some churches are big, and there is nothing necessarily wrong with a church of either size. But we must not make a virtue out of smallness. God wants to be worshipped by large crowds who are united by something far bigger than their intimate fellowship with one another. He wants people who are

[3]John 4:23

[4] Revelation 7:9.

[5] This is of course quite different from an English-speaking church that embraces people from many nations. There are many great churches which operate around the world in non-indigenous languages.

united through intimate fellowship with him, no matter what their differences of race, language, age, class or education.

God wants those crowds of worshippers to be *specific* in their praise. Most of us have experienced the deadness of worship when it is all head and no heart, but we must not exchange it for mere exuberance and emotionalism. God wants our worship to be substantial, based on real truth which stirs real emotion. That is why we find the redeemed singing *"the song of Moses and the song of the Lamb"*.[6] They sing specific songs of praise about what the Lord has done for them, such as triumphing over Satan, sin, death and darkness through the cross of Jesus like he triumphed over Pharaoh and his army through the Red Sea. They sing specific words of praise which glorify God for what he has done and for who he is. Note the words which they use here, telling God that his deeds are *great, marvellous, just, true* and *righteous*, and that he himself is *holy, eternal, King* and *Almighty*. God loves us to be specific in our worship, telling him why his deeds are so praiseworthy, and who exactly we confess him to be.

Another thing which delights God is when we worship him *by faith*, not quite knowing what he is about to do. This crowd of worshippers see seven angels fly out from the presence of God carrying bowls filled with his wrath to pour out on the nations. As they look to the Temple to see some assurance from God's face, he deliberately covers himself with the smoke of his glory so that they cannot see him until the bowls have been poured out. Why would God do such a thing? We can see the answer in the Psalms and Prophets. There we find a God who calls his People praise him in the midst of confusing times, deliberately choosing to trust his character and to sing his praise on the basis of his Word alone. God is truly glorified when we pray:

---

[6] Moses actually sang three songs in the Old Testament: Exodus 15:1–18; Deuteronomy 32:1–43; Psalm 90. Since the redeemed sing by the sea of glass and Moses sang the first of his songs on the far side of the Red Sea, most readers assume that this is the song John has in mind.

Though the fig-tree does not bud and there are no grapes on the vines, though the olive crop fails and the fields produce no food, though there are no sheep in the pen and no cattle in the stalls, yet I will rejoice in the Lord, I will be joyful in God my Saviour.[7]

This united, specific, faith-filled, joyful worship is what God deeply desires from us, and what Satan and his demons so desperately want to silence. If you think it sounds difficult to generate for yourself, and well-nigh impossible to generate as a whole church, you have arrived at the place where Revelation 15 wants to take you, and you are ready to receive the greatest promise that it offers you.

Note the way in which the redeemed worship God in verse 2: *"They held harps given them by God."* They are not harps we make for ourselves. They are harps which the Lord gives us. He does not merely seek a certain kind of worshipper; he seeks people that he can turn into those worshippers. He is not asking us to work up the kind of worship he seeks, as if we creatures have anything of our own to bring to our Creator. He is asking us to let him fill us with his Holy Spirit, so that through him we may be united, through him we may be reminded of specific reasons to worship him, and through him we may be filled with faith to worship in the midst of trouble.

God wants us to understand that his name is so far *"exalted above all blessing and praise"* that we can never generate for him the kind of worship that he desires.[8] Instead, he wants us to let him fill us with his Spirit and give us *"the harps of God"*. He wants to change us on the inside so that we want to worship and are able to worship him in spirit and in truth.[9]

You will worship like this in the midst of God's People for all eternity. Therefore take some time today to worship him in

[7] Habakkuk 3:17–18.

[8] Nehemiah 9:5.

[9] Philippians 2:13.

spirit and in truth, calling others to join you too. Then, when you have worshipped him with all your being, remember to worship him for enabling you even to worship him at all. Remember to thank him for giving you *"the harps of God"*.

Armageddon (16:12–16)

Then they gathered the kings together to the place that in Hebrew is called Armageddon.

(Revelation 16:16)

One of the most famous words in the book of Revelation occurs only once in its pages. Regardless, it has become a common word in the English language. Reporters warn of financial *Armageddon*, nuclear *Armageddon* or environmental *Armageddon*. Bruce Willis fights off an earth-destroying meteor in the movie *Armageddon*. The word has even found its way into the dictionary as *"a final war between good and evil at the end of the world, as described in the Bible, or, more generally, any event of great destruction"*. There's no doubt about it: Revelation 16:16 is a very famous verse.

When I was first introduced to Christianity in the 1980s, I was taught confidently from the Bible that there was going be a great Battle of Armageddon, just before the return of Jesus, where a coalition of nations led by the Soviet Union would invade the nation state of Israel and precipitate a massive nuclear holocaust. I think I had probably stumbled across the stranger end of the Church spectrum, but that was nevertheless my entry point to the Christian faith, and it was not a pleasant one. It made me quite scared. It made me deeply suspicious of the Soviet Union, Arab nations and any other country which might be part of this global anti-Israeli alliance. But most of all, it made me think that the return of Jesus simply could not be as imminent as John, Paul, Peter and the other New Testament writers suggested. After all, if Armageddon needed to happen before the end, then the BBC news told me every morning that the Second Coming was still quite some way off. Looking back now, I think that the teaching I received about Armageddon actually had the exact opposite effect on me to the one which Revelation has in mind.

Have you noticed that Jesus deliberately prevents us from viewing Armageddon as a literal place in Israel? *Armageddon* is the Greek form of two Hebrew words: *Har Megiddon*, or *Mount Megiddo*.[1] Now that's interesting because Megiddo was not built on a high mountain at all, but overlooked a great flat plain. It's the first clue Jesus gives us to see Megiddo as something spiritual rather than geographical – a bit like Babylon in verse 19. Another clue is that the Old Testament prophet Joel talks about a very similar end-time battle in the third chapter of his book and tells us that it will take place in *the Valley of Decision*, which he also calls *the Valley of Jehoshaphat* (or literally *the Valley of the-Lord-Will-Judge*).[2] Add to this John's statement that the battle will take place outside Jerusalem,[3] over sixty miles south of Megiddo, and we have some very strong reasons to see Mount Megiddo simply as a picture of "the battlefield where God judges". It was, after all, where the Lord had used the Hebrew Barak to defeat a great Canaanite army, and the Egyptian Neco to defeat King Josiah when he foolishly supported the Babylonians.[4]

Have you noticed that Jesus also deliberately prevents us from viewing Armageddon as one single, end-time battle? The events he reveals here with the sixth bowl repeat what happened in 9:13–21 with the sixth trumpet, and he repeats them again in the battle of Gog and Magog in 20:7–10. Jesus works very hard to make sure that we cannot pin down any exact chronology to

---

[1] The Hebrew word *har* means *mountain*, as distinct from the word *gibe'ah* which means *hill*.

[2] Joel 3:2, 12, 14.

[3] Zechariah 14:1–5 probably places it outside Jerusalem too.

[4] Judges 4–5 and especially 5:19. 2 Kings 23:28–29; 2 Chronicles 35:20–25.

the Battle of Armageddon.[5] Since we know that there will be many antichrists throughout AD history leading up to one great Antichrist at the end of history,[6] it also appears that there will be many armageddons throughout AD history leading up to one great Armageddon at the end. *Armageddon* appears to be a spiritual name for any battle which takes place when Satan and the Spirit of the Antichrist stir up the people of the earth to oppose the Lord, and this has taken place many times over history and will do so increasingly towards the end.[7]

Hopefully you have also spotted the other thing which eluded the Christians I met in the 1980s. John does not tell us that Armageddon spells a great disaster for the People of God. He actually tells us that Armageddon is very good news! It is God (not Satan) who dries up the Euphrates River so that the armies can cross it, and he does so in order to bring together those who hate him for *"the great day of God Almighty"*.[8] Similarly, it is God who releases the army to come in 9:13–15, and who reveals in 20:7–10 that he does so in order to gather all of his enemies into one place so that he can wipe them out with fire from heaven. Winston Churchill wrote in his memoirs that there came a point when he began to hope that the Nazis would try to invade Britain because he felt it was the best and surest way for him

[5] Note that John tells us here that the Beast and False Prophet inspire Armageddon, but in 20:7–10 he tells us that the battle happens *after* they have been thrown into the lake of fire. Jesus does this deliberately to ensure that we grasp that Armageddon is a series of spiritual events, and not just something to put at the end of an end-time flow diagram.

[6] 1 John 2:18.

[7] The Spirit of the Antichrist united all people against God in 13:11–18. Armageddon is therefore not talking about the Soviet Union or any other nation uniting the world into a global super-state, but about the Spirit of the Antichrist uniting the divided nations of the world all together (whether or not they realize it) under one banner of opposition to God.

[8] The Babylonians crossed the Euphrates to destroy Judah in 586 BC, so this picture symbolizes spiritual Babylon on the move under the inspiration of the Spirit of the Antichrist.

"break the teeth" of their armies.[9] That is the plan God describes here, as Armageddon symbolizes Babylon's foolish venture into the *Valley of Decision*, the *Valley of the-Lord-Will-Judge*.

Can you see the great difference that this makes to our outlook as Christians? If the Battle of Armageddon is a one-off, end-time attack on Israel, we will fear the future, fear certain nations, and not fear the return of Christ. However, if we realize that in every armageddon leading up to the great Armageddon the Lord is luring Satan and his followers into a trap which will advance the Kingdom of God, we will be confident, eager to reach all nations with the Gospel, and vigilant for Christ's imminent return.

If the newspapers talk about financial Armageddon, they are usually describing bad news, but when John talks about Armageddon here he is trying to tell us some very good news indeed. He is telling us that Satan and his antichrists will repeatedly attack the Church and that they will repeatedly lose. As surely as ancient Babylon destroyed ancient Jerusalem, the Lord will make sure that the New Jerusalem defeats spiritual Babylon.

So be encouraged. Even when the forces of Satan lay siege to the Church, God is still on the Throne.

---

9 The Old Testament account of the battle of Gog and Magog in Ezekiel 38:14–16 also makes this point.

Still Unrepentant (16:9–11, 21)

They cursed the name of God, who had control over these plagues, but they refused to repent and glorify him.

(Revelation 16:9)

There is a view in Christian circles that if only God would discipline the nations of the world, they would turn to him in a great revival. Unfortunately, it's not true. Repentance and revival are much more complicated than that.

At 8:46 and 9:03 a.m. on Tuesday 11th September 2001, two passenger jets crashed into the Twin Towers of the World Trade Center in New York and brought them crashing to the ground. Nearly 3,000 people were killed, and the Western world was changed in a moment. Borders were sealed, troops were sent to war, and a coalition of world leaders gathered to survey the new world landscape. In Britain, *The Times* newspaper dubbed it as *"The Day that Changed the Modern World"*, while the *Daily Mail* predicted that *"history will never be the same again"*. All were agreed on one thing: national disasters don't come much bigger than 9/11.

One of the immediate responses to the attacks in America was a significant surge in church attendance. Some congregations doubled in size on the Sunday after 9/11, and many Christian leaders spoke of their hopes for a national wave of repentance. However, within a month, prayer and Bible reading in America was back down to pre-attack levels, and by January 2002 church attendance was back down too. One researcher commented in

August 2006 that *"Now, five years removed from that fateful day, spiritually speaking, it's as if nothing significant ever happened."*[1]

This is not to say that disasters and setbacks never bring nations to repentance and revival. God often uses terrible events to revive nations. But it is certainly not automatic that times of trouble bring people to repentance. Ten plagues on Egypt made Pharaoh more determined to destroy the Israelites, not less. Three and a half years without rain made King Ahab and Queen Jezebel all the more determined to oppose the Lord and promote their false god Baal.[2] Even the miracle at Mount Carmel and the return of rain to Israel only led to a half-hearted and very short-lived revival.[3] So it should not surprise us when Revelation tells us that discipline and disaster do not automatically generate repentance. It tells us in 6:15–17; 9:20–21, and 16:9, 11, and 21 that God's judgment upon the nations of the earth can actually cause them to harden their hearts, curse the Lord and blaspheme his Name. In fact, even when Jesus returns in indisputable power and glory, there will still be many who would rather die than welcome his rule.

That is why it is foolish for us to hope that those who are sent to hell might be granted early probation and an upgrade to heaven once their suffering brings them to their senses. Hell is the place where God gives people completely over to the sinful desires of their hearts, and so it is where people become more and more twisted in their rebellion against God, not more and more repentant. C.S. Lewis wrote that *"I willingly believe that the damned are, in one sense, successful, rebels to the end; that the doors of Hell are locked on the inside."*[4] Similarly, it is mere

---

[1] This quotation is from David Kinnaman, director of a study by the Barna Group in August 2006. He adds that *"People used faith like a giant band-aid... and it was discarded after a brief period of use."*

[2] 1 Kings 18:4–5, 17.

[3] 1 Kings 19:4, 10.

[4] C.S. Lewis, *The Problem of Pain* (1940).

sentimentalism to hope that those who have not fully repented before they die will pass through "Purgatory" so that suffering can prepare them for heaven. If they refused to be justified freely by God's grace in this life, no amount of torment will change their mind in the next.[5]

The truth is that repentance and revival are not primarily the fruit of God's judgment, but the fruit of his work of *regeneration*. To quote C.S. Lewis again, pain may be *"God's megaphone to rouse a deaf world"*, but the world will only hear his megaphone if God raises them spiritually from the dead so that they can hear him.[6] The Bible tells us that unbelievers are *"dead in their sins"*,[7] and that no matter how loudly we shout in their cadaverous ears, they will never hear and respond until they are regenerated, or born again.

Several years ago, my route to work was flooded by torrential rain and my office was cut off from where I live. I spent hours sitting in traffic trying to find a route around the flooding, and it was only when I finally gave up that I noticed that my mobile phone was switched off. As soon as I turned it on, I received a message from my manager warning me not to come into work because the office was not open. Had I turned my phone on earlier, I could have saved hours of wasted effort. The message had been sent but my phone was turned off.

The Gospel is God's message of salvation. Trouble and pain often make the ringtone sound more loudly, but this makes no difference at all if the phone is turned off. We need to preach the Gospel (the ringtone) and be sensitive to God's work in a person's life (the megaphone), but we must also pray that he will switch them on to receive the incoming message.

---

[5] Revelation 7:13–14 shows us that those who place their faith in Christ are made completely white through his blood alone. Purgatory simply cannot be real or else the Bible would mention it at least once by name, and would not teach like this against the very principle upon which it is based.

[6] C.S. Lewis, *The Problem of Pain*.

[7] Ephesians 2:1, 5; Colossians 2:13.

Paul puts it this way in 2 Corinthians 4:4–6:

> *The god of this age has blinded the minds of unbelievers, so that they cannot see the light of the gospel of the glory of Christ... [but] God, who said "Let light shine out of darkness", made his light shine in our hearts to give us the light of the knowledge of the glory of God in the face of Christ.*

Jesus gives us this vision of the nations continuing their rebellion, their cursing and their refusal to repent, even in the face of great judgment, because he does not want us to be naïve and assume that suffering leads to repentance. He wants us to perceive the supernatural work of the Holy Spirit in repentance and revival, and to call us to pray fervently for him to regenerate the hearts of believers so that his message will get through, whether the ringtone is quiet or loud.

Let's pray for our friends, our neighbours and our nations, and let's not give up until our message gets through. We have now finished reading the fifth overview of AD history, but there is still time to lead them to repentance before we see it fulfilled.

The Sixth Overview of AD History

The Fall of Babylon (17:1 – 18:24)

After this I saw another angel coming down from heaven. He had great authority, and the earth was illuminated by his splendour. With a mighty voice he shouted: "Fallen! Fallen is Babylon the Great!"

(Revelation 17:1–2a)

One of the most ingenious military manoeuvres of all time took place in October 539 BC. The Persian army was camped outside the city of Babylon, but it lacked the necessary firepower to breach the city's massive walls and mighty gates. Even the Persian King Cyrus admitted that *"I am unable to see how any enemy can take walls of such strength and height by assault."*[1] But he was one of the greatest strategists of the ancient world, and he found a fatal flaw in Babylon's defences. The words of the prophet Jeremiah were about to be fulfilled that said *"I set a trap for you, O Babylon... Babylon will suddenly fall and be broken."*[2]

It was a Babylonian national holiday, and as the sound of celebration and laughter wafted over the great city walls, Cyrus made his move. The River Euphrates passed under the impregnable walls of Babylon, and this gave the Persian king his opportunity. As darkness fell and the sound of partying grew louder, he passed the signal to his troops upriver and they sprang to work. They activated the makeshift dams which they had constructed to divert the river away from the city, and

---

[1] Xenophon, one of the greatest historians of the ancient world, reports this in his *Cyropaedia*, VIII.5.7.

[2] Jeremiah 50:24; 51:8.

the Persian army watched with astonishment as the riverbed emptied and exposed two broad and undefended passageways underneath the city walls. Cyrus' lateral thinking had completely outwitted the Babylonians, and his troops eagerly poured into the city. By the time Belshazzar and his drunken generals even realized that their walls had been breached, it was too late for them to fight back.[3] Babylon, the most populous, most powerful, most secure city in the world, had fallen.

It is difficult for us to grasp today the intense shock and awe which reverberated around the ancient world at the news that Babylon the Great had been conquered overnight. There is simply no modern event to which it can compare. The impossible had happened, just as the Lord prophesied in Jeremiah 50–51. He had promised that Babylon would fall suddenly, unexpectedly, and decisively, and the Lord always does what he promises.

This sixth and final overview of AD history therefore begins with a promise that what the Lord did to physical Babylon through Cyrus, he will do again to spiritual Babylon through Christ.[4] The sixth overview describes the destruction of Babylon (17:1 – 19:10), of the Beast (19:11–21), of Satan (20:1–10), and of those humans who side with them (20:11–15). Like the previous five overviews, the sixth describes what will happen throughout AD history and increasingly towards the end of the age.[5] More than any of the previous five overviews,

[3] You can read about Belshazzar's final party in Daniel 5. You can also read about it in the writings of the ancient historians Xenophon (*Cyropaedia*, VIII.5.1–32) and Herodotus (*Histories*, I.191).

[4] Note that there are six overviews of AD history in Revelation, and not seven. It may be that six is the number of man and therefore of the history of this age. My personal explanation is that Jesus wants his recreation of the earth to mirror his original creation. In Genesis 1 there are six days of work followed by a day of rest in Eden. In Revelation there are six overviews of this age and then a description of our rest in the age to come.

[5] Spiritual Babylon has fallen in this way throughout history – as Sodom, Egypt, Babylon, Rome, and many more – but this will culminate in one great fall at the end of time.

however, this sixth overview speaks particularly of the end of AD history in order to prepare us for the grand finale to Revelation in the last two chapters of the book, which grant us a vision of the age to come.

We have already seen in the chapter on "A Tale of Two Cities" that the spirit which was behind ancient Babylon was also at work in Sodom, Egypt, Jerusalem and every other nation of the past which set itself up against the Lord.[6] We saw that she is still active today, seducing the nations of the earth with her promises of money, sex, power, fame and man-made religion. She is *"the Great Prostitute"* who is determined to destroy the New Jerusalem, *"the Bride of Christ"*.[7] She inspires governments to kill Christians, she entices nations to worship idols and embrace the occult, and she deceives people into rejecting the Lord and looking for happiness in her fleeting wares. Babylon and Jerusalem are at war, and there will be no peace until one of them is destroyed.

In the chapters since we first met Babylon in Revelation 11:8, we have been impressed by her impregnability. She draws her power from the great Spirit of the Antichrist as she rides on its back to victory,[8] and she manages to seduce every nation on to her side.[9] When she decides to slaughter the People of God no one can resist her,[10] and repeatedly throughout AD history she looks to be on the brink of destroying the New Jerusalem as easily as Babylon destroyed Jerusalem in 586 BC. She boasts confidently that she will never fall,[11] but she has forgotten one important factor: God has already passed sentence over her, just as he did when she worked through ancient Babylon so many

---

[6] Revelation 11:8.

[7] Revelation 21:2, 9.

[8] Revelation 17:3, 7. Compare 17:3 with 13:1.

[9] Revelation 17:15, 18.

[10] Revelation 17:6; 18:24.

[11] Revelation 18:7.

centuries ago. God has prophesied her doom, and when the Lord speaks, he always does what he promises.[12]

This is why Jesus begins his sixth overview of AD history with a long account of the fall of Babylon. He wants us to understand that the Spirit of Babylon only wields her power over the nations of the earth because he permits her to do so,[13] and that, just like physical Babylon, he will suddenly withdraw his permission and make her fall *"in one day"* and *"in one hour"*.[14] He will suddenly set division between the Spirit of Babylon and the Spirit of the Antichrist upon which she rides. It is not called *the Beast* for nothing, and when God turns Satan's kingdom in on itself, the Spirit of the Antichrist will devour and destroy Babylon.[15] This has already happened many times throughout AD history to each successive New Babylon, but at the end of history it will happen once and for all.

The grip of Babylon on the cultures of our world often appears to be as impregnable as the mighty walls which faced the Persian army, but our God has spoken. He is the one who can dry up the Euphrates at a simple command, and who can outwit her even better than King Cyrus.[16] He will always ensure that Satan's attacks on the New Jerusalem fail in the end, and that they always backfire on to Babylon. He will silence the songs of Babylon and fill the world with the song of the New Jerusalem.[17] He will end the sound of bride and bridegroom in Babylon so that the world can hear the sound of Christ coming to meet his Bride.[18]

After chapter 18, the name of Babylon is whispered no more. The rest of Revelation will focus on the New Jerusalem,

---

[12] Revelation 14:8; 16:19.

[13] Revelation 17:12.

[14] Revelation 18:8, 10, 17, 19.

[15] Revelation 17:16.

[16] Revelation 16:12.

[17] Revelation 18:22; 19:1–8.

[18] Revelation 18:24; 19:9.

and the last two chapters will be dominated by her victory and her beauty.

When Jesus Christ calls time on Babylon, "the Tale of Two Cities" will be over. There will only be one city in the age to come: Jerusalem, the City of God.

King of Kings and Lord of Lords (17:14)

They will make war against the Lamb, but the Lamb will overcome them because he is Lord of lords and King of kings.

(Revelation 17:14)

The Spirit of Babylon has never invented anything. Like Satan her master, she is a mere creature who can only steal, pervert, corrupt and pretend. She inspired the rulers of Babylon to steal a name which was not theirs to bear when they first commanded their subjects to hail them as *"King of kings"*. The Babylonian king Nebuchadnezzar claims this title in Daniel 2:37 and Ezekiel 26:7 as a boast that all the kings of the nations must submit to him, and the Persian king Artaxerxes does the same in Ezra 7:12. In fact, Revelation 17:8 tells us that this title is always at the top of Babylon's wish-list. Babylon longs for the nations to praise and worship her as their King of kings and Lord of lords.

Unfortunately for her, that name already belongs to another: one far, far greater than she can ever be. Paul tells us in 1 Timothy 6:15 that the Lord God Almighty is *"the blessed and only Ruler, the King of kings and Lord of lords"*. He is the true Monarch of the Universe who hires and fires every king, president and prime minister as he chooses. He is the one who, when *"the kings of the earth take their stand"*, is able to laugh and rebuke them in his anger.[1] Babylon simply cannot compete with him.

This is the title that the Father conferred upon Jesus

[1] Psalm 2:2–4.

because he suffered and died in obedience to him. Paul tells us that

> *therefore God exalted him to the highest place and gave him the name that is above every name, that at the name of Jesus every knee should bow, in heaven and on earth and under the earth, and every tongue confess that Jesus Christ is Lord, to the glory of God the Father.*[2]

This is why he is able to ride out in Revelation 19:16 with the title *"King of kings and Lord of lords"* emblazoned across his clothes and on his thigh, and why the angel tells us that this is his name in 17:14. This is no throwaway verse in the midst of the account of the Fall of Babylon. It states the reason for her fall, for she has stolen a name which belongs to Jesus Christ, and she is about to be humbled.

A few years ago, I went paintballing with twenty-five friends. We prepared well in advance for victory and arrived at the competition full of bravado. We wore army camouflage. We had given each other call signs and worked out a clear strategy for battle. We invested heavily in ammunition. In short, we were brimming with confidence and had convinced ourselves that we were genuinely the best trained outfit in the competition. However, within seconds of the start of the first battle, the other team had pinned us down to our positions. A few moments later we were in disarray, and in an embarrassing sixty seconds we were all out of the game. Stunned and amazed, we stepped forward to shake hands with the team who had annihilated us, and discovered that they were a group of Royal Marines enjoying a day off work. We had been playing at soldiers and looking the part, but sixty seconds with some real soldiers was enough to expose us for the office boys we really were. Babylon always postures as *"King of kings and Lord of lords"*, but when

[2] Philippians 2:9–11.

Jesus Christ the true King of kings appears, her empty boasts are instantly silenced.

This was important perspective for John on the Isle of Patmos and for the members of the seven churches of Asia. They were under intense persecution from the Roman Emperor Domitian, and many of them had been imprisoned, exiled, and even executed.[3] Rome was deeply influenced by the Spirit of Babylon,[4] and Domitian's rule seemed all-powerful. Only a few months earlier, he had started to demand that people refer to him as *"Our Lord and God"*.[5] Jesus wanted the churches in Asia to know that however loudly the Spirit of Babylon postures, she will instantly fall when the real King of kings appears. This was graphically illustrated in September 96 AD, very soon after John received Revelation, when the Emperor Domitian was assassinated by his courtiers and his corpse was unceremoniously cremated as if he were a pauper.

It is important perspective for us too, because Babylon still postures and preens herself in our own lands. In the totalitarian regimes of the Middle East, South-East Asia and Africa, there are rulers who effectively claim to be *"King of kings and Lord of lords"*, and appear to be unassailable. Jesus assures us that they will fall in an instant when he appears on the scene. In the freer regimes of Europe and North America, there is a dominant and very intolerant worldview which has a near monopoly on the media and arts, and which will tolerate no dissent from her strident views. She is as much Babylon trying to be *"King of kings and Lord of lords"* as the dictators of the developing world. Babylon wants the praise of democracies too, and she knows how to get it. Jesus announces to those who live in the God-

[3] See, for example, Revelation 2:10, 13.

[4] John's first readers would have immediately understood the city on seven hills in 17:9 as a reference to Rome. Rome was influenced by the Spirit of Babylon, but 11:8 tells us that she is not restricted to any one city.

[5] Suetonius, *Life of Domitian*, chapter 13. *Dominus* and *Deus* were the two names which Roman Christians used to describe the true *Lord* and *God*.

hating cultures of the West that their Babylonian worldview will also tumble in a moment when he gives the word.

As far as we can tell, the first ruler in history ever to use the title *"King of kings"* was Pharaoh Rameses II of Egypt.[6] I have visited his great Mausoleum in Luxor, Egypt, and have seen the inscription on the base of one of his statues in which he makes his arrogant boast. Ironically, all that is left of this statue is the base, a leg and a pile of eroded rubble, standing as testimony to the empty claims of Babylon. It prompted the poet Horace Smith to pen the following sonnet:

In Egypt's sandy silence, all alone,
Stands a gigantic Leg, which far off throws
The only shadow that the Desert knows:
"I am the great Ozymandias," saith the stone,
"The King of Kings; this mighty City shows
The wonders of my hand." The City's gone,
Nought but the Leg remaining to disclose
The site of this forgotten Babylon.[7]

Babylon's rulers – whether tin-pot dictators or sophisticated media-machines – will always claim to be *"King of kings and Lord of lords"*, and they will appear to be all-powerful. Jesus wants us to grasp that Babylon is merely an impostor who claims a title which is truly his. He has unmasked her as a fraud repeatedly throughout history, and he will unmask her once and for all on his return.

As Daniel said to Nebuchadnezzar, the so-called "King of kings" who ruled over ancient Babylon: *"[God] sets up kings and*

---

[6] This ties in with Revelation 11:8, which tells us that the Spirit of Babylon was at work in ancient Egypt.

[7] *Ozymandias* was a throne-name of Rameses II. In that same year, 1817, Horace Smith's friend Percy Shelley wrote another, more famous, poem of the same name.

deposes them... the Most High is sovereign over the kingdoms of men and gives them to anyone he wishes."[8]

We need to remember this in the face of the Spirit of Babylon. Jesus Christ is the true King of kings, and he is on the Throne.

[8] Daniel 2:21; 4:17, 32.

Babylon's Last Hope (18:4)

Then I heard another voice from heaven say: "Come out of her, my people, so that you will not share in her sins, so that you will not receive any of her plagues."

(Revelation 18:4)

Babylon launches two attacks against you, not one. She is wily and flexible, the master of disguise, and you need to be on guard against both of her ploys. Her city has not yet fallen, and she will fight dirty to the bitter end.

The Spirit of Babylon's full-frontal attack is to embed herself so deeply within a culture that Christians still think her way, even after conversion. She is in the slave business, and she is determined to recapture those whom Christ has freed from her clutches.[1] She will whisper promises of sex, wealth and pampered luxury – whatever it takes to catch their eyes and ensnare their hearts. If necessary, she will put on religious clothes, driven on by her unquenchable thirst to replace living faith with dead religion. She will turn Christian ministry into a springboard for power, fame and self-fulfilment, and she will even trick the most passionate builders of the New Jerusalem into laying bricks for Babylon. Her dirty fingerprints stain 2,000 years of Church history, and her feet still trample the Church as Jesus predicted in 11:2. No wonder God cries out at this point fervently from heaven: *"Come out of her, my people!"*[2] Christians

---

[1] Revelation 18:13; Colossians 2:8; 2 Timothy 2:26.

[2] This must be the voice of God rather than that of an angel, since he refers to ***"my** people"*. God also calls his People to come out of Babylon in Isaiah 48:20 and 52:11–12, in Jeremiah 50:8; 51:6 and 51:45, in Zechariah 2:7, and in 2 Corinthians 6:17. We dare not ignore this repeated command.

need to resist her full-frontal attack, because if they share in her sins, they will also share in her judgment.

But the Spirit of Babylon also has a second attack with which she ambushes those who resist her first assault. It is an attempt at damage limitation, and it is very effective. She tries to convince Christians that Babylon is the *same thing* as their culture, and that to separate themselves from Babylon means to withdraw from the world. Those who most zealously repulse her first attack are often most easily snared by her second, and soon they are in full retreat, rejecting their nation's media, television, music and schools in favour of a Christian subculture of their own. Most of them are not even aware that they are under attack, and they actually think they are pleasing the Lord with their Christian isolationism. They convince themselves that they have *"come out of Babylon"*, when in fact they have simply withdrawn from the world and cleared the way for Babylon to rule in their stead.

We must not forget that the cultures of the world are neutral ground, which God himself created at Babel as a way of limiting the power of the Spirit of Babylon.[3] She loves to sit on the waters of the world's cultures,[4] polluting their flow and enslaving those who drink from them, but her position is very fragile. The New Jerusalem has a river too, the River of the Holy Spirit, and Revelation 22:1–2 tells us that its leaves *"are for the healing of the nations"*. The clear water of Jerusalem's river will always defeat *"the maddening wine of Babylon's adulteries"*,[5] which is why she is so desperate for the Church to withdraw and leave the world at her feet. She knows that the Lord has power over her river,[6] and that her only hope is to trick the Church into an unnecessary retreat.

That is why we must be ready for Babylon's second attack

3 Genesis 11:6–9.

4 Revelation 17:1; Jeremiah 51:13.

5 Revelation 14:8; 17:2; 18:3.

6 Revelation 16:12.

as well as her first. It's why Jesus prayed for us on the night he was betrayed, telling the Father that *"My prayer is not that you take them out of the world but that you protect them from the evil one... As you sent me into the world, I have sent them into the world."*[7] He wants us to grasp that every culture on earth is a neutral space which will just as readily drink from the river of Babylon or the river of Jerusalem. We must not withdraw from the polluted waters of our world – whether media, the arts, politics or schools – but must take our place at the source of the river, so that the healing River of God feeds, heals and transforms the nations in which we live. Through the River of the Holy Spirit, the Church brings life-giving hope to the world. We cannot yield to Babylon's bid for monopoly. The nations of the earth belong to Jesus.

God calls his People to withdraw from the *contamination* of Babylon so that they will not share in both her sins and her judgment, but he then calls them to a strategy of *infiltration*, not *isolation*. He calls us to take our place within our towns, cities and communities, and to build Jerusalem instead of Babylon at the heart of our nations.

The New Jerusalem is doing well. When John saw the great crowd of the redeemed in Revelation 7, the Church was nowhere near her goal of uniting together people from every culture in the worship of the Living God. The Gospel was still largely contained to Southern Europe, Northern Africa and the Middle East. Today, over 1,900 years later, local churches exist in almost every culture on the earth, from Alaska to Australia and from Venezuela to Vladivostok.

Yet there is still much for Jerusalem to do. Over 2,200 of the world's language groups do not have a single verse of the Bible available in their own language.[8] Babylon still has many people groups to herself, and even in the historic Christian heartland

---

[7] John 17:15, 18.

[8] This is 2008 data from the website of Wycliffe Bible Translators. This represents a third of the world's spoken languages, and nearly 200 million individuals.

of Europe and North America Babylon's attacks have been very successful. She is confident that she sits on their waters and that Western culture lies at her feet.

She hates what Jesus tells us in Matthew 13:33: *"The kingdom of heaven is like yeast that a woman took and mixed into a large amount of flour until it worked all through the dough."* The New Jerusalem has been very successful in previous generations at spreading her yeast throughout the cultures of the world and redeeming the nations for Christ. Babylon's only hope for our own day lies in her twin-pronged offensive, determined either to pollute us or to drive us from the world.

Let's resist contamination and isolation, and take up our calling of infiltration. We are able to withdraw from Babylon and yet advance into the world with the River of God. Babylon's Empire must fall and the world must know that Christ's Kingdom has come.

Thank God that He Judges (19:1–10)

And again they shouted: "Hallelujah! The smoke from her goes up for ever and ever."

(Revelation 19:3)

My mother-in-law's garden is stunningly beautiful. It has a perfect lawn, a feature pond, an old oak tree, a walled vegetable garden, and – best of all – an unbroken view of the rolling fields of Dorset. It is an amazing garden, and she absolutely loves it. Even so, on the day that my father-in-law created it by rotovating her old garden and uprooting its hedges, she went upstairs, crawled under the duvet, and cried. Today her garden is one of her greatest joys, but she simply could not bear to watch the old garden destroyed and its soil laid bare. She sobbed under her covers at the price she had to pay for the garden of her dreams.

Many Christians act like that when they read about God's judgment. They love to read about the glories of God's Paradise in the last two chapters of Revelation, but they are horrified by the Judgment which precedes it. The blood, the fire and the smoke make them want to hide their faces so that they don't have to watch. They feel offended that God should act in such a brutal and intolerant manner. Why can't he move straight on to the delights of the New Jerusalem without forcing us to endure this savage prelude? Jesus knows that many of us ask that question, which is why he chooses to stop at the halfway point in his bloody sixth overview of AD history in order to give us a glimpse of the People of God in heaven. They are not hiding their faces under the duvet – in fact, quite the opposite. They are worshipping God with boisterous excitement over the Judgment that they see.

One of the most common Hebrew words in Christian worship choruses is *Hallelujah!*, or *Praise the Lord!* We find it several times in the Old Testament Psalms, but few people realize that it only occurs four times in the New Testament and that all four of them are in the song of Revelation 19.[1] This word which features in so many of our own worship-songs, and which inspired Handel's "Hallelujah Chorus", is the word which dominates this song of the redeemed and the angels in heaven. They watch the blood, guts, judgment and vengeance of chapters 17–18, and then they erupt into one of the greatest praise parties in the whole of the Bible. Since God personally calls us to join in with their worship in 19:5, we need to realign our view of God's Judgment so that it stops being a source of discomfort or embarrassment, and starts to fuel us in our heartfelt worship.

One way to do this is to imagine we are already dwelling in the new heaven and new earth which is described in the last two chapters of Revelation.[2] Imagine that AD history has long since ended, and we now inhabit God's great Paradise. We are strolling together down the golden main street of the city, basking in the presence of God and the beauty of his new creation. We turn around the corner, and suddenly our faces drop. There, right in front of us, are a number of advertising hoardings. One of them advertises the opening of a new lap-dancing club in the city where drinks are free and guests can take advantage of the in-house call girls. Another promotes the ultimate in home-security systems and promises that it can save us from falling victim to one of the armed robberies which have recently gripped the city. The others offer free tarot readings, discount

[1] The word *Hallelujah* only occurs in the New Testament in Revelation 19:1, 3, 4, 6.

[2] We will explore what this will be like in much greater detail in a few chapters' time.

breast enlargements, and a free trial of the new adult movie channel which launched last weekend. You look at me with pain in your eyes and complain, *"We've been deceived! How can God call this Paradise?! What happened to all his promises?!"* We both feel cheated, deceived and betrayed, because we expected God's new creation to be much better than this.

That imaginary scene helps us understand why the People of God rejoice in heaven when they see God judging the earth. They see that he is doing what it takes to create new world that he has promised. They grasp what eluded my mother-in-law when she wept over the destruction of her old garden. They understand that the eradication of the old is the price which always has to be paid for the advent of the new. Those advertising hoardings represent what the new heaven and new earth would be like if God did not judge and destroy Babylon and her followers. We are told in verse 2 that she *"corrupted the earth by her adulteries"*, and if God were to let her live, she would most certainly corrupt the new heaven and new earth with them too. We are also told in verse 2 that she hates and murders the People of God, so if God allowed her to survive into the age to come, he would be about as loving as a man who asks a local paedophile to babysit his children for the weekend. God loves his children enough to root out the evil of this age so that, through the purifying blood of Christ, they can enjoy his pure and unblemished Paradise with him forever.

Do you see now why this halfway mark in the sixth overview of AD history describes one of the loudest worship parties in the whole of Scripture? The People of God rejoice that he has not stayed his hand in weakness, but has treated sin as radically and diligently as a surgeon who removes cancerous cells from his patient's body. God has destroyed the Spirit of Babylon so that *"the smoke from her goes up for ever and ever"*, and he is about to go on to destroy the Beast, the Devil, and all those who follow them. He *"has begun his reign"* and has not left any vestige of fallen humankind to pollute his Kingdom.[3] Because he is the God who destroys both sin and the sinner, the People of God celebrate that in the age to come there really will be no more death, no more sickness, no more cancer, no more rape, no more theft, no more racism, no more child abuse, no more war, no more ethnic cleansing, no more loneliness, no more hunger, no more tears, no more hatred, no more pain, no more suffering, and no more complaints that God is too harsh in his judgment. They rejoice that the new heaven and new earth are going to be perfect, because God has been willing to pay the price.

We need to watch the redeemed worshipping God in heaven, rising like an excited football crowd to applaud his judgment, and to let it change our perspective. We need to be stirred by their *Hallelujahs* to obey God's command and join in with their celebration. We need to learn how to praise God for his judgment now, because we will praise him for it forever when we witness his Final Judgment.

It is time for us to see what heaven sees and to step up to our place in the great choir of worshippers. It is time for us to grasp that unless God destroys every trace of this fallen world and its unrepentant inhabitants, there will never be room for the new heaven and new earth which he has promised.

It is time for us to come out from under the duvet to marvel with gratitude at God's destruction of the old world order. It's time for us to thank God that he judges.

---

[3] Note that the verb *ebasileusen* in v. 6 is an aorist tense and therefore means *he has begun to reign*, just like in 11:17.

The Wedding Supper of the Lamb (19:7–9)

Then the angel said to me, "Write: 'Blessed are those who are invited to the wedding supper of the Lamb!'" And he added, "These are the true words of God."

(Revelation 19:9)

World history will not end with a funeral, but with a wedding. It will not end tragically through nuclear holocaust, climate change or any other natural disaster. It will end when Jesus Christ the King returns from heaven to marry his Bride, the Church.[1] Revelation tells us that the whole of world history is one long love story, the tale of a Father preparing the perfect Bride for his Son, and that the Gospel is his invitation to become part of that Bride. Think about that for a moment. Is there any other religion or philosophy which dares to suggest anything so glorious?

It's not simply that God looked at human marriage and decided it would make a good illustration for how his Son would receive the Church. That's the wrong way round. God planned even before he created the world that history would end with his Son marrying the Church.[2] He planned that wedding first and then created human marriage so that we might understand its meaning. That's why Satan wants to twist, corrupt and destroy

---

[1] Ephesians 5:22–33 tells us that the Bride of Christ is the Church. Revelation 21:2 clarifies that she is the New Jerusalem, which includes all those saved throughout BC history too.

[2] See the chapter on "Before the Foundation of the World".

marriage, and why a godly marriage is one of the greatest ways to glorify Christ and declare his Gospel.

The book of Revelation will not end with the Great Prostitute Babylon on centre stage. She has fallen, and the focus shifts to the New Jerusalem walking down the aisle as the Bride of Christ. It is fitting that the last few chapters should celebrate *"the wedding supper of the Lamb"*, because this is the great romance behind world history, the reason that God created a world in the first place.

This picture of a wedding feast declares God's intense *love* for his People. I will never forget the moment on my wedding day when the church doors opened and in stepped my bride. My eyes filled with tears, but my love for Ruth is nothing compared to Christ's love for the Church. You see, Revelation never refers to the wedding of the Son, but only ever to the wedding of the *Lamb*. It emphasizes that the wedding is only possible because the Bridegroom gave up his life to pay a hefty bride price. Jacob worked fourteen years to marry Rachel, and Boaz risked his inheritance to marry Ruth, but Jesus gave up his very life to be able to marry you and me.[3] That is why the greatest Old Testament promise that we are the Bride of Christ comes in Isaiah 54:5–6, immediately after Isaiah 53 and the greatest Old Testament chapter on the atoning death of Jesus for his People. The *"wedding of the Lamb"* shows us the depth of Jesus' love for us, a love which is stronger than death.

This picture of the wedding feast also speaks of God's great *joy* and *celebration* over his People. There is nothing reluctant or half-hearted about weddings. They are happy, noisy affairs, and so is the wedding of the Lamb. Jesus endured the cross because of *"the joy set before him"*,[4] and he was so excited about his wedding day that he filled his teaching with illustrations of brides and bridegrooms.[5] It is just as he promised in Isaiah

[3] Genesis 29:15–39; Ruth 4:1–13.

[4] Hebrews 12:2.

[5] For example, in Matthew 9:14–15; 22:1–14; 25:1–13.

65:18–19: *"I will create Jerusalem to be a delight and its people a joy. I will rejoice over Jerusalem and take delight in my people."* Jesus is over the moon about marrying us.

The picture of the wedding feast also emphasizes God's *commitment* to share his riches with us. The traditional wedding vows contain a promise that *"All that I am I give to you, all that I have I share with you"*, and Jesus pledges to do all this and more. A bride adopts her husband's name, and Jesus promises in 3:12 that he will put his name on us.[6] If the bridegroom is a king, the bride automatically becomes queen, and God promises in Jeremiah 3:17 that *"at that time they will call Jerusalem 'The-Throne-of-the-Lord'"*. If she marries someone very wealthy, she instantly becomes very wealthy too, and so God promises us in Luke 15:31 that *"everything I have is yours"*. Many guys find it hard to get excited by the wedding of the Lamb, as if they ordered an action movie and were given a rom-com, but they have missed the point. The wedding is what gives us the authority to sit next to Christ and to reign with him forever. Being the Bride of Christ couldn't be a manlier calling.

The picture of the wedding feast also reminds us that we have a *choice* to make with our lives. The four most important words in any wedding ceremony are *"Will you?"* and *"I do"*, and those are the words which Jesus wants to hear from you. Will you forsake all others to be part of his Bride? Will you give your life to being part of a local church and to playing your part within the wider Church of Christ?

If your answer is *"I do"*, Jesus calls you to do two things in verse 8. He calls you first to put on the pure white clothes of righteousness which he gives you as a gift of grace. When you accept them and are declared righteous, he calls you second to work with his Holy Spirit to be made righteous. He calls you

---

[6] See the chapter on "God's Signature".

to get ready for your wedding day and to be *"without stain or wrinkle or any other blemish, but holy and blameless"*.[7]

Imagine a wedding where the bride sauntered down the aisle, stopping to flirt with one or two of the guests, and surreptitiously passing her phone number to a good-looking groomsman. It would make a mockery of marriage itself. Jesus gives you this picture of the great Wedding Supper of the Lamb in order to tell you of his love, joy and commitment towards you, and to invite you to reciprocate with your own love, joy and commitment too. No other response will do.

Paul puts it this way in one of his letters:

> *I am jealous for you with a godly jealousy. I promised you to one husband, to Christ, so that I might present you as a pure virgin to him. But I am afraid that just as Eve was deceived by the serpent's cunning, your minds may somehow be led astray from your sincere and pure devotion to Christ.*[8]

Let's not be deceived. World history will end with a wedding, and we will be the Bride.

[7] Ephesians 5:27.

[8] 2 Corinthians 11:2–3.

What Angels Can't Do (19:10)

> *At this I fell at his feet to worship him. But he said to me, "Do not do it! I am a fellow-servant with you and with your brothers who hold to the testimony of Jesus. Worship God! For the testimony of Jesus is the spirit of prophecy."*
>
> (Revelation 19:10)

The angels of God are very, very strong. God needed to send only one angel to destroy Jerusalem when David sinned.[1] Three centuries later in 701 BC, he needed to send only one angel to slaughter 185,000 trained Assyrian troops and rescue Jerusalem.[2] Angels are awesome in their strength, which is why their standard greeting in Scripture is not *"Hello"* or *"Peace"* but *"Do not be afraid"*.[3] John had seen Jesus appear in his glory at the start of Revelation, but the sight of this angel was still enough to make him fall down and worship.

Which leads to the most startling thing about this verse. It's not that John should foolishly sin by trying to worship an angel.[4] It's that the mighty angel should tell John that there is something that we can do that they can't. There's something that you can do – even if you've only been a Christian for a few

---

[1] 1 Chronicles 21:15–17.

[2] 2 Kings 19:35; Isaiah 37:36; 2 Chronicles 32:21.

[3] For example, three times in Luke's account of the nativity alone. See Luke 1:13, 30; 2:10.

[4] Some people believe that John tried to worship an angel for a second time in 22:6–9, but I believe that a better reading of those verses is to see them as John referring back to his earlier error here in 19:10.

days, and even if you feel like you're the weakest Christian in the world – there's something that you can do that the mightiest angel can't.

The angel tells John that although he and his kind are *fellow-servants* of God alongside Christians, they are not their *brothers*. Christians, the angel says, are not *our brothers* but *your brothers*, and they have authority to do something that is denied to angels. It's one of the reasons why angels serve us and not the other way round,[5] and it's this: We have been entrusted with the Gospel of Jesus Christ.

Now I know that most modern English translations assume that the angel is telling John that Christians *hold to* the testimony of Jesus, but the most straightforward translation of the Greek word here is simply that we *have* the testimony of Jesus in a way that the angels do not. That's how the older English translations understand his words, and it's how many non-English translators understand them too.[6] We have the testimony of Jesus, which John makes clear in 12:17 and 20:4 refers to the Gospel. We possess the Gospel with authority to proclaim it to sinners and lead them to salvation, and angels do not. It's that simple.

We can see this at work in the book of Acts. Jesus told those around him on the night of his arrest that he had more than *"twelve legions of angels"*[7] at his disposal to enforce the

---

[5] Hebrews 1:14. Our authority comes from the fact that, unlike the angels, we are part of the Family of God.

[6] The translator of the Latin Vulgate understood the Greek this way, which is one of the reasons why the King James Version, Young's Literal Translation and a whole host of non-English Bibles such as the French Louis Segond Version also understand it this way. For example, the same Greek word *echō* simply means that Jesus *has* the keys of Death and Hades in 1:18, that God's prophets *have* authority to perform miracles in 11:6, and that we *have* ears in 13:9.

[7] Matthew 26:53. Since a Roman legion contained as many as 6,000 foot soldiers and cavalry men, this equates to about 72,000 angels, but since there were twelve tribes of Israel and twelve disciples this number is almost certainly a symbolic way of referring to many more than this.

Kingdom of God, but he chose instead to commission twelve apostles to preach the Gospel in Acts 1. In Acts 5:19 we read of an angel breaking these apostles out of jail so that they could keep on preaching the Gospel, but at no point do we read that the angels did their job for them. In chapter 8 the time comes for God to save an Ethiopian official and to spread the Gospel to black Africa, but the angel's role is simply to find the Christian leader Philip and to tell him where he can find the man to share the Gospel with him. Even more strikingly, in Acts 10 when it is time for the Gospel to go powerfully to the Gentiles, an angel appears to the Roman centurion Cornelius to tell him that he needs to hear the Gospel, but he instructs him to send messengers to fetch Peter if he wants to find out what the Gospel is.

So let's just stop and consider this. God decides that it is time for the Gentiles to be saved in large numbers. He gets Cornelius' attention through such a powerful angelic visitation that even a leader in the mighty Roman army is filled with fear. And then at the very moment when he has Cornelius' complete attention, he tells him that he can't hear the Gospel for another forty-eight hours until Peter comes to his home and shares it with him! That truly is remarkable. It's remarkable restraint on the part of the angel, and it's why the angel tells John to get up and stop worshipping him. It's time for him – and us – to recognize that Christians have authority to share the Gospel in a way that the angels simply don't.

Perhaps it's because they are mere spectators of the Gospel rather than recipients of the Gospel. Perhaps it's because God wants to train us for the age to come through us being his Gospel preachers rather than the angels. Perhaps it's simply that no one would believe that God accepts sinners and extends mercy to wretches if they heard the message from a pure and holy angel, but – let's face it – the message of grace is a whole lot more believable when it comes from flawed messengers like us! We don't know exactly why it is, but the angel tells us that it just is. It's a fact which conveys dignity upon every Christian, and a grand purpose upon every Christian's life which, if grasped properly, should transform our lives.

It means that evangelism is not a chore but a great honour. It isn't something for specially gifted Christians, but something for each one of us. It isn't something for us to do in our own strength, but in the power of the Holy Spirit. So much so that the angel assures John that the Gospel itself *"is the Spirit of prophecy"*.

The angel is making the scandalous statement that, when we share the Gospel, we speak with the same power that the Old Testament prophets did when they proclaimed their words of Scripture.[8] We speak the word of God with such power that, just as God spoke *"Let there be light"* and caused light to shine on day one of creation, so too we speak the Gospel and the Holy Spirit causes a spiritual light to turn on in people's hearts so that they are saved.[9] We have been entrusted with the Gospel of Christ and given such great power and authority that even the feeblest Christian can speak the Good News of Jesus' death, resurrection and victory, knowing that the whole power of heaven will rush forward to back up what he or she says.

Angels can't proclaim the Gospel. They are part of heaven's army which backs up the Gospel when it's proclaimed by us. That's why the angel told John that Christians are *"brothers who have the testimony of Jesus"* and that they speak the Gospel as *"the Spirit of prophecy"*. That's why the angel told John to stop worshipping him and to understand that he and all heaven's

---

8 This is different from saying that we speak with the same inspiration as them, since unlike us they spoke God-inspired Scripture (2 Peter 1:20–21). Yet Peter is very clear in 1 Peter 1:10–12 that those who share the Gospel today are backed up by the Holy Spirit so that they speak with the same power as them. Interestingly in view of the title of this chapter, Peter ends this statement with a comment that *"angels long to look into these things"*.

9 Paul explains this principle in 2 Corinthians 4:1–6.

army are at hand to back up Christians when they tell people the Good News.

So let's take this to heart and do what the angel said. Let's get up off the floor to share the Gospel every day, in every place and in every way. To paraphrase God's command in Isaiah 52, let's wake up, let's shake off our dust and let's proclaim the Good News of Christ's Kingdom to every man, woman and child before Jesus comes again. For *"how beautiful on the mountains are the feet of those who bring good news, who proclaim peace, who bring good tidings, who proclaim salvation, who say to Zion, 'Your God reigns!'"*[10]

More beautiful than the feet of angels.

[10] This was originally a prophecy about Jesus coming to save humankind, but Paul deliberately changes the singular participle in the Hebrew and Greek Old Testaments into a *plural* when he quotes this verse in Romans 10:15. He does so to make it clear that this verse now applies to all Christians too, as explored in the earlier chapter on "The Iron Sceptre".

Jesus Christ Rides Out to War (19:11–21)

> *I saw heaven standing open and there before me was a white horse, whose rider is called Faithful and True. With justice he judges and makes war.*
>
> (Revelation 19:11)

This is the moment you have been waiting for. Better than the moment when Superman appears to save Lois Lane. Better than the scene in *Commando* when Arnold Schwarzenegger finally puts on his camouflage and weapons to save his kidnapped daughter. Better than the moment when the ace poker player smiles and reveals his winning hand. This is the moment when Jesus Christ rides out to war.

Up until this moment, eighteen chapters of anticipation, tribulation and expectation have gripped our stomachs with righteous indignation. With each succeeding chapter of blasphemy and injustice, we long more and more for Jesus to rise up from his Throne and assert his powerful rule. Revelation is deliberately structured in the run-up to this passage to make us cry out like David: *"Arise, O Lord, let not man triumph; let the nations be judged in your presence. Strike them with terror, O Lord; let the nations know they are but men."*[1] Suddenly our prayers are answered. The darkness clears. This is the moment that God plays his trump card and silence falls. This is the moment that Jesus Christ rides out to war, and nothing can resist him.

This is very good news if you are sick and tired of all the pain and suffering on Planet Earth. There are many good

[1] Psalm 9:19–20.

answers to the question *"Why does God allow suffering?"*, but none of them answer it as completely as this. The bottom line is that God will not allow suffering to go on forever. He has set a day when Jesus will ride out on a white charger to slaughter the Antichrist-Beast, the False Prophet, and all those who follow them. He has ridden out many times throughout AD history, but he will do so fully and decisively at his Second Coming.[2] Paul describes the destruction of this Antichrist-Beast in 2 Thessalonians 2:8 by simply telling us that *"the lawless one will be revealed, whom the Lord Jesus will overthrow with the breath of his mouth and destroy by the splendour of his coming"*. I have reached the age where the breath of my mouth can only just blow out all the candles on my cake. When Jesus Christ blows, however, the Beast's rule will crumble.[3]

Many people are surprised by this scene because they have been fed a sanitized version of Jesus which is only half true. They have been told that he is the *"Prince of Peace"*, but not that he establishes his peace by destroying those who threaten it.[4] They have heard about the parable-telling, donkey-riding meek man of Galilee, but not about the sword-wielding captain of the armies of heaven who rides out on a white charger to destroy Satan's work and renew the universe. They have worshipped the Jesus who wore a crown of thorns and shed his own blood,

---

[2] Like all of the six overviews of AD history, Jesus tells us that this will happen in miniature throughout history but will happen fully at his Second Coming. However, the sixth overview particularly focuses on the end of history. See references to Jesus returning with his angel army in Matthew 16:27; 25:31; Mark 8:38; Luke 9:26; 2 Thessalonians 1:7.

[3] We are not meant to see Jesus destroying Babylon *then* the Beast, *then* Satan, *then* the wicked. He deliberately prevents us from doing so by telling us that the kings of the earth gather to fight in 16:12–16; 19:17–21 and 20:7–10. They are destroyed but reappear each time, which is a big clue that Jesus is simply showing us how the same event will judge Babylon, the Beast, the devil, and unbelieving humans.

[4] Many Christians know the description of Jesus in Isaiah 9:6, but miss the fact he reappears in Isaiah 63:1–6 to trample the wine-press of God's wrath and to stain his clothes with the blood of the wicked.

but they have not learned to worship him wearing many kingly crowns[5] and spattering his clothes with the blood of his enemies. This is the *"Revelation of Jesus Christ"*, the revelation of Jesus as he really is.[6]

Perhaps our confusion is caused by our failure to grasp God's plan of salvation. Jesus the Messiah was born at the start of AD history to perform God's work of salvation and to call the world to submit to him. He will appear again at the end of AD history to close his offer of salvation and to judge those who refused it. The Jews largely rejected him because they expected a Messiah-Judge who would deliver them from the Romans, and because they were offended by the meek Messiah-Saviour. Tragically, many people reject the real Jesus today because they expect nothing more than a Messiah-Saviour, and because they are offended by the Messiah-Judge. The demons understand that God's Messiah will both save and judge, and they beg Jesus not to *"torture us before the appointed time"*.[7] Sadly many people – even Christians – do not grasp this at all.

The one who told the crowd in Jerusalem that *"I did not come to judge the world, but to save it"*, will end AD history by riding out to judge those who refused his offer of salvation.[8] The one who told Pontius Pilate that *"my kingdom is not of this world"*, will one day appear with a troop of angels to establish the fullness of his Kingdom on earth.[9] On that day, when he has fulfilled all God's promises about the Messiah-Who-Saves, he will arrive to fulfil all God's promises about the Messiah-Who-Judges. Jesus was the Word of God in Bethlehem, Galilee, and

---

[5] These are not *stephanoi*, or "victory crowns", but *diadēmata*, or "crowns of royal authority". The only other two uses of this word in the whole of the New Testament are in Revelation 12:3 where Satan wears seven diadems and in 13:1 where the Beast wears ten diadems. We are meant to grasp that Jesus has much, much more power than either of those impostors.

[6] Revelation 1:1.

[7] Matthew 8:29.

[8] John 12:47.

[9] John 18:36.

Jerusalem at the start of AD history,[10] and he will still be the Word of God when he rides out to end history.[11] The difference is simply that he came once to fulfil the promise that God saves, and will come a second time to fulfil the promise that he judges.

We can see both of these promises in the two dinner invitations which Jesus issues in chapter 19. We talk most about the salvation invitation which he sends out in verse 9 and which calls the world to come to his Wedding Supper and become part of the Bride of Christ. We must not forget that he also offers a judgment-invitation in verse 17 to all those who refused him the first time. It summons them to the Great Supper of God, and is very different from the first invitation. The Wedding Supper is a call to sit and eat because the blood of the Lamb has turned us into a pure Bride. The Great Supper is a call to come and be eaten, because if we reject the blood of the Lamb, we will be turned into food for the vultures. Whoever refuses the Wedding Supper will be summoned to the Great Supper. Whoever refuses Jesus the Saviour will meet Jesus the Judge.

We must grasp this full revelation of Jesus Christ for our own sake, because this is our true Husband. We are betrothed to one who is perfectly pure and who wants us to share in his hatred for sin. On that day we will wield the iron sceptre with him.[12]

We must also grasp it for the sake of those who have not yet accepted the wedding invitation of the Gospel. If we present them with a sanitized, half-true shadow of the real Jesus, we are responsible for their destruction. The Lord warns us in Ezekiel 33:8 that *"When I say to the wicked, 'O wicked man, you will surely die', and you do not speak out to dissuade him from his ways, that*

---

[10] John 1:1, 14; 1 John 1:1.

[11] Revelation 19:13.

[12] John's quotation here from Psalm 2:9 is exactly the same passage that Jesus applied to us in 2:26–27.

wicked man will die for his sin, and I will hold you accountable for his blood."

This is the real Jesus, the glorious Jesus who appeared to John on Patmos. We preach a pretend Jesus at our peril.

The Millennium (20:1–10)

They came to life and reigned with Christ for a thousand years.

(Revelation 20:4)

OK, take a deep breath. This is the least understood and most debated passage in the whole of Revelation. Some Christians find it so confusing that they ignore it altogether, while others see it as fascinating fuel for their fantasy and speculation.[1] I want to save you from both extremes.

Most of the debate centres on how we understand the *"thousand years"* which John mentions six times in these ten verses. Depending on our interpretation, we become – wait for it – *postmillennialists, amillennialists, historic premillennialists* or *pretribulational premillennialists.* As if these titles were not confusing enough, some people also refer to *historic premillennialism* as *classic premillennialism,* and to *pretribulational premillennialism* as *dispensational premillennialism*. Yes, theologians really are quite geeky.

Post- basically means *after-*. Postmillennialists believe Jesus will return *after* the *"thousand years"*, and that this simply refers to the last years of AD history. God will bind Satan and allow the Church to see massive revival and to Christianize world culture, and this utopia will only end when God releases Satan to reassert himself. This will simply be the prelude to Jesus' Second Coming, and he will suddenly return to destroy Satan, raise the dead to life and execute his Final Judgment.

---

[1] Tim LaHaye's best-selling *Left Behind* series draws heavily on this passage. I personally think his novels are very entertaining fiction, but quite muddled in their understanding of this passage.

A- means *not-*, although *amillennialists* do not deny that there will be a millennium, rather they see it as simply a symbolic way of referring to *the whole of AD history*. They argue that 1000 is simply 10^3, and that it therefore symbolizes the whole period between Christ's ascension and his return, rather like the *"forty-two months"* of 13:5.

Pre- means *before-*. *Historic* or *Classic* premillennialists believe that history will culminate in a short period of "tribulation",[2] and that Jesus will return to end this tribulation *before* the *"thousand years"* begin. He will "rapture" his followers away into the sky, and will then descend to earth with them to rule together on the earth for a thousand years. This will mean righteous rule and revival, but at the end of those thousand years God will release Satan to muster all those who have resisted the revival to fight in a great battle against Christ. Satan will lose, and Jesus will then usher in the age to come by raising dead non-Christians to life, by judging them and by throwing them into hell with Satan.

Pretribulation or *dispensational* premillennialists believe that Christ will begin his return by whisking believers away in a "secret rapture" up to heaven, and that he will do this not only before the thousand years begin, but also before the tribulation begins. He will do this to spare them from the tribulation,[3] and their seven-year absence in heaven will enable God to convert the Jews en masse to Christ, then use them to rebuild Jerusalem and convert the nations to their new-found Messiah. Jesus will then complete the Second Coming he began with the "rapture", and he will reign on earth for a thousand years with the converted

---

[2] This term is taken from Jesus' words in Matthew 24:21, 29 in the King James Version.

[3] The key verses used to support this idea of a "secret rapture" are Matthew 24:40–41, hence the name of the *Left Behind* novels. Other verses used to support the idea of a "rapture" in general are 1 Thessalonians 4:16–17 and Revelation 3:10; 11:12–13.

Jewish race. At the end of this, he will defeat Satan's rebellion, raise unbelievers to life, and issue their Final Judgment.

If you find all this confusing, you are not alone. I have actually only described a simplified version of the debate, but enough for you to take a viewpoint of your own. Jesus revealed this for a reason, and that means we mustn't just ignore what he says, so in the very brief space I have here, let me make a few suggestions to help you navigate these different opinions.

If we assume that Revelation consists of six overviews of AD history, it is only logical to assume that these *"thousand years"* refer to the whole of AD history, just like the all the others. 20:1–10 cannot take place chronologically after the destruction of Babylon in chapters 17 and 18, since God-hating human society is still very much available to Satan in verse 8 when he musters them to war.[4]

It should concern us that no other passage of Scripture talks explicitly about Jesus ruling on the earth for a thousand years before the Final Judgment. On the contrary, the Bible consistently talks of one Second Coming and not two, of one resurrection for both the believer and the unbeliever,[5] and of terrible times rather than utopia in the last years of AD history.[6] The idea that Christ might return to reign on the fallen earth before the Final Judgment seems to me to stem from a wrong view of *Israel*,[7] and from an incomplete view of the *age to come*.[8]

[4] Gog and Magog is a reference back to Ezekiel 38–39 and to the Battle of Armageddon in Revelation 16:12–16.

[5] John 5:28–29; Acts 24:15; Daniel 12:2.

[6] For example, Matthew 24:15–31.

[7] Dispensational premillennialism is an attempt to explain how God can still fulfil his promises to ethnic Israel. It fails to grasp that he will do so through their faith in Christ and their salvation into the People of God. See Ephesians 2:11–22 or the chapter on "True Jews". John tells us only a few verses later in 21:2 that *"the city he loves"* in 20:9 is not geographical Jerusalem but the *"New Jerusalem"*.

[8] If we assume that our eternal home is "up" in heaven then we need to force-fit a number of promises about the earth into this present age. The chapter on "The New Creation" shows that we may not need to force-fit them at all.

Even though Satan is still free in AD history to blind the minds of unbelievers,[9] Jesus has nevertheless bound him so that the Church can plunder his possessions through the Gospel.[10] We must not underestimate Christ's power: no one will be able to dwell on earth in rebellion against him once he returns in glory.[11]

Rather than viewing the *"thousand years"* as a golden age in the future, we should be encouraged that they describe our here-and-now. If we have been born again spiritually, we have already received the *"first resurrection"* which is referred to in verse 5, a resurrection which even death itself cannot kill, and we are able to reign with Christ on earth right now as his kings and priests.[12] We refuse to be distracted from prayer and action today by promises that an easier utopia is on its way, or that the Jews will be converted without our help and will evangelize the nations for us.

That is the opposite of what Jesus is trying to show us in this passage. He is telling us that Satan has been bound and that he himself is on the Throne as the Ruler of the Universe. Ever since Jesus' death and resurrection, Satan has been bound and has lost his grip on the pagan Gentile nations of the earth. The Church has spread to almost every race, tribe and language, but there are still more nations to prise from Satan's chained hands. Now is the time for us to rise up and reign with Jesus. Now is the time to do as he commanded us before he ascended to heaven: *"All authority on heaven and on earth has been given to me. Therefore, go and make disciples of all nations."*[13]

---

[9] 2 Corinthians 4:4.

[10] Revelation 20:2 is therefore linked to Luke 11:21–22 and Matthew 28:18. Satan is both bound and unbound, which is why he is given a key to the Abyss in Revelation 9:1 but then is restricted again and again in the rest of the chapter as to how he uses it.

[11] 2 Thessalonians 2:8.

[12] Revelation 1:6; 5:10.

[13] Matthew 28:18–19.

The Final Judgment (20:11–15)

And I saw the dead, great and small, standing before the throne, and books were opened. Another book was opened, which is the book of life. The dead were judged according to what they had done as recorded in the books.

(Revelation 20:12)

God answers prayer. He answers prayer each day of our lives, but on the Last Day of history he will answer the deepest prayers of humankind in a full, complete, and glorious manner. In these, the last five verses of the six long overviews of AD history, Jesus reveals to John what will happen when he finally blows the whistle on this age and ushers in the next. They describe what will happen at the Final Judgment, and they are a magnificent showcase of answered prayers.

The Final Judgment brings the answer to the prayer of the *Christian martyrs* back in 6:9–11. It seems a long time ago that we read about the Seven Seals and the second overview of AD history, but at that time the martyrs cried out *"How long, Sovereign Lord, holy and true, until you judge the inhabitants of the earth and avenge our blood?"* They were told to *"wait a little longer"* until the full number of martyrs had been killed and the sin of the earth had reached its full measure. Now their request is granted, and the Lord sits on a great white Throne to judge every single man, woman, and child.[1] No one is able

[1] The one who sits on the Throne in 20:11 is probably God the Father, since he is the one who sits on the Throne in Revelation 5:13 and 7:10, and in Daniel

to escape the judgment, because neither the sea nor even the grave itself can grant immunity. All humanity will be judged, and the martyrs will have what they prayed for.

The Final Judgment brings the answer to the Old Testament prophet *Habakkuk*'s prayer. His short book is an emotional complaint that the wicked seem to escape their just deserts, and he asks *"How long, O Lord, must I call for help, but you do not listen?... The law is paralysed, and justice never prevails."*[2] If there is one think we hate almost as much as bad things happening to good people, it is good things happening to bad people, and these five verses promise that this injustice will not go on forever. God's Throne is white as an expression of his utter impartiality and justice, and John stresses that he will judge both the *"great and small"*. In Shakespeare's *Hamlet*, even the wicked uncle recognizes that *"In the corrupted currents of this world offence's gilded hand may shove by justice, and oft 'tis seen the wicked prize itself buys out the law; but 'tis not so above. There is no shuffling."*[3] Here John promises that Shakespeare is right, and that however much the wicked escape justice in this life, they will never escape it at the Final Judgment.

This scene brings the answer to Job's prayer in Job 19:23–24: *"Oh, that my words were recorded, that they were written on a scroll, that they were inscribed with an iron tool on lead, or engraved in rock for ever."* Here we find that his prayers are answered and that God has kept books recording every single deed committed by every single person during their lifetime.[4] All rebels will be thrown into hell, but all will not be punished equally. Since all will be punished *"according to what*

7:9. However, Revelation 22:1, 3 makes it clear that both the Father and the Son sit on the same Throne, so Jesus the Son will also preside over the Final Judgment, as predicted in Matthew 25:31; John 5:22, 27; Acts 10:42; 17:31; 2 Timothy 4:1.

[2] Habakkuk 1:2, 4.

[3] *Hamlet*, Act III, Scene III. Hamlet's uncle is a wicked murderer, but even he recognizes that the Lord will be just at the Final Judgment.

[4] These are probably the same books that are mentioned in Daniel 7:10.

they have done", we can be assured that those who have rebelled much will be punished much, and those who have rebelled less will be punished less. My Gran will be in the same place as Adolf Hitler, but she will not be treated as if she were Adolf Hitler. God will be fair even towards those he punishes.[5]

The Final Judgment even brings the answer to the prayer of *unbelievers* too. Jesus created hell as *"the eternal fire prepared for the devil and his angels"*,[6] not as a place for human beings, but he takes seriously even the prayers of those who reject him. When people spend their lives telling him that they have no need for him and no desire to know him, he actually grants them their foolish wish. He will raise them to life so that no one misses out on the fulfilment of their desire,[7] and he will consign those who sided with Satan and his Beast to the destiny they have chosen. As C.S. Lewis puts it: *"There are only two kinds of people in the end: those who say to God 'Thy will be done,' and those to whom God says, in the end, 'Thy will be done.' All that are in Hell choose it."*[8]

Lastly, the Final Judgment brings the answer to *our own* prayers too. We long for God to end all suffering and for his Kingdom to come fully on the earth with no pain, no sickness, no tears, no death and no curse of sin. Verse 11 tells us that God's Final Judgment will cause even the earth and sky to flee from his holy presence like Adam hid from him in the Garden of Eden, and this paves the way for the new earth and sky at the start of chapter 21.[9] We also long for many of our friends, family, neighbours and colleagues to respond to the Gospel and

---

[5] For more on this, see Matthew 10:15; 11:21–24; Luke 12:47–48; 20:47.

[6] Matthew 25:41.

[7] John 5:28–29 speaks about the resurrection of *unbelievers* as well as believers from the dead. Jesus will raise every single person from the dead and seal their eternal destinies according to their earthly choices.

[8] C.S. Lewis, *The Great Divorce* (1945).

[9] The Greek word *ouranos* means both *sky* and *heaven*, so the words used in 20:11 for *earth* and *sky* are the same words that are used in 21:1 for the *new heaven* and *new earth*.

be saved, and this passage promises us that if anyone's name is written in the Lamb's Book of Life, they will be saved on the basis of his works in spite of the sinfulness of their own works. Peter tells us that the reason why Jesus has delayed so long in answering our prayers that he would return is that *"he is patient with you, not wanting anyone to perish, but everyone to come to repentance"*,[10] and this double mention of the Lamb's Book of Life is a promise that, before he returns, he will indeed save many of the people for whom we are praying and with whom we are sharing the Gospel.

Let's resist the urge to complain about the Final Judgment or to point the finger at God for sending people to hell. The scene which John describes here is of God answering the prayers of all people over history in one glorious moment. What are the big things which you are praying that God will do in the world? Praise God, you are going to receive your answer.

---

[10] 2 Peter 3:9.

The Vision of the Age to Come

The New Creation (21:1)

Then I saw a new heaven and a new earth; for the first heaven and the first earth had passed away.

(Revelation 21:1)

On 30th April 1975, the city of Saigon fell to the Viet Cong and the Vietnam War ended. For twenty-four hours before the city fell, swarms of people covered the roof of the American Embassy in hope of becoming one of the lucky few who were airlifted away to American warships and to freedom. As the sound of tank fire grew louder and louder, many people in the crowd panicked, and fights broke out for the last few seats on the helicopters. People left their possessions and even their families behind in their desperate rush to abandon the Vietnam nightmare and exchange it for the American dream.

Many people live as though the Christian life should be like that terrible day in Saigon. They throw up their hands at the state of the world and praise God that one day they will receive a heavenly airlift away from its trouble. They fail to notice that their attitude is the exact opposite of Christ's when he left heaven and came to earth to save the human race, and they even manage to convince themselves that God is pleased with their disdain for the earth. They may fall into this trap through the "rapture theology" of the previous chapter, but it is just as easy to do so if we fail to grasp what Jesus shows us in Revelation 21–22.

Scripture tells us that all who die go straight to heaven

or to hell, even before history ends with the Final Judgment.[1] Christians are welcomed into what theologians call *"the intermediate heaven"*, which is why Jesus told a dying thief that he would be with him today in Paradise,[2] and why Paul was happy to die early so that he could *"be with Christ, which is better by far"*.[3] It is also why Revelation often shows us what dead Christians are currently doing in heaven.[4] Yet Scripture also tells us that this is not the Christian's final home. In the words of Tom Wright, it tells us that there is *"life after life after death"*, when we will be raised to life with new resurrection bodies.[5] We will not always be disembodied spirits in heaven who have effectively *"fallen asleep"* to life on Planet Earth.[6] When Jesus returns, he will re-create a new heaven and new earth for us, and that is what he shows John in the last two chapters of Revelation.

Perhaps the reason why many of us assume that the Christian hope is a disembodied eternity in heaven is that 2 Peter 3:10 tells us that *"The heavens will disappear with a roar; the elements will be destroyed by fire, and the earth and everything in it will be laid bare."* We assume that this means that the earth will be obliterated because we will ascend to heaven, but the rest of the Bible tells us that this is not what Peter is saying at all. Jesus will destroy the earth like a farmer who burns stubble

[1] For example, in Luke 16:22–31. This means that the Final Judgment is not so much the declaration of guilt or innocence as it is the passing of sentences.

[2] Luke 23:43.

[3] Philippians 1:23. See also 2 Corinthians 5:8.

[4] One example is Revelation 6:9–11.

[5] Tom Wright's book *Surprised By Hope* (2007) and Randy Alcorn's book *Heaven* (2004) both cover this topic brilliantly and in far more detail than I can here. Both books help us to return to the historical Christian understanding of our eternal home, and are excellent next steps if you want to explore this theme further.

[6] Note how the New Testament repeatedly uses this phrase in Matthew 9:24; John 11:11; Acts 7:60; 13:36; 1 Corinthians 11:30; 15:6, 18, 20; 1 Thessalonians 4:13–17. The last passage links this *sleep* to being *woken up* when Jesus returns and raises the dead.

in his field, as the preparation for sowing a fresh harvest, and so he refers to the *"rebirth"* of the universe in Matthew 19:28,[7] and Peter refers to God *"restoring"* the universe in Acts 3:21. The Lord promised in the Old Testament that he would create a *"new heaven and new earth"* out of the destruction of this current universe,[8] and his promises in the New Testament are exactly the same.[9]

Revelation 21 gives us clear detail about what will happen at the end of time. After the Final Judgment,[10] God's People will *not* be whisked away to heaven. Instead, heaven will come down to earth, and the new heaven and new earth will be fused together into one glorious place where God dwells. There will be no more pain, mourning, crying, death, or danger in this New Creation.[11] It will be Paradise Restored because the Last Adam has dealt with the curse through which the First Adam infected the earth.[12] We will not ascend to heaven to live on clouds and play endless tunes on heavenly harps. Heaven will descend to us, and we will live forever with God on earth, ruling with him and working together in perfect fulfilment without any toilsome labour.[13]

A few years ago I went to the funeral of a very godly

---

[7] The Greek word *palingenesia* means literally *"being born again"*. It is the same word that Paul uses for a person being born again in Titus 3:5.

[8] Isaiah 65:17; 66:22.

[9] 2 Peter 3:13; Romans 8:19–23.

[10] Revelation 20:15.

[11] One of my friends is a retired Royal Naval officer and is very upset that v. 3 promises there will be no sea on the new earth. He can be comforted that Revelation is simply using *the sea* here as a picture of a *danger* and *division*. It actually tells us in 4:6 and 15:2 that something like the sea is not incompatible with the new creation. After all, Jesus chose to minister on Lake Galilee with a group of fishermen.

[12] Compare Genesis 3:17–19; Galatians 3:13; Revelation 22:4.

[13] Genesis 2:15 and 3:17–19 tell us that work is *not* part of the Curse but only the hard labour that makes work a hassle rather than a joy. Revelation 22:5 and Luke 19:11–27 tell us that there will be plenty to do in the new creation. We will not get bored.

ninety-five-year-old woman. Those who loved her sobbed with great tears of anguish, not because she had died young or unforgiven, but simply because deep down we know that death does not belong on this planet. When I pray for sick people to be healed, I regularly find myself breaking down in tears over their situation, because deep down we know that sickness does not belong here either. Every time we fight against injustice or complain about the failures of our politicians, we also show instinctive awareness that this planet should be different. That is the fantastic news of Revelation 21 and 22. Our instinct is right. Jesus is coming back, not to take us away from earth to heaven, but to bring heaven down to earth and to recreate our universe.

This news is so thrilling that it must affect the way we live as Christians. When Paul writes about it he urges the Thessalonians to *"encourage each other with these words"*.[14] We must not buy into the quasi-religious planet worship of many environmental groups, but nor must we write off our planet in the hope of a one-way ticket to heaven. Instead, we must do what Christian churches have normally done with this hope over the centuries. Because we know that one day God's Kingdom will come fully on earth as it is in heaven, we work by his grace and his power to make his Kingdom come in small ways today.[15] Because one day there will be no poverty, pain or injustice, we work hard to eradicate them here and now as an expression of God's coming Kingdom. Because the new earth will one day resound with a unified song of worship to King Jesus, we work hard today to call the nations to worship him together. Because a day is coming when the Lord will declare *"I make all things new"*, we work hard today to bring the hallmarks of the age to come into this present age.

This, and nothing else, is the great Christian hope for

---

[14] 1 Thessalonians 4:18.

[15] Matthew 6:10.

"life after life after death". Jesus is coming back because he has not finished with his work of creation. We will not be airlifted away from Planet Earth to consign it to its fate. We will receive resurrection bodies to live on a renewed earth for an eternity of adventure with him.

God With Us (21:3)

And I heard a loud voice from the throne saying, "Now the dwelling of God is with men, and he will live with them. They will be his people, and God himself will be with them and be their God."

(Revelation 21:3)

Once upon a time, God lived with his People on the earth. His main home was heaven, but every evening at supper time he would go for a walk in the Garden of Eden with his friends Adam and Eve. He treasured their face-to-face chats so highly that one day, when Adam failed to show up for their time together, he called until he found him.[1] You know the rest of the story. Adam and Eve believed the words of a talking snake over the words of their Creator, Friend, and God, and their relationship broke down. Adam hid and God threw him out. God's intimate, face-to-face Paradise was lost.

The last two chapters of Revelation describe God's new Paradise in the age to come. The tree of life is there, just as it was in Genesis 2, but this time it is watered by a better River. God's People are there, but now so numerous that they are not merely a husband and wife but a whole city. There is no curse, no sin, no pain and no death, but none of these things are what makes it Paradise.

Towering far above these lesser joys is the promise that *"Now the dwelling of God is with men, and he will live with them. They will be his people, and God himself will be with them and be their God. He will wipe every tear from their eyes… They will see*

[1] Genesis 3:8–9.

his face."[2] The thrill of the new creation is that once we receive our resurrection bodies and have our home in a restored and sinless universe, we will finally enjoy the face-to-face intimacy with God which Adam knew and lost. When King Solomon finished his magnificent Temple, he asked despairingly, *"Will God really dwell on the earth? The heavens, even the highest heaven, cannot contain you. How much less this temple I have built!"*[3] John's excitement about the new earth is linked to Solomon's question. He tells us: *"I did not see a temple in the city, because the Lord God Almighty and the Lamb* ***are*** *its temple."*[4] The city will be Paradise because the Father and the Lamb will dwell there with their people, and because the River of the Holy Spirit will pour forth from their Throne.

This vision should make us look forward eagerly to the delights of the age to come. Some Christians have a very strange and twisted view of what eternity will be like, imagining disembodied harp-playing on clouds "up there" instead of God giving us resurrection bodies and then dwelling with us "down here". They complain that heaven sounds boring, but it is a heaven of their own making. The new earth will be a thrilling place where we see God face to face and enjoy walking, exploring, learning, working and ruling together with him. We will only find it boring if we can get bored with God, and even eternity will not be enough time to get to know the exquisite depths of his character.

This vision should also make us profoundly grateful. The patriarchs were so aware of their own sinfulness before God that after one encounter Jacob exclaimed, *"I saw God face to face, and yet my life was spared."*[5] Moses often spoke with God *"face to face"*,[6] and yet God even told him on one occasion that

---

[2] Revelation 21:3–4; 22:4.

[3] 1 Kings 8:27.

[4] Revelation 21:22.

[5] Genesis 32:30.

[6] Exodus 33:11; Numbers 12:8; 14:14; Deuteronomy 5:4–5; 34:10.

"you cannot see my face, for no one may see me and live".[7] Unless we grasp the great gulf which sin places between us and God, we will never know John's excitement that God should deign to dwell with us. The only reason he can do so is that when he has cast all unbelievers into hell, he will purify, glorify and give sinless resurrection bodies to those he has redeemed.[8] We will only see God face to face because Jesus, the true Temple of God, will fully redeem both us and our planet from the curse as a result of the fact that he *"became flesh and made his dwelling among us"*.[9]

This vision of the new earth should also make each of us treasure the intimate presence of God every day of our lives. Jesus prayed that *"this is eternal life: that they may know you, the only true God, and Jesus Christ, whom you have sent"*,[10] and he expects us to embrace eternal life here and now by laying hold of his presence. He told his disciples that *"It is for your good that I am going away"*, and that it would enable him to pour out his Holy Spirit at Pentecost on all who follow him. Those who truly rejoice in the face-to-face intimacy which is to come, show it by letting God dwell inside of them as they drink daily of his Holy Spirit.[11]

Finally, this vision of the new earth should make us treasure the presence of God corporately in our churches. The distinguishing mark of God's People in eternity will be that God dwells among them as a city,[12] and it has always been the mark of God's chosen People.[13] He promised to mark out Old Testament Israel with the promise that *"I will put my dwelling-place among you, and I will not abhor you. I will walk among you and be your*

---

[7] Exodus 33:20.

[8] Revelation 21:27.

[9] John 2:19–22; 1:14.

[10] John 17:3.

[11] John 16:7. See also John 14:16–18; 14:23.

[12] Ezekiel 48:35.

[13] Exodus 33:16; Ezekiel 48:35.

God, and you will be my people."[14] He promised to mark out his New Testament Church in the same way when he told them that *"I will live with them and walk among them, and I will be their God, and they will be my people."*[15] At a time when most churches have their own mission statements and their own philosophy of ministry, the Lord lays down what must be at the core of them all. The number one calling of any church is to experience the presence of God and to let others experience it through them. We must not be like the church at Laodicea and not even notice that God's presence has left us.[16]

John's vision of the new earth reminds us that heaven is nothing less than God dwelling with us face to face, and that the Christian life is nothing less than his dwelling with us in our hearts today. We are those who follow *Immanuel*, or *God-With-Us*,[17] and who value God's presence above all else. That presence is ours today by grace through the Holy Spirit, and it will be ours by grace forever in the face-to-face City-Paradise of God.

---

14 Leviticus 26:11–12.

15 2 Corinthians 6:16.

16 Revelation 3:20.

17 Isaiah 7:14; 8:10; Matthew 1:23.

Courage (21:8)

But the cowardly, the unbelieving, the vile, the murderers, the sexually immoral, those who practise magic arts, the idolaters and all liars – their place will be in the fiery lake of burning sulphur. This is the second death.

(Revelation 21:8)

God likes to surprise us. He loves to hide morsels of unexpected truth in the verses of Scripture, ready to spring out and catch us unawares. Many Study Bibles ignore them or attempt to explain them away, but I think this misses the point. These are the places where God shows us that our thinking is out of step with his own. They are a call to stop, to reflect and to adjust the way we think.

Take, for example, Revelation 21:8. I find this verse very surprising. I can understand why murderers, sorcerers, idolaters, liars and those who are sexually immoral should be barred from God's City and thrown into hell. I can even understand why unbelievers should be with them too. But *cowards*? I find that shocking and pretty troubling. After all, I get scared sometimes, and so do you. What does God mean when he talks about the fate of the *cowardly*?

He is certainly not telling us that we should not be afraid. The repeated message of the Old Testament – in the Pentateuch, in the History books, in Wisdom Literature and in the Prophets – is that we must fear God. Jeremiah prophesied that this would also be one of the hallmarks of the New Covenant, and so we find the same command to fear God in the New Testament –

in the gospels, Acts, the letters and Revelation.[1] God does not forbid fear. He simply tells us to stop fearing man and to start fearing him.

Fear of man made Abraham lie to Pharaoh and let him take Sarah to be his wife, but fear of God made him obey the Lord and sacrifice his son Isaac.[2] Fear of man made Aaron lead the Israelites into idolatry with the Golden Calf, but fear of God had made him stand before Pharaoh and demand that he let the people go.[3] Fear of man was why ten spies gave a bad report about the Promised Land, but fear of God gave Joshua and Caleb faith that they could conquer.[4] Fear of man made Elijah flee before Queen Jezebel, but fear of God empowered him to stand before King Ahab.[5] True Christian courage is therefore not a lack of fear; it is simply fearing God with such reverent awe that no other threat can be heard above the presence of his terrifying glory.

If it were not for verses such as Revelation 21:8, we might fool ourselves that cowardice is a weakness rather than a sin, a simple human frailty which God understands and accommodates. God uses this verse to shock us and convince us that it is a deadly sin. Cowardice makes people flee when they should fight, shrink back when they should advance, and run away from God when they should run towards him. It couples with *unbelief* to bring forth *disobedience*,[6] and it could not be more serious. That's why Jesus warned his disciples that he would disown cowards before his Father at the Final Judgment, and that they needed a true vision of God-the-Judge if they were ever to stand firm before men.[7]

[1] For example, in Deuteronomy 6:24; 2 Chronicles 19:7; Psalm 34:9; Isaiah 8:13; Luke 12:5; Acts 9:31; 2 Corinthians 5:11; Revelation 14:7.

[2] Genesis 12:10–20; 22:12.

[3] Exodus 32:21–24.

[4] Numbers 13.

[5] 1 Kings 18:15–18; 19:1–3.

[6] Matthew 8:26; 14:30–31; Mark 4:40.

[7] Matthew 10:28–33.

Peter was a textbook example of cowardice on the night that Jesus was arrested. One dictionary defines cowardice as being *"too eager to avoid danger, difficulty and pain"*,[8] and that was Peter all over when his Master was arrested and led away. It only took a slave girl and her friends to make him deny Jesus three times in rapid succession.[9] He feared man (or girl) and in doing so showed that his faith in Christ was all too superficial.

Yet Peter is also a textbook example of how God can turn cowards into faithful followers and spare them the judgment of Revelation 21:8. I find his turnaround very encouraging, because by God's grace it can happen to us too. Only a few weeks after his terrible denial of Jesus, this same Peter stood up before the Jewish Sanhedrin and *"when they saw the courage of Peter and John and realized that they were unschooled, ordinary men, they took note that these men had been with Jesus"*.[10] Luke tells us that this new-found courage came through his being filled with the Holy Spirit and spending time with Jesus,[11] but Peter himself explains it still further. He commands us in 1 Peter 3:14–15: *"Do not fear what they fear; do not be frightened. But in your hearts set apart Christ as Lord"*. He therefore tells us the same thing that Jesus taught, that the great antidote to the fear of man is simply recognizing Christ for who he really is. Only genuine fear of God can truly silence the fear of man.

Do you see now why we must not rush past Revelation 21:8 before letting God ambush us with this warning? He tells us that cowardice and conversion cannot walk hand in hand, and that no one who is *"eager to avoid danger, difficulty and pain"* can become a disciple of Christ. Following Jesus means by definition taking risks, tasting hardship and suffering loss for the King and his Kingdom. True subjects of King Jesus care more about what

---

[8] The *Cambridge Advanced Learner's Dictionary* (Cambridge University Press).

[9] Luke 22:55–62.

[10] Acts 4:1–20, especially v. 13.

[11] Acts 4:8, 13.

he thinks than they fear the empty threats of the world. Those who do not are counterfeit subjects and will be excluded from the New Jerusalem.

If you know that your life is more shaped by what people think of you than it is by what Jesus thinks of you, you need to take very seriously what he says in this verse about cowards. You need to grow in your fear of God, so that you can be free from the fear of man.

Jesus said:

> *Do not be afraid of those who kill the body and after that can do no more. But I will show you whom you should fear: Fear him who, after the killing of the body, has power to throw you into hell. Yes, I tell you, fear him... I tell you, whoever acknowledges me before men, the Son of Man will also acknowledge him before the angels of God. But he who disowns me before men will be disowned before the angels of God.*[12]

Be afraid, be very afraid, but make sure that your fear is placed in the right person. Fear the Lord, and then you have nothing else to fear.

[12] Luke 12:4–5, 8–9.

The New Jerusalem (21:9–27)

And he carried me away in the Spirit to a mountain great and high, and showed me the Holy City, Jerusalem, coming down out of heaven from God.

(Revelation 21:10)

In August 70 AD, the future Emperor Titus breached the walls of Jerusalem and destroyed the city. The Jewish historian Josephus was there, and he estimates that as many as 1.1 million people were slaughtered when the Romans torched the Temple and razed the city to the ground.[1] Such carnage drew even the pity of Titus himself, and he is said to have refused to accept a victory-wreath because he saw *"no merit in vanquishing people forsaken by their own God"*.[2] The destruction of Jerusalem was a colossal Jewish national tragedy.

John knew and loved Jerusalem, so his vision of the New Jerusalem over twenty years after its destruction is very surprising. He does not interpret the prophecies about a New Jerusalem in Ezekiel 40–48 and Isaiah 60 as if they were Old Testament promises for the physical city. Instead, he treats them as a spiritual picture of the *People of God*, just as he used Babylon as a spiritual picture of rebellious human society. He emphasizes that the *New Jerusalem* is spiritual by echoing Ezekiel's account of an out-of-body visit to a *"great, high mountain"*, even though

[1] Josephus Flavius, *The Wars of the Jews*, VI.9.3.

[2] Philostratus II, *The Life of Apollonius of Tyana*, VI.29.

there is no such mountain near Jerusalem.[3] He confirms this further by giving us dimensions for the city which are clearly spiritual.[4] Finally, he stresses that the city is the Bride of Christ, the united People of God, which includes both Old Covenant Israel and the New Covenant Church. John does not call for his readers to rebuild the ruins of Jerusalem, because this vision describes something far better through the Gospel: a New Jerusalem which is gloriously different.

John tells us that the New Jerusalem is *very big*. The mainly Jewish People of God in Old Covenant times is intermingled with the international People of God in New Covenant times (one gate for each of the twelve tribes of Israel and one foundation for each of the twelve apostles).[5] John's New Jerusalem is nearly a thousand times as wide and long as the one which Ezekiel saw, with walls as thick as forty grown men lying head to foot, which surround 2.75 billion cubic miles of city.[6] These huge numbers are meant to rid us of any "remnant theology" which assumes that the number of people God has destined for salvation is small. Jesus wants us to know that his People will be very large, and that we need to proclaim his Gospel to all nations with this image in mind.

John tells us that the New Jerusalem is *full of God's presence*. Ezekiel ended his prophecy with the climactic statement that

---

[3] Ezekiel 40:1–2; Revelation 21:10. Ezekiel received his apocalyptic vision in 573 BC, and it is remarkably similar to John's vision. Compare, for example, Ezekiel 40:3; 43:2 with Revelation 21:15, 23.

[4] Each side of the city measures the distance from London to Athens!

[5] Ezekiel merely saw the twelve gates for the twelve tribes of Israel in Ezekiel 48:30–35, but John has a better vantage point to see the scope of God's plan of salvation. The *twelve foundations* in Revelation 21:14 probably refer to the base of each of the twelve sections of wall between the twelve gates, so the BC and AD People of God are intermingled as one People of God and not two.

[6] Ezekiel saw the length and breadth of the New Jerusalem as a very reasonable 2.3 km. John sees it as an outrageous 2,200 km, which is a picture of God creating a huge People through the Gospel of Christ: 144 cubits is simply 12^2 and 12,000 stadia is simply 12×10^3, so they seem to represent the completely-gathered-in People of God.

the name of the New Jerusalem would be *The-Lord-Is-There,*[7] and John expresses this same theme in a number of different ways. He tells us that the whole city is a perfect cube like the Old Covenant Holy of Holies, and that there is no temple in the New Jerusalem because God the Father and Jesus the Son dwell everywhere in the city.[8] The New Jerusalem is not *heaven* but the *People of God*, and so the absolute purity of God's sanctified People will enable him to dwell in every part of the city.[9]

John also tells us that the New Jerusalem is *pure* and *beautiful.* The city is a pure jewel. Its gates are pearls, its foundations are gems, and its main street is gold. The whole picture is breath-taking, defying the brushwork of the greatest artist, as John uses superlative after superlative to convey the pure beauty of what he saw. The city is beautiful because it has been given the glory of God, and because it is the Bride who reflects her Bridegroom's glory as the moon reflects that of the sun.[10] It is a city fit to be the Lord's eternal dwelling place, and it is made fit through the blood of the Lamb.

Jesus wants to encourage us through this vision that the Church will one day look like this, but he also wants us to grasp that the Church is *already* like this in heaven. She will come down from heaven looking like this, but she is already like this in heaven as she awaits the day of her great Wedding Feast. When we pray *"Your kingdom come, your will be done on earth as it is in heaven"*,[11] we are asking the Lord to conform the Church-on-Earth to the likeness of the Church-in-Heaven, and we are asking him to speed the day when Babylon will be thrown down so that the New Jerusalem might then come down.

[7] Ezekiel 48:35.

[8] The Holy of Holies was the small room which housed the Ark of the Covenant. It was 5 m^3 in the Tabernacle and 9 m^3 in the Temple.

[9] This will completely fulfil what we partly enjoy today through 1 Corinthians 3:16 and 2 Corinthians 6:16.

[10] See 2 Thessalonians 1:10 and then compare Revelation 4:3; 21:11.

[11] Matthew 6:10.

Jesus wants this vision to transform all the hopes, plans and activities of his Church on earth so that she will be a ready Bride for whom he can return as Bridegroom.[12] He wants us to evangelize, plant churches, reach nations and change cultures out of our faith that the New Jerusalem will be big and that the gates of hell shall not prevail against her. He wants us to be so filled with his Spirit that the whole world can see that God is real, accessible, and mighty to save. He wants us to be so pure and spotless that the world can see God's character in us and long to be part of his new creation.

John was very attached to the Old Jerusalem which Titus destroyed, but one glimpse of the New Jerusalem melted his heart and evaporated his desire for lesser things. John was captivated and energized by his sight of the New Jerusalem, and Jesus wants us to be too. Then we can work shoulder to shoulder with him, pouring out our lives to lay more and more bricks in the beautiful and eternal walls of the coming City of God.

[12] Revelation 19:7; 21:2.

God's Private Treasure Collection (21:19–21)

The foundations of the city walls were decorated with every kind of precious stone.

(Revelation 21:19)

By anyone's standards, Cheryl Cole is a very beautiful woman. In 2009 alone, the *Girls Aloud* singer, footballer's wife, and *X Factor* judge was voted the *"World's Sexiest Woman"* by *FHM* magazine, and *"Style Icon of the Decade"* by The Style Network. To top it all, she was also chosen in February of that year to pose on the cover of *Vogue* magazine. Surely this would be enough to convince any woman that she was beautiful? Apparently not. She confessed in *Vogue* that

> *I remember being in Selfridges and taking these size 28s into the changing room and not being able to get them on, and then getting on the scales and crying because I was nine and a half stone. Nine and a half stone when I'm only 5 foot 3 inches!... I remember I ate the same thing from room service – chicken in cream sauce with a couple of carrots – every night, for weeks, and I just felt horrible.*[1]

While the nightclubs of London were full of unattractive people convinced that they were beautiful, Cheryl Cole was starving herself in a hotel room convinced that she was ugly.

This ironic reversal can happen spiritually too. Many

[1] Interview in *Vogue UK*, February 2009.

people who are unattractive spiritually convince themselves that God thinks that they are beautiful. The Pharisee did so when he prayed *"God, I thank you that I am not like other men..."* and discovered that *"what is highly valued among men is detestable in God's sight"*.[2] Large numbers of people in every nation convince themselves that their good deeds have endeared them to God and have made them beautiful in his eyes, yet the truth is that *"all of us have become like one who is unclean, and all our righteous acts are like filthy rags"*.[3] There are many smug and self-deluded people who have a tremendous shock waiting for them at the Judgment when they will discover that the New Jerusalem is far purer and far more beautiful than they have ever imagined. All their spiritual preening and self-confidence will evaporate when they see that *"Nothing impure will ever enter it, nor will anyone who does what is shameful or deceitful, but only those whose names are written in the Lamb's book of life"*.[4]

It is the second group of people whom Jesus wants to address in Revelation 21:19–21. He wants to lay hold of the spiritual Cheryl Coles, beautiful yet unwilling to accept it, and to show us how we look in his eyes. Here we see the twelve apostles represented as precious gems of *jasper, sapphire, chalcedony, emerald, sardonyx, carnelian, chrysolite, beryl, topaz, chrysoprase, jacinth* and *amethyst*. Doubting Thomas is one of those gems, as is Peter who denied Jesus three times, both transformed into exquisite jewels in God's great city. Here we see the twelve tribal leaders of Israel represented as *pearls*. Reuben who slept with his father's concubine, Simeon who slaughtered a city in his anger, and Judah who slept with his daughter-in-law because he thought she was a prostitute at the shrine to a false god. This motley assortment of roguish patriarchs has been transformed by God's power into pearls large enough to serve as the great gates of the New Jerusalem. Amazingly, as we

---

2 Luke 18:9–14; 16:14–15.

3 Isaiah 64:6.

4 Revelation 21:27.

saw when we looked at the *twenty-four elders* in Revelation 4, we are also included among those represented by these twelve apostles, which means that even the very least believer is a precious stone in the wall.[5]

Ancient kings used to honour themselves by creating something called a *segullah* in Hebrew or a *peripoiēsis* in Greek. It was their *private treasure collection*, and both David and Solomon refer to their own in 1 Chronicles 29:3 and Ecclesiastes 2:8. God wants you to understand that he has a *private treasure collection* too, and that every single believer is part of it. He told the Israelites that he had decided to turn them all into his *segullah*,[6] and he tells the Church that he has decided to turn them all into his *peripoiēsis* too.[7] Not just the best of us, not just most of us, but *all* of us, turned into precious gems in God's private treasure collection. He is so determined that we should grasp this great fact that he instructed the high priests to wear jewels on their breastplate engraved with the names of the twelve tribes of Israel,[8] and he pictures all believers as jewels in the walls of the New Jerusalem both here and in Isaiah 54:11–12. The question over each of our lives is whether we will believe the accolade he bestows upon us, or whether we will give in to Satan's accusations and believe that we are still tainted, impure and vile through our sin.

Many Christians live as if self-loathing and low-level depression were part of the fruit of the Spirit. They hear the Gospel and accept God's forgiveness, but they never truly accept his declaration that they have been transformed into precious stones in his private treasure collection. They are more conscious of their own sin than they are of the power of Jesus' blood, which is tragic since his blood is the most powerful

---

[5] 1 Peter 2:5; Isaiah 54:11–12.

[6] Exodus 19:5; Deuteronomy 7:6; 14:2; 26:18; Psalm 135:4; Malachi 3:17.

[7] Ephesians 1:14; 1 Peter 2:9. Paul also uses a very similar word in Titus 2:14.

[8] Exodus 28:15–21.

detergent which wipes any sinner completely clean.[9] The blood of Jesus can make the murderer Moses, the adulterer David and the persecutor Paul into precious stones in his treasure collection, and we honour the blood of Jesus not by grovelling in persistent guilt but by revelling in total acceptance. God tells us to stop listening to the recriminating voice of self, Satan, or even well-meaning saints. He tells us to listen to him and the verdict which he passes over our lives.

Jesus taught that *"The kingdom of heaven is like a merchant looking for fine pearls. When he found one of great value, he went away and sold everything he had and bought it."*[10] Jesus saw a great jewel in you with his eyes of grace, and he gave up everything he had when he died on the cross to purchase you for his treasure collection.[11] His price was sufficient to secure the deal, and now your filth has been cleansed and your spiritual ugliness turned into dazzling beauty. All that remains is for you to admit your filth, receive that beauty by faith, and give up everything to follow him.

What a God. What a Gospel. What a Saviour.

[9] Revelation 7:14.

[10] Matthew 13:45–46.

[11] Revelation 5:9.

The River of God (21:1–2)

Then the angel showed me the river of the water of life, as clear as crystal, flowing from the throne of God and of the Lamb down the middle of the great street of the city.

(Revelation 22:1–2)

Great cities have great rivers. In the ancient world Rome had the Tiber, Nineveh had the Tigris, Babylon had the Euphrates, and Thebes had the Nile. In the modern world, London has the Thames, Paris has the Seine, New York has the Hudson, and Shanghai has the Huangpu. Thames Water, the water company which serves London, delivers 2.7 billion litres of water to the city every day. Great cities consume great amounts of water, which is one of the reasons why they are built on great rivers.

But Jerusalem was different. Unlike the other great cities of the world, it had no great river; in fact, it had no river at all. It was forced to rely on the Gihon spring outside the city walls for its water supply, and this made the city weak. David managed to capture Jerusalem and make it his new capital by sending his men up the water shaft to surprise the unsuspecting Jebusites.[1] King Hezekiah was so worried that a besieging army might cut off Jerusalem's water supply that he built a special secure tunnel to bring water from the Gihon spring into the city.[2]

So there it was – an urban anomaly, a town-planning headache, a source of military embarrassment – until one day the sons of Korah suggested something radical. Since the Lord

---

[1] 2 Samuel 5:8.

[2] 2 Kings 20:20.

had chosen Jerusalem,[3] he had purposefully chosen a riverless city to express a spiritual truth. Jerusalem did have a river, but that river was God himself. The surging, rushing, powerful river which served the city of Jerusalem was none other than the Holy Spirit of God.

Imagine that we are both among the worshippers at the Temple on the day that the sons of Korah first played their new worship chorus, known to us now as Psalm 46. Imagine the look on our faces as partway through the song we sing *"There is a river whose streams make glad the city of God, the holy place where the Most High dwells. God is within her."* Suddenly we both stop and look at each other. We're thinking the same thing. *No there isn't! Don't the sons of Korah know Jerusalem?!*

Now fast forward several centuries to the Feast of Tabernacles in 29 AD. Imagine that we are both in a different crowd in those same Temple courts, this time listening to the preacher Jesus. It is the last day of the Feast, the day each year when the altar is drenched with jugs of water from the Pool of Siloam, the place inside the city walls to which Hezekiah's water tunnel brings the water of the Gihon spring. We hear Jesus shout out his startling interpretation of the ceremony: *"If anyone is thirsty, let him come to* ***me*** *and drink. Whoever believes in me, as the Scripture has said, streams of living water will flow from within him."*[4] Again we look at each other with confused faces. *Which Scriptures?!* There simply aren't any clear Old Testament Scriptures which come to mind. Unless, of course, he means the words of the sons of Korah, words which Ezekiel later echoed in his vision of a great river pouring out from the Temple of God.[5]

---

[3] 2 Chronicles 6:6; Zechariah 3:2.

[4] John 7:38–39.

[5] Ezekiel 47:1–12. Note that the temple which Zerubbabel rebuilt between 537 and 516 BC did not reflect Ezekiel's description of the new Temple in Ezekiel 41–46. The Temple which Ezekiel saw was a picture of the People of God, just as the city the sons of Korah described was also a picture of the People of God.

Aren't you glad that we're not in those crowds and that we have the benefit of John's commentary on the River of God? Aren't you glad that we have John 7:39, which explains that *"By this he meant the Spirit, whom those who believed in him were later to receive"*? Aren't you glad that we have John 4:14 and Jesus' promise that *"whoever drinks the water I give him will never thirst. Indeed, the water I give him will become in him a spring of water welling up to eternal life"*? Aren't you glad that we have Revelation 22 and John's vision of God's great river, clear as crystal, flowing from the Throne through the middle of the New Jerusalem?

If you are a Christian, you are part of that city, and today God wants you to get your drinking water from his river. It's a costly river. It flows not from God and the Son but from God and the *Lamb*, because it's a river which is only yours to drink through Jesus' death, resurrection, and ascension.[6] It's a pure and wonderful river, called the *"river of delights"* by David,[7] and producing love, joy, peace, patience, kindness, goodness, gentleness, faithfulness and self-control in the hearts of those who drink it.[8]

So drink deeply of the river. It will never run dry because *"God gives the Spirit without limit"*.[9] The question isn't whether you are charismatic or non-charismatic, a holy-roller Pentecostal or a staunch evangelical. The question is whether you are drinking daily and deeply of the Holy Spirit of God. Everybody drinks something, and those who are part of the New Jerusalem drink from the River of God. It's as simple as that.[10]

Drink for your own sake, but drink also for the sake of those

[6] Acts 2:33; John 7:39.

[7] Psalm 36:8.

[8] Galatians 5:22–23.

[9] John 3:34.

[10] The Lord complains about his own People in Jeremiah 2:13 that *"my people have committed two sins: They have forsaken me, the spring of living water, and have dug their own cisterns, broken cisterns that cannot hold water."*

who don't yet know Jesus. There's a strange reference here to the River of God causing a tree to bear leaves *"for the healing of the nations"*. Some readers wonder what this means, since in the new creation the nations will either be saved into the City or cast into hell. John is telling us that we are *already* part of the New Jerusalem above, and that we need to drink from this river today for their sake as well as our own. The nations will be saved when through the Holy Spirit we become Christ's witnesses.[11] The nations will be saved when through the Holy Spirit they see Christ in us and therefore know that the Gospel must be true. The nations will be saved when the dam of spiritual self-centredness is broken down and the current of God's River is able to flow through our lives. That's what Jesus meant when he told the crowd that the Scriptures promise that *"streams of living water will flow out from within"* each Christian.

Are you ready to drink deeply from the River of God? Are you ready to become so filled by God's River that you actually become the River of God to those around you?

Let's be heavy drinkers from the River of God. It's a desert out there.

[11] Acts 1:8.

The Choice (22:6–19)

Let him who does wrong continue to do wrong; let him who is vile continue to be vile; let him who does right continue to do right; and let him who is holy continue to be holy.

(Revelation 22:11)

Last summer, my wife and I took an asylum seeker into our home. Her conversion story sounded plausible and her tears seemed genuine, so we gave her a door key, set her up in our spare room and made her part of the family. She ate with us, played with our children and became part of our lives – then we discovered that she was lying to us. One of the hardest things I have ever done was to confront her with her lies and forged documents, and to force her to leave. I like being nice to people. I like extending grace to people. But I had to throw her out for the sake of my wife, my children and my home.

Jesus faces the same situation here, but many, many times worse. He *"wants all people to be saved and to come to a knowledge of the truth"*,[1] yet he knows that his new creation can only stay pure and perfect because *"nothing impure will ever enter it, nor will anyone who does what is shameful and deceitful"*.[2] Therefore he ends the book of Revelation, and the Bible itself, with a fourteen-verse appeal for us to make our choice and decide which side we are on. His staccato series of exhortations and warnings reminds us that Jesus will not force his Kingdom upon us, and that he is committed to letting each one of us decide how we

[1] 1 Timothy 2:4.

[2] Revelation 21:27.

respond to his Revelation. He is the Alpha and Omega, the one who raised the curtain on world history and the one who will lower the curtain to signal its end. He calls us to choose sides, because the curtain is already beginning to fall.

The book of Revelation is full of terrible judgments, but I find this final ultimatum more chilling than them all. While God disciplines us for our sin, there still remains a glimmer of hope,[3] but hope is snuffed out when God endorses our wrong choices and abandons us to our fate. The most terrible words which Jesus ever spoke to Judas Iscariot were *"What you are about to do, do quickly,"* and *"Friend, do what you came for."*[4] The most terrible words which Jesus utters in Revelation are *"Let him who does wrong continue to do wrong; let him who is vile continue to be vile."*[5]

Jesus calls us in verse 12 to choose either to respond to the Gospel and receive *"**his** reward"* by grace, or to be judged *"according to what **we** have done"*.[6] He urges us in verses 14 and 15 to *"wash our robes"* in his blood and enter the New Jerusalem, or else to persist in evil and be thrown into hell. He warns us in verses 17–19 to choose the Holy City and its River of Life instead of plagues of judgment and the horrors of hell. Again and again he stresses that there are only two choices to make, and that there is no third option for the undecided. It is time for us to choose, and choose quickly.

A few months ago, I took my wife away for a romantic weekend without the children. When our hand luggage was searched before boarding the flight, the security staff told us

---

[3] See Revelation 3:19.

[4] John 13:27; Matthew 26:50.

[5] Revelation 22:11. There is some confusion over who is speaking in vv. 6–19. The key is to understand that vv. 8–9 is a reminder of what happened in 19:10 rather than a second act of folly by John. The speaker from v. 6 onwards is Jesus as he personally ends *"the Revelation of Jesus Christ"*.

[6] Jesus' words echo Isaiah 62:11 which also emphasizes that the Saviour will come with *"**his** reward"* and *"**his** recompense"* as a grace-gift for undeserving sinners.

that we could not take some of our possessions onto the plane. I was rather put out, but the choice was simple. Either we gave up our possessions or we forfeited our holiday, so of course we waved the offending items goodbye. Jesus presents us with a similar choice here at the end of Revelation, commanding us to turn from our sin and commit ourselves wholeheartedly to him so that we may dwell in his City-Paradise.

Some people complain at Jesus' stark choice, but they simply forget that heaven is only heaven because its citizens submit to Jesus. We cannot enter the City unless we leave behind everything which is impure. Other people fool themselves that the can smuggle their sin past the fiery eyes of Jesus, but he warns us that *"appearances don't impress me. I x-ray every motive and make sure you get what's coming to you."*[7] Instead, we must throw ourselves fully on God's grace towards us, believing the promise of Scripture that *"He who conceals his sins does not prosper, but whoever confesses and renounces them finds mercy."*[8] Jesus forces us to choose, but he hopes that every one of us will choose the Gospel.

The last word of the Old Testament in Hebrew is *herem*, which either means *a curse* or the action of *being cut off from the People of God*. The last words of the New Testament are very different. Jesus warns us with curses and threats, but he ends with a promise of unmerited *grace*. Choose God's blessing, not his curse. Choose his forgiveness, not his judgment. Choose to become part of the New Jerusalem, not to burn with fallen Babylon.

Verse 17 pictures the Holy Spirit, the Church, Jesus and John himself, all crying out for us to *"Come!"* and respond to what we have seen. They remind us that the message of Revelation is both the best news and the most terrible news ever given to humankind. Jesus states the options clearly, then steps back and simply lets us choose.

---

[7] Revelation 2:23 in *The Message.*

[8] Proverbs 28:13.

I Am Coming Soon (22:20)

He who testifies to these things says, "Yes, I am coming soon". Amen. Come, Lord Jesus.

(Revelation 22:20)

Jesus promised to come back soon. Two thousand years ago. Many people find that confusing.

Actually, when we read Revelation more closely, we see that this promise sits within a wider context. Jesus tells us three times in 22:7, 12, and 20 that *"I am coming soon"*,[1] but he deliberately sets this statement alongside the teaching of the rest of Revelation. *"The time is near"* for his return,[2] but it will only take place when the events he predicts have been completed. He will return after a period which will last figuratively for *"a thousand years"*,[3] and which will require believers to display patient endurance as people from every nation, tribe and language come to salvation.[4] That's why he described the gap between his ascension and his Second Coming as *"a long time"* in many of his parables.[5] His return will be soon but it will also require us to be patient, as Peter explains in 2 Peter 3:3–15.

Peter wrote his second letter in about 65 AD, almost three decades before John received the book of Revelation, yet even within thirty-five years of Jesus' ascension many people were laughing at the idea that Jesus might come back soon. They sneered *"where is this 'coming' he promised? Ever since our*

---

1 Jesus also says this in Revelation 3:11.

2 Revelation 1:3; 22:10.

3 Revelation 20:1–10.

4 Revelation 1:9, 13:10; 14:12 and Revelation 7:9; 14:6.

5 Matthew 24:48, 25:5; 25:19; Luke 20:9.

fathers died, everything goes on as it has since the beginning of creation." Peter therefore sets out to give an answer to their – and perhaps our – cynical complaint.

His first comment is that people felt exactly the same way before Noah's Flood destroyed the earth. There was considerable delay between God's promise of judgment and Noah's completion of the ark, and this made people ignore Noah's frequent warnings and assume that they were safe.[6] Peter points out that the delay did not make the Flood any less sudden or certain, since one day God simply gave the word and his judgment immediately fell. He will give the word again when Jesus returns, and it will be soon, sudden and urgent, in spite of the long delay.

Peter's second comment is that *"With the Lord a day is like a thousand years, and a thousand years are like a day."* The book of Revelation describes both AD history and the age to come. Of course 2,000 years seems a very long time in the confines of earthly history, but placed alongside the unending age described in chapter 21 it is a mere heartbeat in God's adventures with his People. Two millennia or more of AD history will only appear *"light and momentary"* when they give way to *"the eternal glory"* which is to come.[7] In the words of C. S. Lewis at the end of his *Chronicles of Narnia*:

> *All their life in this world and all their adventures in Narnia had only been the cover and the title page: now at last they were beginning Chapter One of the Great Story which no one on earth has read: which goes on for ever: in which every chapter is better than the one before.*[8]

---

[6] 2 Peter 2:5.

[7] 2 Corinthians 4:17.

[8] C.S. Lewis, *The Last Battle* (1956).

Jesus tells us that he is coming soon because this age is not the end of the story. It will be over very soon, and he will turn over the page for chapter one of the age to come.

Third and finally, Peter tells us exactly why Jesus is taking so long to blow the whistle on this present age. It is linked to the great vision of Revelation 7 where John saw people from every nation, tribe and language worshipping the Lord as part of the global People of God. Peter tells us disarmingly that *"He is patient with you, not wanting anyone to perish, but everyone to come to repentance."* The reason why Jesus is coming soon-but-not-yet is that he has still has many more people to save from the nations of the earth. He will not come back prematurely and lose anyone whose name has been written in his Book of Life.

So don't be confused by the promise in Revelation 22 that *"I am coming soon"*. Jesus will come back suddenly, unexpectedly and imminently, just as soon as the last one of his Elect surrenders to him. Peter warns us not to grow complacent, but to *"speed his coming"* through active evangelism and prayer, playing our part in taking the Gospel to the nations. He reminds us that people who know that Jesus is coming soon must live holy, spotless and blameless lives as they wait. He is coming when we least expect it, so we need to live ready.

This is also what Jesus says to us here as he ends the book of Revelation, and it is the reason why he repeats his warning that *"I am coming soon"*. Even though non-Christians deny it, and many Christians live as if it were not true, we must take it to heart and let it shape the way we live. His words are *faithful and true*, even as he himself is *Faithful and True*,[9] and this warning could not be more relevant to our lives.

"Behold, I am coming soon! My reward is with me, and I will give to everyone according to what he has done." Blessed are those who take the words of Revelation seriously, and live with that great Day in view.

---

[9] Contrast Revelation 21:5; 22:6 with Revelation 3:14; 19:11.

Conclusion: God is on the Throne

The twenty-four elders and the four living creatures fell down and worshipped God, who was seated on the throne. And they cried: "Amen, Hallelujah!"

(Revelation 19:4)

When Handel's *Messiah* was first performed in London in March 1743, his depiction of Jesus' Second Coming melted the hearts of his audience. King George II was so moved when he first heard the "Hallelujah Chorus" that he famously stood to his feet in honour of the King of kings – a tradition which is still followed when the piece is sung today. Shortly after that performance, the Earl of Kinnoul visited Handel and congratulated him on having created *"a noble entertainment".* Handel was mortified and quickly shot back his reply: *"My lord, I should be sorry if I had only entertained them, I wished to make them better."*[1]

As we draw this book to a close, my concern for you is the same as Handel's. You have read to the end of this book, and I hope that you have enjoyed its sixty chapters, but my aim was not simply to educate or entertain you. I wish to make you better.

Therefore let me close with four things which you should sense in your heart if you have truly understood the message of Revelation.

First, you will want to *worship*. More than any other book of the Bible, Revelation reveals the God Who Sits on the Throne and his Son Jesus the Lamb who reigns at his side. This vision

[1] G. Hogarth, *Musical History, Biography and Criticism* (1838).

of God should stir your heart to worship, and if it doesn't, I urge you to talk to a Christian friend who can pray for you. You owe God the praise of your heart,[2] and he promises to turn your heart of stone into a heart of flesh if you ask him to.[3] Each of these sixty chapters sounds a different note from the pages of Revelation, but each note joins with the others to lift you up into one great song of worship: God is on the Throne.

Second, you will see the world with a *different perspective*. Last week I received some terrible news by email, just as I was leaving to meet with a group of Christian friends. I didn't tell them about the email, but as we began to worship together, the presence of God fell in the room and I was convicted by a real sense of his power and his majesty. Suddenly I found that I could laugh at the news I had received, confident that God was on the Throne and that all would be well. Sure enough, as I brought the news to Jesus in prayer and told him that I was leaving it at his feet of burnished bronze, I received a second email the following day which told me that the problem had been miraculously resolved. Jesus does not just call us to display patient endurance.[4] He also shows us the heavenly realities which enable us to do so.

Third, you will want to *deal with sin* and all that hinders your walk with God. No one who has truly looked Satan, the Beast and Babylon in the face through the pages of Revelation can willingly harbour sin and rebellion in their hearts. No one should read about the Seven Seals, the Seven Trumpets or the Seven Bowls without fearing God's judgment. God is on the Throne and we are not, which means we must repent and surrender our lives to King Jesus. Anyone who reads Revelation and still clings to cherished sin runs the great risk of hearing

---

[2] Revelation 4:11.

[3] Ezekiel 11:19; 36:26.

[4] Revelation 1:9; 13:10; 14:12.

Jesus tell them on his return that *"I never knew you. Away from me, you evildoers!"*[5]

Fourth, you will *pour out the rest of your life* into building Christ's Church and proclaiming Christ's Gospel. You will be gripped with the vision of chapter 7, which speaks of God saving people from every nation, ethnic group and dialect. You will be spurred on by the vision of chapter 21, which promises that God's People will not be a tiny remnant but a vast City. You will feel like David Livingstone, the great Scottish missionary to Africa, who expressed his heart to a gathering of students after seventeen years of mission work in Africa:

> *For my own part, I have never ceased to rejoice that God has appointed me to such an office. People talk of the sacrifice I have made in spending so much of my life in Africa. Can that be called a sacrifice which is simply paid back as a small part of a great debt owing to our God, which we can never repay?... It is emphatically no sacrifice. Say rather it is a privilege. Anxiety, sickness, suffering or danger, now and then, with a foregoing of the common conveniences and charities of this life, may make us pause, and cause the spirit to waver, and the soul to sink; but let this only be for a moment. All these are nothing when compared with the glory which shall be revealed in and for us. I never made a sacrifice.*[6]

The twenty-four elders see God as he really is, seated on the Throne and in complete control over the events of history, and it causes them to worship and to cast down their crowns at his

---

[5] Matthew 7:21–23.

[6] David Livingstone made this speech to students at Cambridge University on 4th December 1857 during a brief return visit to England. He spent all but two years of the rest of his life in Africa, and he died there of malaria and dysentery in 1873.

feet.[7] Revelation also helps us to see what they see, and if we have truly grasped its message, we will do the same. Take time, if you need to, to re-read John's vision very slowly before you rush to another part of the Bible. *"Blessed is the one who reads the words of this prophecy, and blessed are those who hear it and take to heart what is written in it, because the time is near."*[8]

It helps us to see that God is on the Throne, God is in control, and God will prevail. It is the Revelation of Jesus Christ which changes everything.

---

[7] Revelation 4:9–11; 19:4.

[8] Revelation 1:3.